Inside The Red Zone

Physical and Spiritual Preparedness Against Weapons of Mass Destruction

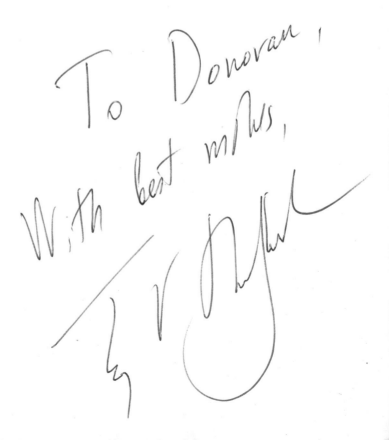

To Donovan,
With best wishes,

Inside The Red Zone

Physical and Spiritual Preparedness
Against Weapons of Mass Destruction

Igor V. Shafhid, MD
with
June Summers

Global
Strategic
Resources

Global Strategic Resources

Inside The Red Zone

Published by
Global Strategic Resources
1725 S. Rainbow Blvd. Suite 2, Box 171
Las Vegas, NV 89146

First Printing 2004
Second Printing 2004, Revised

Printed in the United States of America

Library of Congress Number: 2004105717

ISBN 0-9754214-9-2

Table of Contents

ILLUSTRATIONS

This book is dedicated to
Star, our beloved daughter

Preface

This book contains three stories. The primary story is about weapons of mass destruction—biological, chemical and nuclear—in today's world. Where do they come from, how are they used, and what is their significance to you?

The second story is what you can do to defend yourself and your family against outside threats. There are many basic techniques you can learn and steps you can take to keep you and your family safe.

The third story is mine—my journey from a godless Soviet nation to finding God and freedom in the United States. It's a love story—acknowledging my love for Jesus and then finding the love of my life in June who has become my wife.

The Red Zone has dual meanings for me—the stern country where I grew up under the thumb of Soviet communism, and the hot center of turmoil caused by the accidental or purposeful use of destructive agents, such as I witnessed during my military service.

Our world is threatened daily by mass stockpiles of weapons of mass destruction and current developments of nuclear bombs and biological/chemical weapons. Because any disaster will result in loss of lives, this book would be incomplete if I did not include the importance of spiritual preparedness as well as physical preparedness. Both are equally important when facing a terrorist attack or war.

My expertise with WMD comes from my ten-year service in the Soviet Army. As an officer and medical doctor I was involved in large-scale exercises on the principles and tactics of biological, nuclear, and chemical warfare. All too often real chemicals were used during those drills. I worked with limited protection around highly contagious diseases in both civilian and military hospitals, including irradiated victims from the Chernobyl Nuclear Plant incident. In all these instances, Russia never winced at the cost of losing military doctors or soldiers to live pathogens or nerve agents. What better way for them to learn and understand the effects of the biological and chemical weapon than by human experience?

My unit was part of the Strategic Rocket Force, where we trained in weapon deployment for all types of WMD. Our goal was to be ready and in position to eliminate Russia's greatest enemy—the United States of America. To prepare against a biological or nuclear U.S. attack, the Soviet Union built powerful offensive weapons and a solid civil defense system.

What defense can America have against these monster weapons? A good one, if it knows the strategies of the ones who created them. Within the pages of this book I "borrow" some of those ingenious strategies from the Soviet military to give the American people the answers necessary to prepare against any unexpected invasion.

After 27 years of being pinned under the communist fist and hating every minute of its encroaching evil upon my life, I took a giant step against it in order to find out who I really am. I had been programmed by the Soviet ideology for so long, it had dominion of my thoughts and attitudes. I knew that coming out from under such a one-sided delusion could only be wrought through a miracle. That miracle came when I began to acknowledge what I secretly had suspected—that God did exist.

Communism did not allow for extra relationships outside its dogma. Thus a belief in God was unacceptable. Believers in Christ were imprisoned for their faith, and many were tortured and killed. Sure, Soviet Russia's constitution declared freedom of religion, but this was a front for the world's eyes. Russia was not threatened by "religion" (a few churches and "loyal" communist pastors); it was good for their public image. But Russia *was* threatened by the intimate relationship many people had with Jesus Christ. "Religious" people could be molded and programmed, but it was impossible to beat out the faith and belief of those who had a close relationship with Christ.

Freedom and democracy, born from a Biblical foundation, are health and hope to the heart and mind. Without them men crumble and deteriorate, as did I during the Soviet rule. Having the ability to reason, think and choose as individuals should never be taken for granted.

Therefore, not only do I talk in depth about the international black market, radiation incidents, and the mass amounts of biological/chemical/nuclear weapons threatening this world today (and how to prepare against them), but I also discuss the deadliest weapon of all, mind control. This weapon goes farther than killing the body; it seeks to destroy the human soul.

Coming out from under this "weapon" in my own life took the power of God to set me straight. I quickly discovered the difference between having a *relationship* and having *religion*. A relationship with God guides you to the truth; religion takes you away from it.

Getting back my mind was something I couldn't do alone; I needed to know someone big enough to help me—I needed a relationship with God.

Communism is a far greater weapon of mass destruction than all the nuclear arsenals still sitting in the New Russian Federation territory today, because the shadow of communism is still moving rapidly, like a cancer, throughout the world.

Separate from my story, at the end of the book, I have written three appendices, to offer specific detailed "how-to" reference sections for you and your family, and for responders and health care professionals in the event of a WMD disaster.

Based on what I learned in the Soviet military, I have compiled the quick-find emergency key points and graphs to provide civilian instruction on what to stockpile in the home, how to evacuate, and the process of decontamination.

Emergency responders will glean important rules and tips on safe work methods inside hot zones, how to process contaminated victims through the decon stations, and what equipment is necessary to do the job right.

For hospitals, a proper decontamination plan set up outside a hospital during a catastrophic biological release will ensure that the inside hospital setting stays free from contamination.

Whatever the spiritual viewpoint of the reader, the detailed information on how to handle and respond to a WMD attack in the pages of this book is invaluable.

—Igor Shafhid, MD

Chapter One
Behind the Iron Curtain

SOVIET ARMY RESEARCH
COMMUNIST LIFE EXPLORED
BIOLOGICAL WEAPONS
CHEMICAL WARFARE
NUCLEAR THREAT

My ballooned cheeks ached, and my engorged eyelids left me with only oozy bloody slits to see through. A red rash raced down my torso, seeming to purposely avoid clashing hues with the yellow-green splotches marring my arms and legs.

The fall weather kept temperatures inside the 200-year-old observation ward cool, but I did not notice; the fever kept me sweating. Thirteen of my comrades lay sick with the same thing, tossing and turning in sterile beds alongside me. The first few weeks had been a blur of needles, eye-drops, bedpans and inspecting physicians, generals and colonels, all donned in protective wear. I felt like a speck under a microscope.

A high-ranking military physician entered the room right after the nurse bit my arm with another shot of anti-serum. The doctor sped down the two rows of occupied beds and stopped near mine. He flipped through the pages of my medical chart while the nurse continued shooting up the last row of patients. "I have good news," he said, his eyes avoiding us. "You have only a mild case of measles. But you will still need to remain here in bed for at least four weeks." Before any of us could complain, he added, "The boys downstairs in the isolation unit will be staying a lot longer." Without waiting for questions, he was gone.

I kicked the sheet off my body. *A mild case of measles, how can that be?* It was 1983 and I was in my second year studying medicine at the prestigious Leningrad Military Medical Academy. Although our class had not yet studied infectious diseases, my bloody urine, yellow skin, swollen face, "rabbit" eyes, and puffy gray-mushroom tongue seemed odd for measles. Nurses and orderlies seemed to be taking plenty of blood tests in between sandwiching thermometers under both armpits. Afraid our spleens might burst, they did not allow us to get out of bed at all the first week. To top that off, everyone who had contracted the disease two weeks before me left the hospital looking as if they had been punched in the face by the Hulk.

In the Soviet Army you didn't argue with commanders, nor did you question what they said. If they said green was black, green *was* black. And so it was documented: we had measles— and that was final.

I looked up at the iron-barred window as tiny wet drops began to pound against the glass. The rain reflected my mood. All I could do was settle back against the pillow with a sigh. It was going to be a long month. As I watched the icy droplets pelt the window, my mind wandered from my diagnosis to my parents. Today I felt angry with them for pushing me into the military academy. Without their determination and sacrifice I would not have been accepted, yet my current woes, added to the hardships of military life, wouldn't let me see past the disease now bullying my body. My goal had been to enroll in the Leningrad University and study archeology—which meant skipping full time military service for part-time active reserve duty. Mom was a professor of history at the university and I had a good chance of getting accepted. But my parents had worked hard to get me into the academy since only those from upper-class families found their way in, with some exceptions, as was my case.

Preparation had to take place well before high school graduation. My parents had joined the Communist Party while I was still in grade school to ensure I would have a promising career, despite the fact neither one embraced communist ideals. My mother's family despised communism; her father spent most of his life as a fugitive in Siberia fighting the regime. And so my mother Albina did not see him much. But his beliefs for a free democracy remained a part of her. Except for her older sister, Lucia, Mom's past would have never allowed her access into the Communist Party. Lucia, a stunning dark-haired beauty, captivated Anatoly Sitzeen, the chief of the secret police force KGB in the Kronach Region of Siberia. Their marriage secured my mother's future and enabled her to leave Siberia and study at the Leningrad State University.

My father's grandfather Isaac, of Jewish descent, was an avid revolutionary for the communists. My original given name was Yoffe, not Shafhid, but my great grandfather changed his name to elude the czar police in 1917. Years later he and my great grandmother Mary settled in Belarus. At the beginning of the Great Patriotic War, the summer of 1941, they were trapped inside the synagogue by the German army and burned alive with 50 other Jewish people. He left behind three sons who followed his footsteps and became dedicated communists.

The youngest son, Mendel, became my grandfather. During World War II he was a major in the Soviet Army and a *politruk,* which means, a trusted political leader whose job is to ensure that soldiers are fed a constant diet of communist ideology. He held a prestigious position as second to the commander of his unit, meaning the party put great trust in him. Mendel was reported missing in action a few months after his only son, my father, Vladimir was born in 1940 to Mendel's Russian wife— my grandmother Valentina. Mendel's body was never found and his death left my father to butt heads with a cruel step-dad, a man also fanatical to the philosophy of communism. It was no wonder it took years for my mother to convince Dad to join the party. Guess that is why I never intended to join the party.

What really solidified my chances as a doctor came through my mother's friendship with Joana Kolesnekov, an outgoing head nurse at my academy who was married to the respectable two-star General Anatoly Kolesnekov.

"Hey, Igor." Leonyd, my lanky friend from Moscow, burst through my thoughts. "You know we were all vaccinated for measles. What's going on?"

In the 1930s the Leningrad Military Medical Academy was the first place Joseph Stalin ordered new laboratories for study and research of biological weapons. Before World War II, typhus was one of many bio-weapons studied at the academy, because typhus was one of the main infectious diseases killing Russian soldiers and civilians in mass numbers during World War I and the Russian Civil War. Besides the laboratory at the academy, labs were constructed on the Solovetsky Islands in Ladoga Lake. Researched pathogens consisted of Q-fever, melioidosis, glanders and leprosy (although leprosy was later removed from the list of potential operational biological weapons). A leper colony lived on one of the islands, and thousands of crippled World War II veterans were secreted away from society, by Stalin's decree, on another.

In 1941 research programs from both Leningrad and the Solovetsky Islands were moved to Kirov at the Red Army Scientific Research Institute of Epidemiology and Hygiene. This move guaranteed shelter from possible Nazi German takeover.

During the cold war, building an effective resistance in bio-weaponry became mandate and extremely classified. Billions were spent creating labs and procuring equipment. The Soviet Army worked tirelessly to create the greatest sophisticated level of weapons of mass destruction (WMD)—and they succeeded. Years passed, and no other country came close to the vast quantity produced or the ingenious technology developed.

The U.S. and Britain began developing an offensive biological weapons (BW) defense program during WWII when intelligence sources revealed Nazi Germany was working hard to

produce BW, a threat that could devastate both countries and
their allies. The research was centered in Frederick, Maryland,
which became known as "Fort Detrick." After the war, the
American BW development strategies continued in order to
counter the Soviet threat. The U.S. Army weaponized both
incapacitating and lethal biological agents prior to the end of
the U.S. offensive program. When President Nixon stalled the
biological research program in 1969, the Soviet Union became
the running wheel of WMD in the world.

It is ironic how Nixon's statement on November 25, 1969
completely butted heads with the Soviet Union's lack of sympathy for humankind: "...the United States of America will re-
nounce the use of any form of deadly biological weapons that
either kill or incapacitate." Despite the 1972 Biological and
Toxin Weapons Convention that officially banned the development and possession of such weapons in the United States, the
Soviet Union, and other countries, the Soviet BW development
intensified and continued into the early 1990s. Ken Alibek, in
his book, *Biohazard*, confirms this information as he recounts
his life working inside the Russian labs developing killer bio-
agents. In 1992 Russian President Boris Yeltsin *let the cat out of
the bag* regarding the 1979 anthrax outbreak in the Russian city
of Sverdlovsk, which killed dozens of local citizens.

The term "weapons of mass destruction" is summed up in a
statement given by Soviet Defense Minister Georgi Zhukov to
the Communist Party in Moscow in 1956: "A new war will be
characterized by mass use of air power, various types of rocket,
atomic, thermonuclear, chemical and biological weapons."
Those words reverberate a prophetic chill as today's news media

report on the tragedies and threats of terrorism around the
world. Thus "WMD" has become a familiar term. Zhukov
furnished a clear definition of WMD in his statement—that
weapons of mass destruction consist of destructive weapons
made from nuclear devices or biological and chemical agents.
Although mass destruction can only occur from a nuclear type
weapon (destruction of buildings, animals, and plants, as well as
human life), the WMD term includes chemical and biological
weapons as well. Mass annihilation of human life through
disease can be almost as destructive to cities or countries.

The Leningrad Military Medical Academy was still researching biological/chemical agents for the Ministry of
Defense when I started my service. The Central Military Medical Department in Moscow was involved at that time under the
direction of four-star General Academician F.E. Komarov. They
were working on new immune-prophylactic drugs and vaccines
for troops protection against most biological weaponized agents,
including their own stockpiled agents, such as anthrax, tularemia, plague, typhoid fever, and hemorrhagic viruses. Because
the laboratories were constructed for a level B protection only,
and because virile agents need level A protection, their research remained focused on bacterial and rickettsiae agents
instead of viruses.

My unit in the Soviet army was assigned to the Strategic
Rocket Force in 1982 to be trained extensively, not only on
epidemiological outbreaks of natural forms of diseases, but also
on the know-how of biological weapon deployment and how to
deal with an enemy counter-attack of the same. We were not

naïve about Russia's biological, nuclear, and chemical defense system and what our role as military medical doctors might entail. We knew who "the enemy" was. Propaganda worked on my mind year after year to abhor the United States. In the military, soldiers seldom uttered the word "America," almost fearful that if they were to let it roll off their tongues, the sound of it might somehow debase them. Thus the faceless term "the enemy" stuck. Soviet Russia spent trillions of rubles to procure the most advanced defense system using biological and nuclear weapons, for one purpose: to destroy the United States of America—and become the only superpower in the world.

To understand Soviet Russia's reasoning for ignoring international treaties to dominate as a world military power, one must understand its history and particularly its spiritual state.

I wouldn't come to know the Lord Jesus Christ, my Savior, until 1993, after the Iron Curtain was pulled down and Christian missionaries began coming into St. Petersburg. Even though I avoided joining the party, the system still controlled my mind. Since the first grade, the ideology of the great "Grandfather" Lenin and other Russian leaders was emblazoned into each student all the way through high school. That brainwash continued into our adult years through media, work, college, and the military. Communism was part of everything we did. It was more than just a government. It was a lifestyle, a guiding power forced on some individuals and willingly embraced by others.

I was part of the third generation that did not know what life was before communism. And although I felt it did absolutely nothing for me, a lot of other folks, stripped of God and faith, needed something to believe in, some ideal with which to fill that void inside. Those people turned to Lenin and Stalin, so much so that when Stalin died in 1953 and his body was laid next to Lenin, hundreds of "worshippers" were stomped to death in the rush to pay tribute to him. Believing in Vladimir Lenin and Joseph Stalin kept the communist ideal alive. However no matter how many of those citizens stayed true to their gods, it didn't erase the apprehension on their faces. Without a smile or a nod, they passed each other on busy streets and brushed against one another on crowded subways.

The Revolution in 1917 produced the new USSR with a constitution that proclaimed people would be equal, without class stature. The resources and production facilities would be the property of the entire society rather than individuals. Labor would be shared equally, as well, and the benefits of labor would be distributed according to need. This way of life is contrary to the way God intended people to live. Sad to say, I have heard Christians in America promote this same socialistic idea as something our country needs. The deception begins there, and woefully so.

Scripture says in Proverbs 29: 18, *Where there is no vision, the people perish....* To understand the deception one must understand the heart of this scripture within the frameworks of both a democratic and a socialist/communist government. Capitalism is any economic system that uses capital goods in acquiring or producing consumption goods. Consumption goods would include food and drink, which everyone needs to survive. Capital goods are utilized for producing the consumption goods, and this is where the twist occurs between a free democracy and a communist regime. Every nation needs citizens to produce consumption goods or it will fail. How they go about using individuals to produce those goods is the key to understanding the tremendous differences between governments. America allows the economic system to be owned and controlled by private individuals. This is based on the foundation of God's Word and why America's founders implemented it into the U.S. Constitution. Under socialism and communism, the state owns and controls the economy and not the individuals. Fascism allows private owners to own capital goods, but the state still controls them. Human effort is needed to procure a successful capitalist economy. Without labor, no food and drink will be produced. Soviet Russia used force to produce capital goods, which caused a constant floundering economy, whereas America thrived and prospered because force was not factored into the process.

For example, it was almost impossible for an ordinary Soviet citizen to buy a flat, or apartment. The shortage of housing happened after World War II because Russia would not rebuild enough homes, and for this reason families had to live together. The average wait to get a flat was 20 years. Most of the time people could not even get their names on the list unless they had connections. My parents had only a ten-year wait because my grandfather Mendel was a *politruk*. Those families that couldn't get apartments lived in a *communalka*, a 15-room flat that housed about 50 people. Each person was allowed only 65 square feet. Therefore a family of six got a 400 square foot home, sharing kitchen and bathroom. If the parents died, the children remaining and living in the flat did not inherit the apartment. Despite the fact that the people paid for their homes, the government owned them. Because the government controlled all housing and food, any siblings left behind after the parents' deaths often were forced to accept strangers to live with them. Retired military personnel were more fortunate; after 30 years of service they were honored with a free apartment.

American people had ownership of goods, and that ownership gave them rights to reason and think and make decisions; it all goes back to having a vision. Without goals, aspirations and ambition to spur individuals on, they wither and die inside, emotionally and physically. Russia is proof of this.

The huge reason communism rejects religion is because true democracy is patterned after God's Word, an utter contrast to the socialist lifestyle. We see this confirmed in the Ten Commandments. First commandment: *He is One and no other gods shall be set before Him.* In communism God is not acknowledged.

Second commandment: *God forbids idol worship.* A man-centered system like communism rebels against this command because they demand their government to be a replacement for God.

Third commandment: *Do not misuse God's name.* A socialist and communist regime breaks this rule by their acts of persecution toward God's saints and God's Holiness.

Fourth law: *Remember the Sabbath.* God wants us to rest on one day in remembrance of how He rested after completing six-days of creation (Saturday is the historically correct day, but most Christians use Sunday as their day of rest). This law is ignored under a human government.

Honor your parents, the fifth law is horribly discarded and debunked. Karl Marx, one of communism's founders, proclaimed the co-relation of a parent and child was "disgust-ing." He promoted equality through raising children commu-nally, away from the parent. His views were consistent with the way he lived his life, an unfaithful husband to his wife, and a father who allowed two of his six children to starve to death because of his own contempt for industrious labor. Marx's lack of respect for family eventually pushed his other two children to commit suicide.

It was no wonder Russian law forced all women to work. That way the mother was kept from the child, allowing the system to be the "parent." It is not hard to understand Marx's reasoning to hate family when one is made aware of his member-ship in the satanic church. He once wrote that he wished to avenge himself "against the one who rules above."

A communist/socialist society hates the next three com-mandments: *you shall not murder, commit adultery, and steal.* Such a society is motivated to ignore these three righteous policies. A nation that develops offensive weapons of mass destruction without any concern for the welfare of its own people cannot be righteous. Stalin, the Soviet Union's leader between the late 1920s and early 1950s, gained power by stealing and undermining comrades he had been politically associated with. By 1938, he had executed almost every Bolshe-vik leader he had worked with.

Fourteen million peasants died of starvation because of his greedy laws; others were executed for challenging his order to "collectivise" their farms to the state. At least 20 million people were killed under Stalin's repressive rule, not including World War II. No wonder Stalin's name is translated as "man of steel."

The ninth commandment: *You shall not give false testimony against your neighbor,* could not exist in Soviet Russia. The public had to be cautious of what they said against the Communist Party, especially in front of family and friends. Speaking against the party could mean imprisonment. People were either terrified of the KGB or extremely loyal to communism, and either one was a motivation to turn on their own loved ones. I remember as a boy overhearing some of my parents' friends make wisecracks against the government. My mom enjoyed having dinner parties for friends where she would serve delicious bowls of borscht, meatballs, platters of bread, caviar and vodka. This relaxed people and they would open up. Usually though, not until the vodka disappeared. Since our flat was small with only a few rooms I was able to hear most of the conversations. The next morning my parents would warn me to keep quiet about what I might have heard the night before. They took big risks sometimes with those parties, never knowing if a friend might betray them.

Marx saw unequal distribution of wealth as the cause of the sad state of humanity and blamed the tenth commandment: *Thou shalt not covet thy neighbor's goods,* as a threat to his philosophy. He rejected organized religion, which taught that one person could not take the property of another by force. Everything God is, communism isn't. A socialist nation would never allow the Ten Commandments. Taking God out of the government is the first sign that socialism is coming. There is much to pray about these days.

Since communism prohibited Russian citizens the opportunity to follow their dreams, they had to be satisfied with "equal," which meant little. Equal never brought wealth to the masses. After the revolution the new government snatched land, farms and businesses from the owners—those who had labored hard over many years not only to build a home for themselves, but provide food and jobs for their neighbors. The *kolhoz*, meaning collective organization, was brought in to oversee and run production. The *sovhoz*, a different group, was in charge of all the animals that had been confiscated from the farms. Suddenly those who had years of experience running the farms or businesses were replaced by those who did not carry the same talent, heart, experience, or know-how to make them productive. That "equal to all" idea destroyed lives and caused a domino affect of economic woes to ripple across Russia.

The average citizens woke up each morning knowing they would have the same paycheck and position year after year, and not much more than that. I was more fortunate. Although I did not like the military, marrying General Kolesnekov's daughter in my third year at the academy kept me out of the Afghanistan war where many of my comrades died. I was the only cadet in my unit that got transferred to Poland. The rest of my class ended up in the less desirable places—Afghanistan, Siberia, and Middle Russia. Because of my father-in-law, I had the good fortune to dine with generals and partake of the better life that was not available to the majority of the military and general population. Equality to me was only a mirage, and I saw communism as a creed of contradictions.

God in His wisdom knew the makeup of a man and a woman and what made His creations tick. He set up the Bible in a way that would allow the use of our minds and talents, individually.

His system works. His rules and laws keep us holy and in line with His desires, yet they don't stop us from pursuing our dreams. Christ's parable about the talents in Matthew 25 shows this as He exhorts us to go out and use those God-given talents to produce something better, not bury our gifts in the sand. In fact, God expects us to use what He gave us. Because when we do, we are glorifying Him. It delights the Lord to see us succeed and prosper (and I don't mean only financially). That is why the Lord in the parable got angry with the servant who buried his talent. By doing so he dishonored the One who entrusted him with the gift. Communism can actually be a type of this slothful servant.

I implore every person reading this book and who lives in a free democracy, to grasp that great opportunity available to enrich your lives. Put your talents to use. Double and triple them—go reach for the stars. Brush aside fear and shoo away low self-esteem because what you let flow out of you can bring you and the Lord great joy! There are many still today withering under a communist rule who wish they had the same opportunity to open a bakery, publish a book, sing a song, or raise a child.

The United States, patterned after God's biblical foundation, confirms that what God put together thousands of years ago still works today. Our Heavenly Father knew poverty would remain on earth because we live in a fallen world, yet He wanted to establish a system that would still allow people independence and not stifle their opportunities and desires. He came up with a good workable solution to meet the needs of the poor through the simple and gracious act of tithing.

Tithing was set up in the Old Testament to provide for the Levites (those who did the work of the Lord and received no wages), and for the hungry widows, orphans and strangers. Deuteronomy 14 relays God's heart behind tithing; when we read that chapter (in Deuteronomy), we see how giving consisted of goods such as corn, wine, oil or herds and flocks, rather than money, because food is what people need to live on. The act of tithing was also a reminder to the giver of God's provisions. How beautiful to note in scripture that God intended the tithe to be a blessing to the giver as well.

Verse 26 reads, *And thou shalt bestow that money* (their own tithes held aside from the sale of corn or flocks) *for whatsoever thy soul lusteth after, for oxen, or for sheep, or for wine, or for strong drink, or for whatsoever thy soul desireth: and thou shalt eat there before the Lord thy God, and thou shalt rejoice, thou and thine household*. Tithing was a celebration time.

Today it still should be, not under compulsion, but with love. (I have to interject here how sad today that some churches use tithe money to buy crystal chandeliers, padded pews, gold-trimmed podiums, or a cooler air conditioning system instead of helping the poor families sitting in their pews. Jesus sacrificed horribly for us; we should be willing to endure a few discomforts if it means those less fortunate will have groceries or rent money.) Our Lord never demanded distribution of property equally between families or individuals, just a small percentage from each family so others don't go hungry. Tithing is another proof that God never intended a socialist approach to living.

Socialism and communism did not disappear when Russia became a new federation. Its evil tentacles had already wound deep into the heart of American society, and even more so after the September 11, 2001 attacks. Subtle changes are taking place through new laws that are undermining the constitution under the guise of American safety. The new Patriot Act is one, signed on October 26, 2001, and hastily put in effect after 9/11 to fight terrorism. It undermines the Constitution of the United States by compromising the First, Fourth, Fifth and Sixth Amendment rights of citizens and non-citizens alike with such issues as the FBI's new powers of search and surveillance, the over-broad definition of domestic terrorism, the indefinite detention of both citizens and non-citizens without formal charges. The principles of free speech, due process, and equal protection under the law have been seriously destabilized. This is worrisome because most citizens are either not aware of this or too busy to notice. And since the average American doesn't understand life under communist rule and what socialism entails, many are vulnerable to the deception. Since what constitutes a terrorist is vaguely defined in this law, it could be misused to eliminate certain races, religions or classes. Jews were "terrorists" to Hitler. He had his own "Patriot Act" that gave him license to slaughter millions of Jewish people. He hated the Jews and found a way to get rid of them, and he did so by convincing the masses it was right, it was law.

This new American law now gives the government complete rights to spy on citizens, based simply on suspicion, not facts, and those citizens will not know they are being watched. The government is filtering what we type into the search engines on the Internet and can now scrutinize what we read via the library computers. Cameras stare down at us from streetlights, peeking past our car windshields right into our laps. FBI and CIA can now tap phones and computers without demonstrating that each is even being used by a suspect or target of an order. The government may now serve a single wiretap order on any person or entity nationwide, without showing to a court that the particular information or communication to be acquired is relevant to a criminal investigation. And soon our entire lives, everything including medical records, credit information, political and religious affiliation, military records, and more, will be stored in a computer database under a new program called CAPPS II, a program put into effect under the U.S. Department of Transportation. Every time we go to the airport to travel, our private lives can be displayed and made public by the click of an icon.

What I find most disturbing is that the last head of the Russian KGB of the former Soviet Union, General Yevgeni Primakov, has been hired as a consultant to help put this new program together. Clearly warning flags should be waving for U.S. citizens as to why a prominent Russian general with a history of pro-communist views would be put in this position. A man like that doesn't "get over" his love for communism. My own father-in-law, General Kolesnekov, confirmed this to me over and over with his statement, "Communism is everything I am."

As for me, without God changing my own life and freeing my mind, I would still be under the web of that system.

The United States has remained a safe fortress over the last 200-plus years since the constitution was put forth, despite the effects of a civil war, two world wars, the bombing of Pearl Harbor, a depression, and yes, even the latest 9/11 attack;

through all of this the constitution has been its anchor. The excuse that the constitution is too outdated to deal with this "new" kind of war doesn't make any sense at all. Terrorism has been around since the days before Christ. America has had war touch its soil before, and this nation got through it. It has stood through the worst of the worst *because* of the constitution. The only plausible reason why someone would strive so hard to change what works is to further an agenda to change this government. To believe any other reason is hogwash.

Once the constitution is revised, the structure of our way of life is compromised, and thus a new government can step in. Changes occur gradually at first to condition people to accept them, then rapidly, before they get wind of what is really happening. Someday Christians will be "enemies of the state," and this is not just a maybe. Scripture is clear that an antichrist government will rule and persecute God's people. Communism and socialism is the horn of this evil empire. The disintegration of the Iron Curtain did not end the plans of the evil one; he uses what works. I fear that the disintegration of that curtain was a mini-step to further the goal of a one-world totalitarian government.

Christ has been rejected by the U.S. government and schools, has been removed from homes and the workplace; socialism is just a breath away. God is being removed by the subtle workings of a communist/socialist group which has infiltrated this Godly nation to form a new government of its own.

Repentance is vital for our nation's freedom and our freedom to worship the Lord we love so much. I have not always lived in a free world, and I like it very much. I encourage believers to ask God what they can do for Him and for this nation.

We need to pray for our leaders, because they are subject to error, just like any other human. Following any person can be dangerous. Trusting God will guarantee our safety. The possibility of a communist/socialist takeover should frighten Americans more than any terrorist attack. The United States may lose a city and lives but it can still rebuild and move forward, as it always has after wars in the past. But an America revolutionized by socialism will result in a greater destruction than any WMD incident ever could. If another iron curtain goes up, then terrorism will have won because freedom would be lost.

The first bio-labs ordered by Stalin were soon over-shadowed and moved to greater technically advanced, secured, and classified facilities. They included the Institute of Microbiology in Kirov, The Technological Institute of Biologically Active Substances and the Scientific and Production Base in Berdsk, the Institute of Ultra-Pure Biopreparations in St. Petersburg (then Leningrad), and the Institute of Molecular Biology "Vector" located in Koltsovo in the Novosibirsk region. Thus the Leningrad Military Medical Academy, during the time of my study, focused on WMD readiness, military force preparedness, and nuclear/biological/chemical (NBC) protection.

My seven-year medical studies under the Soviet Strategic Rocket Force sector included large WMD-oriented military field exercises in first and second echelons of medical casualty collection facilities and organization of infectious disease

control at field hospitals. Most NBC exercises were located in
the Red Village area about 70 miles outside Leningrad (now St.
Petersburg) and at the Kapustin Yar Nuclear Test Site in the
Astrakhan Region. I had hands-on experience dealing with most
military chemical agents and their effects on the human body
and I received specialized training inside military infectious
disease clinics on aspects of isolation precautions and contact
work with contagious and non-contagious patients.

My role in the army did not consist of development or
research of biological agents for weapons. I learned defensive
and offensive strategies and tactics of global and local warfare,
including weapons of mass destruction and their effects on
civilian and enemy forces. Training was thorough and intense.
Actual diluted chemical agents were often used during practices, risking soldiers' health in order to accomplish an effective
readiness plan for military forces. Soviet Russia did not compromise on national security and safety during communist rule. If
there were cracks in the system, it meant devastation for Russia,
an end for the military superpower. Soldiers were expected to
risk lives to protect the "Motherland." Of course, an army of five
million undertaking such dangerous training could not protect
military personnel from mistakes and injuries, including loss of
life. In the middle of the 1980s, the usual number of soldiers
and officers who died during military service was between
10,000 and 15,000. Today, due to the reduction in the army, the
number is smaller, around 4,000.

During the first two years in the academy, I bunked with 120
other cadets. Barracks were part of a pentagon-shaped building
located on campus. Our rooms were like a web of elongated

hallways. When the alarm sounded at six a.m., we had less than
five minutes to throw on our exercise uniforms, urinate, and
form a line outside before we began an hour of calisthenics and
two-mile sprints. From there we hastily washed at the sinks and
ran for breakfast. We could only use the *banya* (sauna) or
showers on Saturday evenings, and there was no hot water in the
showers.

After the second year all cadets had the good fortune to earn
more privacy, sharing a room in a five-story brick building
outside the "pentagon" with only three other fellows. The third
year granted us daily showers with warmer water. But rules
remained just as rigid. Classes started at eight a.m. sharp.
Lunch had to wait until three o'clock, and only those students
who were fortunate enough to have parents deliver snacks on
the weekends (sometimes I was one of those fortunate guys)
were able to abate their growling stomachs. Hungry or not, full
attention had to be given to the instructors.

BIOLOGICAL WEAPONS

Without exception, lessons on weapons of mass destruction were
implemented into almost every course subject, such as bio-
chemistry, parasitology, microbiology, and field surgery. Weapons of mass destruction fell under three categories: biological,
chemical and nuclear. Biological weapons were developed to
offensively overpower other nations and render them useless.
This is done by attacking the respiratory tracts through inhalation of the agent, and in many cases causing lethal forms of
infectious diseases, with the potential to cause epidemic in
multiple areas. Bio-weapons are pathogenic microorganisms

which are germinated and purified into a special condition, stabilized with classified ingredients that are intended to deliberately disseminate the pathogen by aerosol techniques in largely populated areas. Dissemination of microorganisms can also be accomplished through vectors (transmitted via live insects or animals). This type of transmission is one of the first generations of bio-weaponry and is outdated compared to the aerosol dissemination. But it is still the cheapest and easiest way for a terrorist to accomplish a mission.

Bio-agents are formed in two types: either a replicating type agent such as bacteria, rickettsiae and viruses, or non-replicating type agents such as toxins, active proteins or peptites. Non-replicating agents can be reproduced either through chemical synthesis, solid face protein synthesis, or recombinant expressive techniques, speaking of genetic engineering of organisms. Most militarized bio-agents are artificial and developed for distribution in aerosol forms so that infection can take place through inhalation. Inhalational pathways for bio-agents produce devastating effects and high mortality rates.

Strategic bio-weapons can infect millions of people, causing aggressive and speedy endemics which bring catastrophic outcomes for affected population and health systems. There is also bio-weaponry categorized as operational agents. These are less contagious and aggressive than the strategic weapons, but still cause some deaths. Generally long-term health problems occur. Debilitating the enemy for short periods enables victory for the dispenser. An entire enemy unit hit with high fever, diarrhea, nausea and vomiting is unable to defend itself. Agents such as tularemia, glanders, VEE, legionella, melioidosis, and

measles were used for short deployment. Starting in the 1950s
they were approved only by the Soviet Government to be used in
their army. These same agents were also readied for deployment
against European pro-capitalist nations.

Some of the most virulent agents (anthrax, plague, Marburg,
Ebola and smallpox) were prepared for long distance attacks
against U.S. territories.

Bio-agents are a great advantage for potential terrorist use.
Not only can they render an army unit helpless, as mentioned
above, but they also can be cost effective depending on the
agent's ability and transformation. They are easy to hide without
detection during transportation from one place to another, and
they are easy to produce if scientists have the proper equipment
and know-how on the subject. Even better, the bio-agents can
copycat a naturally occurring disease with prolonged incubation
periods preceding the onset of illness, or slow onset of symptoms. For instance, inhalational anthrax sometimes takes days
or weeks to show symptoms, and once they occur are similar to
the beginning of a chest cold.

Using a zoonotic disease like plague, as a weapon with
natural transmission through fleabites, would be enough to
create serious epidemiological outbreaks. The various ways in
which humans can be infected using biological agents is another
great plus for a potential terrorist attack. The secondary spread
(from person to person) of infection in populations is a benefit
over using nuclear and chemical warfare, especially since there
are no vaccines available to protect against most of the genetically modified bio-weapons. Whole nations can be halted and
destroyed. If the Russian Federation decided to deploy toward

the United States a multiple number of ballistic missiles with a contagious bio-weapon packed inside the warheads, such as plague, Marburg or smallpox, a potentially catastrophic disaster would occur and end our society as we know it today. Not only would there be a shortage of vaccines (useless against genetically modified bio-weapons), antibiotics, and hospital facilities, but health care workers would become victims themselves.

Bio-warfare eliminates the messiness of burning buildings and a contaminated atmosphere, and the slim chances of catching the guilty culprit make this kind of WMD an effective choice. Agents can be colorless and odorless; by the time a person becomes contagious, days or weeks will have gone by before an investigation begins. Tracking down where the virus came from might be impossible, especially if the strain originated in Africa during an outbreak and was secretly taken into another country with the goal of developing more violent strains of bio-weaponry. The U.S. strain of tularemia called SCHU-4, a lethal bio-weapon strain prepared by the U.S. Army, for instance, was stolen by the KGB in the 1950s and adapted for Soviet use. If an attack were used on American cities using this particular strain, without the knowledge that the Russians had gotten hold of the germ, it would be impossible to trace; Russia would remain anonymous.

Incubation periods can take days and weeks before symptoms go beyond the sniffling or mild aching stage. People go to work, they go to parks, they visit grocery stores—and they can infect many who they come in contact with. The goal for spreading is accomplished as the epidemic expands from city to city, state to state, country to country.

Thus the "act of biological terrorism" can decrease life expectancy and life quality by using different types of harmful techniques involving a live pathogenic microorganism or its toxins. Based on logic and predictability of research and development of bio-weapons by terrorist groups, it can readily be said that small terrorist cells, as long as they don't have possession of extremely contagious pathogens like smallpox, Marburg, plague or anthrax, can potentially develop bio-weapons and create small epidemiological outbreaks of that agent. A state or country that supports terrorists with finances, equipment and facilities to produce biological weapons is a serious threat for other nations because they are able to make a more purified product with a better delivery system, which can be catastrophic for the targeted country. A nation, like Russia, China, Cuba, or North Korea, which has a proven track record of secret bio-programs, is the highest danger to global security.

During World War I in Russia, 60 percent of medical personnel became infected with endemic typhus during contact work with patients. To bring about proper training, America can learn from these past outbreaks. Facts, not fear, can help eliminate complete chaos and save many lives. Responding agencies need solid preparation to work as one unit and understand each other's responsibilities. This takes training and commitment, but it can be done even in large cities.

CHEMICAL WARFARE

Chemical warfare is different than biological weapons in that it is typically artificially made and complicated. This type of terrorism is a threat to the security of humankind because it is a more aggressive weapon than the use of modern firearms. In the world of chemical agents, organophosphates are the most toxic agents used on humans. During a battlefield encounter, chemical agents are a good choice for testing WMD preparedness on the enemies. The chemical weapon (CW) is the mass destruction weapon, the action of which is based upon toxic properties of chemical agents. The main components of CW are warfare chemical agents and means of their application (chemical munitions), as well as vehicles, equipment and guiding devices used for delivery of chemical munitions to targets.

Modern high-toxic chemical substances can fall into a terrorist's hands through a wide range of channels, including theft from Russian military depots and arsenals, where thousands of tons of military chemical weapons are still stored today. Other channels for theft from industrial companies associated with anti-gas equipment, military and civilian storage facilities, include factories for production of high-toxic insecticides, herbicides, pharmaceutical preparations of group A, and so forth.

The CW black market is connected with illegal production of weaponized material from Russian military storage facilities and underground laboratories. These extremely toxic agents are non-living organisms, and processed either through industrial or military means.

Militarized chemicals are environmentally stable, have long hazardous life, and can be a danger for anyone who is exposed to them. Sometimes the danger can last for months or years. For example, traces of the blistering agent mustard, used in World War I, are still found in some places in France. Environmentally unstable chemical agents, such as a gaseous form of hydrogen cyanide, change toxic properties so fast that in a few hours they dissipate and are no longer hazardous.

Most chemical agents that are thermally active and volatile can be distributed in liquid or aerosol forms. They don't need to be dispersed like biological agents where particles must be small, between one to ten microns, to pass through the nasal area, catch into the bronchial tree, and float down to the small parts of the lungs. Chemical agents quickly affect the respiratory tract and irritate mucous membranes.

Military chemicals can have thermal or burning effects on the skin. In many cases a person needs only to be close enough to the chemical cloud to receive enough concentration to harm the respiratory tract and skin. For example only ten milligrams of the nerve agent VX applied on the skin will be a lethal dose to 50 percent who receive that application. VX by quantity of weight is 600 times more toxic then chlorine and is considered one of the most toxic military chemicals on earth. The ricin toxin, produced from rice and beans, is at least three times more poisonous then the VX agent, and botulinum toxin is 15,000 times more toxic. In comparison, most bio-agents are not active on the skin (with one exception, micotoxin-type agents like staphylococcal micotoxin 2 has great penetration into the skin to spread toxins inside the body's vessels). Some chemical agents produce symptoms that are short and can show up in seconds. Hydrogen cyanide or cynogen oxyme will cause this kind of reaction. Mustard agents will have a longer onset time (between six to eight hours) before blistering starts appearing on the skin.

NUCLEAR WEAPONS

Of the three WMDs, nuclear weaponry is the major weapon of "mass destruction." Nuclear weapons have incredible, long-term destructive power that travels far beyond the original target. Detonation of a nuclear bomb over a populated area causes immense damage. The degree of damage is dependant upon the distance from the center of the bomb blast, which is called the hypocenter, ground zero or, what I call, the Red Zone. The closer people are to the Red Zone, the greater the destruction. The damage comes from a wave of intense heat from the explosion, pressure from the shock wave created by the blast, radiation, and radioactive fallout (clouds of fine radioactive particles of dust and bomb debris that fall back to the ground). In this zone the searing temperature (up to 500 million degrees Fahrenheit) causes instant vaporization. Burns from the heat, injuries from the flying debris of buildings, and acute exposure to the high radiation cause many fatalities. The radioactive fallout can be long-term and spread a long distance away from the blast, due to prevailing winds. The fallout particles are either inhaled or ingested through the water supply. Health conditions from the fallout include nausea, vomiting and diarrhea, cataracts, hair loss, and loss of blood cells. These conditions often increase the risk of cancer, infertility, and birth defects.

Strategic thermonuclear weapons are measured by megatons; a one-megaton device is equivalent to one million tons of TNT. High yield devices provide catastrophic results to the enemy site. Even a nation with a strong anti-missile system cannot completely prevent a mass number ballistic missile

attack. This means quite a few multi-megatons of missiles will
break through and hit their targets. Theory has it that if many
nuclear bombs are exploding in different parts of the world a
nuclear winter might occur. The great clouds of dust and radioactive material could travel high into Earth's atmosphere,
blocking out sunlight. The reduced level of sunlight could lower
the surface temperature of the planet and reduce photosynthesis
by plants and bacteria, causing the reduction in photosynthesis
and disrupting the food chain, causing mass extinction of life.
Fortunately, terrorists cannot accomplish this scenario. But
superpowers like the U.S. and Russia can.

The observation room in which I remained quarantined for
four weeks in 1983 was one of three Infectious Disease
Clinics, part of the Leningrad Military Medical Academy built
in 1798. They were used by the army for research and to house
sick military personnel. Since this academy was where Stalin
opened the first laboratories for development and research of
biological warfare, the clinics might have been home to those
first labs because of the classified floors restricted from cadets.
Whether or not bio-weaponry was being studied or developed at
the academy during my military career was not made known to
me. I suspect so because of the unusual bout my unit had with
"measles."

Knowing what I know today I might guess that what we
contracted was a genetically modified microorganism, possibly
endemic typhus with recombinant properties of one of the
hemorrhagic virile fevers. Measles causes rash, bloodshot eyes,
fever, but not extreme hemorrhaging of the eyes, swelling and

bruising of the face, yellowing of the skin, or blood in the urine. How we caught it, I don't know, but with 20 sick cadets, an aerosol transmission would seem logical. We could have been used as guinea pigs because we were too inexperienced to know the difference, or we were simply victims of a tragic blunder. I conclude the latter because of the nervous flurry of high-ranking military personnel scurrying in and out of our hospital room. The mystery remains intact though. In 1991, at the end of the communist reign, those three infectious disease clinics, where I spent one long miserable month in bed, were hastily bulldozed to the ground.

Chapter Two

Behind the Honey

How The Black Market Became a Global Problem

Business in New Russia

Afghanistan War & Oil

N icolai was standing upon the foot of the bed when I walked in, his hands rushing up and down the faded yellow wallpaper. Boris leaned forward in the chair next to the bed and silenced me with one thick finger to his mouth. I lowered myself to the edge of the bed and waited. The November chill was still inside the room.

The room, furnished only with a single bed, worn dresser, small wooden table with lamp, and chair, was inside the Hotel #1, located on Lunechartsky Street near the Central Hospital #17 in the newly renamed St. Petersburg. It was common in Russia for businesses and hotels to be recognized by numbers rather than names. Dedicated to Department #5, one of the KGB sectors during the Soviet rule, the hotel now housed offices for public health officials under the Sanitary Unit #122, Ministry of

Russian Health. It was also the class location of Advanced
Training of Medical Personnel, College #1, where I trained
physicians and nurses on medical therapy. The hotel was once a
meeting place and stopover for the KGB, which explained why
many of the rooms remained bugged.

The five-story hotel looked unpretentious, nestled in between the other red brick buildings on the block. The simple
black iron gates, once guarded, now remained open because of
the change in government during that sobering year in 1991.
Viewing the place from the road you would not know it had
become a hang-out for the new mafia-type businessmen sprout-
ing up inside the newly free Russia.

"It's clean," Nicolai muttered and jumped down beside me.
His unkempt moustache overpowered his dark features and
almost hid his mouth that became visible when he laughed. His
dark eyes seemed jittery and flitted from me to Boris, and back
to me as he patted the lump on the bed behind him. Boris
leaned back smiling, his pocked face a red splotch from the
vodka he was drinking. He grabbed the bottle, took a long swig,
held it up and exclaimed, "Time to celebrate!"

As his partner spoke, Nicolai reached back and threw off
the covers, revealing a jumbled pile of rifles, military optics and
grenades. I stared, stunned. *Military firearms!* My business with
Nicolai and Boris had been to sell bulk containers of honey from
Moldova.

My Dad and I had conducted decent business with
Uzbekistan, Moldova, Ukraine and local regions in St. Petersburg, selling fruits, vegetables, liquor, and wood since the
change in government. We had met Nicolai and Boris at the

Hotel #1 through other business acquaintances and had agreed
to help them sell honey from Moldova. We had no idea Nicolai's
honey business was a front for illegal smuggling of military
weapons. Because of my ten-year career in the army, I immediately recognized that pile on the bed to be military armory.

"Nicolai, what is this?" I asked, brushing my hand briskly
through my hair, hoping my widened eyes didn't match the
nervous blues I suddenly felt. I scanned the weapons.

Nicolai grabbed the bottle of vodka from Boris and chugged
for a while before slurring out, "In Moldova we have conflicts
with Prednistrovia because they want to be independent. The
Russian army sold us lots of junk before they left Moldova ...
AK-47 rifles, field mines and grenades ... including propelled
rocket grenades. They penetrate tanks like butter. Good stuff."
He slapped my knee and kept talking. "Boris and I pack the
guns behind the honey. This is where the money is, my friend."

"How do you cross the borders?" I asked, suddenly wanting
a drink myself.

Boris laughed and replied, "Money." He handed me the
vodka.

Everyone's lives changed on that overcast day on August 21,
1991. Crowds had massed throughout Red Square in
Moscow, the majority supporting the leadership of Mikhail
Gorbachev against the stringent communist coup trying to
overthrow his New Russian Federation government. Those who
remained inside glued to their television sets watched the sea of
jubilant demonstrators cheer as military tanks crept stealthily
past them to barricade and protect the White House. Boris

Yeltsin balanced atop one tank with his arms swaying high, waving the new three-color flag. After 74 years of Soviet power, Russia lost her Red. An era of oppressive ideology had been smothered by aspirations for independence. The once-great rolling train of communism that shattered hopeful minds, pilfered faith, and robbed values had run out of fuel. Or had it? Few people were aware that another train was ready to roll in carrying another kind of evil.

The Russian people emerged as adventure seekers, reeling under the thrill that wealth was now possible. They had worked hard all their lives without luxuries, some always hungry, others just getting by. They hoped the new government would bring an end to two-hour waits in line for bread and meat, and bring in more fruit to buy. Young people looked forward to the opportunity to buy American jeans and music. Those who did not have the comforts of the upper military and political classes now faced new opportunities to achieve something better for the first time in their laboriously worn-out lives. New businesses opened and flourished.

However, the rush to get rich overrode vexed consciences and, with no government constitution to control and direct the people, illegal racketeering became a moneymaking venture. The criminal elements found ways to make money from fraudulent sales and by robbing honest business dealers. Those people that opened small kiosks near the subways were forced to pay high percentages to the newly formed criminal-minded bullies or face beatings and torched businesses. Ex-KGB officials and those leaders who had held powerful positions during the Soviet reign became dominant figures in organized crime.

Soviet rule had dominated the country with a strong thread of dictatorship and lies, mind control and false propaganda; tearing down the iron curtain did not unravel the mindset of the masses. It was an every-man-for-himself attitude that prevailed, especially as prices soared and jobs were lost. Factories that once built machinery and equipment for the military screeched to a standstill. The already stunted economy took a tailspin, and even good people did what they had to do to feed their families. And now that their communism "god" was shattered and gone like the wind, there was no moral groundwork to hang onto, nothing left to lean on. Thus the people leaned on the only other god they knew—themselves.

It became clear in the new Russia that once-honest people, friends, and co-workers who were becoming corrupt were being killed; only experienced people with ties to the KGB or police departments lived longer. I didn't want to end up dead. And I worried about my father. We finished up our deal with Nicolai after the experience with the honey sale, and became cautious with whom we did business. But the criminal elements had become a cancer inside Russia. We had to be on guard with everyone; no one could be trusted. Scamming and cheating were profitable. We knew that to continue doing business we had to learn how to deal sensibly with the *mafia* and use them for our benefit without compromising our integrity.

As it was, Nicolai was arrested a few weeks later for throwing a hand grenade at Chechen patrons inside a busy restaurant. Innocent people died from his lack of restraint. I didn't want to become part of that lifestyle. I was a doctor simply trying to supplement the low wage I was being paid.

Organized crime groups flourished and, in some states, became uncontrollable. The high-ranking ex-KGB officials, some educated men with Ph.D.s, ran most of the large criminal organizations that included the sale of oil, gas, precious stones, alcohol, sex and drugs. These groups became so efficient and wealthy that they controlled the borders by paying off Customs workers. In Russia it seemed anyone and everyone could be bought off. The fall of the Soviet State, combined with the escalating poverty, ushered in an evil more dangerous than communism—the international black market.

The weapons Nicolai and Boris had in their possession were sold to Chechnya fighters. Much of the military equipment in those years between 1991 and 1993 was sold at a cheap price to whomever would buy it. Neither the security of the nation nor the results of selling armory to other countries or enemy states concerned the seller. Businessmen emerged from Dagistan hiding automatic machine guns and grenades in 100-pound bags of flour, all purchased from Russian military bases to be resold to Chechnya guerillas, along with large quantities of radioactive material.

When Russia's army pulled out of Poland about the same time, military equipment including short-range missiles and helicopters were left behind and sold on the black market by high-ranking military personnel. I know about this because my unit was the last to pull out of Poland the year before I resigned. Brokers who sold precious metals were soon in business selling radiological and nuclear material. They had no problem getting those materials for trade from underpaid employees working at nuclear plants, military bases and military stockpiles.

Black market business negotiations seldom happen without a *middleman* to oversee the deal. Because most sellers are employees from nuclear plants or nuclear warhead production companies, usually scientists and technologists working around radioactive or chemical sources, they want to ensure their identity is kept secret. The middleman (or "ventilator" as Russians call them) keeps the buyer and seller from knowing each other's identity. Like a real estate agent, he makes sure the transaction is processed smoothly, especially because sales are taking place inside and outside Russia. He "trades air" between the two parties, becoming the mediator to ensure the seller gives quality product and the buyer finalizes the deal. Today these illegal business people have become masterminds at smuggling WMD and drugs. The middleman takes grave risks, knowing he can lose his life if too much information is let out about the buyer, or he becomes embroiled in the sale of bad material. The money outweighs the risks—and risks don't end there.

Transporting toxic military agents on the black market can be very dangerous. Material may be transported in powder or solid pieces inside low-grade stainless steel pipes instead of the lead containers necessary to protect against ionizing gamma waves. Or different radiological isotopes, such as cesium-137 or cobalt-60, can be delivered in the wrong containers. If such material has a strong radiation field, the person transporting the material might receive unnecessary doses of radiation. The transporter then develops acute radiation syndrome and ends up in an emergency room. The Russian FSB (Federal Security Bureau) will investigate if the transporter cannot explain the exposure to high levels of radiation.

Chloropicrin, a vomiting agent and a highly toxic military chemical partially formulated for usage as a pesticide, delivered in aerosol form, can spread and contaminate a city from over two miles away. To understand the potency of this agent: if it was delivered using a correct dispersal device, it would cause tens of thousands of casualties from simple inhalation. Selling on the black market is a hazardous risk to every city and town that finds itself a backdrop to an illegal chemical or biological weapon convoy. Bigger organizations use protective equipment and take the steps for proper delivery. Still, they are even more dangerous, selling and buying for terrorists and states desiring to do more than destroy one city.

On June 24, 2003 two Russian businessmen were caught by the FSB transporting Chloropicrin into the city of Kursk. This was the second time in one year that private businesses purchased or stole military agents from military stockpiling areas and transported the highly toxic agents cross country, with the goal to sell them to the Chechnya Republic. Muslim militants, on a quest to secure independence from the New Russia, relocated to the big Russian cities and opened unlawful businesses to help build up their network to fight against Russia. Many Russian citizens who felt Russia was discriminating against the Chechnya Republic worked willingly to help them. So it was that these two Russian men were part of those citizens who wanted to liberate Chechnya. The arrests occurred during the time the men were pulling the 150-liter container out of their truck.

The concentration of this chemical in 0.01 milligrams per liter will irritate nasal and bronchial mucous membranes as well as make the eyes feel as if they were filled with sand. Concentration level of 0.05 milligrams per liter will cause intense nausea, vomiting, and stupor. In a few hours possible pulmonary edema and alveolar hemorrhaging can occur in the lungs. A concentration of about 20 milligrams per liter for one person is lethal; 150 liters of this agent properly dispersed in correct concentration levels can kill several thousands of people. In the Soviet Army this agent was used to train soldiers during exercises to learn the efficiency of gas masks. Although the dosage used was minimal, many soldiers got sick during training.

The Russian Ministry of Internal Affairs agrees that 60 percent of the Russian economy is controlled by criminal organizations. The amount of money misused from Russia could amount to as much as $100 billion dollars over the four-year period from 1990 to 1994. Over four trillion rubles ($800,000,000) were misappropriated from Russian banks alone between 1993 and 1994. Since 1991 these criminal groups have become a dominant and sophisticated force, causing a serious threat and concern to many nations. Today selling weapons of mass destruction goes beyond making money; the sales are being used for political manipulation and economical influence. Countries that have material and technology to develop weapons of mass destruction become confident enough to dictate threats to other nations.

As I write this, over 20 of Russia's largest crime syndicates are estimated to operate in the United States. Around 300 cases are under investigation for illegal business, such as auto theft rings and insurance scams. A handful are involved in international black market.

One example of an international criminal business that dodges the legal system comes from Hungary. A powerful man, Boris Mogilevich, known as "Brainy Don," who is tracked by the FBI, works illegal business within the United States, Russia, Israel, Ukraine and some African countries. An influential man with four citizenships, "Brainy Don" traffics nuclear materials, drugs, prostitutes, precious gems, and stolen art. His personal wealth is estimated at over $200 million cash. His contract hit squads operate in both Europe and America, and he controls everything that goes in and out of Moscow's Sheremetyevo International Airport. He was able to legally purchase almost the entire Hungarian armaments industry, jeopardizing the war against terrorism. In 1994 he procured a license enabling him to buy and sell weapons, thus making him a legitimate armaments manufacturer. His connections continue into the U.S. Two of his Russian buddies from New York City met in Los Angeles to plot the dumping of American toxic waste in Russia, proposing that the Red Mafia would dispose of the toxic waste in the Chernobyl region through "payoffs" to the decontamination authorities there.

Criminal groups work daily in the black market for the best profits, because they know they have a good chance of getting away with it. Police arrest only ten to 15 percent of the black market dealers. There have been over 160 known attempts to smuggle radioactive material out of the former Soviet Union since 1992. Who knows exactly how many more attempts were made, and how many succeeded?

The U.S. government has documented one of the largest known transactions ever made in the history of the WMD radiological/nuclear black market—one that happened in the capital city of Vilnius, Lithuania in May 1993. The police department was alerted to high numbers of unexplainable killings in the city. Using their local contacts within the different mafia groups, they discovered a shipment had come into Vilnius and was being hidden by outsiders (other organized criminal groups). Soon after that, a mysterious caller told the police department to look in the basement of the Lithuanian Joint-Stock Innovation Bank.

The police found, stacked in one dark corner, 27 wooden crates, all greenish-gray in color with unusual markings stamped on the side. Because Lithuanian police had been a part of the Soviet Union, they could read from the text that the shipment came from Russian military bases. When the crates were opened, the contents revealed thousands of peculiarly shaped parts made from a gunmetal-gray material. Shipping papers inside identified the parts as a radioactive material called beryllium.

Beryllium is used as an efficient neutron reflector in modern bomb designs to greatly increase the weapon's explosive power and reduce the amount of fissile material the bomb designer needs. The explosive power of fission trigger is boosted to several kilotons by the use of a beryllium reflector. In the late 1980s, countries such as India were trying to develop the hydrogen bomb; the Indian government was searching hard for beryllium. Based on the close relations India had with the USSR, it might have been easy for them to acquire this type of material. Today the biggest purchases of WMD are occurring in pro-communist and pro-Islamic nations.

The total amount of material found that day in Vilnius was 4.4 metric tons. Partial shipment of that amount was found in another bank basement in the city of Kaunas. This incident marked the first evidence of how fast criminal organized groups were smuggling nuclear related materials out of Russia. Multiple countries were involved in the investigation, including the United States. The conclusion was that the material had come from one of the classified military bases located in Sverdlovsk, Siberia. The smuggling process of such a hefty quantity of material shows how organized different criminal groups can work together. The starting point of this venture began with local mafia who were in close contact with the main criminal syndicates from Moscow and St. Petersburg. Locals in Sverdlovsk had purchased the material using phony orders from the Institute of Physics and Power Engineering located in Yekaterinburg in the Sverdlovsk region. Obviously there were internal connections, and it was discovered that the deal also involved trading firms in Yekaterinburg.

As the deal progressed, the material was transported by truck from Yekaterinburg to Moscow. Yuri Alexeyev, who was responsible for shipment and one of the racketeers handling the payment, received the material in Moscow. Unable to sell the stuff, it was transported back to Yekaterinburg, and in June 1992 they found a buyer. The beryllium then was flown to Vilnius. Destination was to be Switzerland. The buyer, H-Kontor, a company in Klagenfurt, Austria, was ready to purchase this shipment for $2.7 million. But this company was only the middleman. They were planning to resell the beryllium for $24 million to the final buyer, probably from the Middle East region. Interpol (International Police) found there was a partner working with the H-Kontor firm—called ATRACO—thought to be based in the Italian city of Brescia and who knew the buyer in Zurich. Interpol was unable to identify the final buyer. Mafia from four countries were involved in this sour deal. But the scary point is that they managed to transport the large shipment across several borders without any problems.

The Russian government refused to accept the material as theirs, despite the markings on the boxes. Major General Andrei Terekhov, head of the Russian Interior Ministry and directorate responsible for guarding nuclear facilities, simply said, "It is impossible to speak of the existence of mafia groups specializing in the theft of radioactive materials."

America's solution was to confiscate the shipment. But Lithuania had no laws controlling beryllium. In March 1994, the Lithuanian Prime Minister Slezevicius wrote an official letter to then Russian Prime Minister Victor Chernomyrdin asking Moscow to take charge of that shipment. Russia refused. In May 1994, the Lithuanian government returned the beryllium to the bank. In 1997, after the Joint-Stock Innovation Bank went out of business, about four tons were transported to an undisclosed location.

Soon after Nicolai was arrested, my father and I put in a bid to purchase, as part holders or corporate owners, a three-story factory that had recently gone onto the government auction list. The factory, called the Fortune Factory, sat beside the Kalimaga Railway Station in the southern area of St. Petersburg. During Soviet rule, the 50,000-square-foot depot was storehouse for large containers of fruits and vegetables brought in daily on the trains. The tan brick complex, divided inside to separate the offices from the storage area, was dotted with a few windows strategically located on the office side of the second and third floors. The ground floor beneath the offices housed a giant high-tech "laser eye" developed by Major Romanov of Leningrad. The stainless steel laser scanned tons of products daily to ensure spoiled vegetables or fruits were not delivered into the city. On the storage side, stainless steel shelves ascended three stories high from the concrete floor.

When my Father and I won the bid, only 30 people re-mained working inside the factory, a handful compared to the hundreds who had been employed before the new Russian Federation took over. The slow moving trains no longer carried in products. The offices were vacant, the "laser eye" inane in a warehouse that echoed the emptiness of steel. Business had come to a standstill. Our plan was to bring it back to life, renting the storage space and using the train system to build up production for private businesses. Our excitement was growing as we procured new clients to fill up the warehouse.

The "Tombovsky" mafia is part of the OCG (Organized Criminal Group) in Russia. Birthed in the city of Tombov in the early 1980s, this polished group controls parts of St. Petersburg ports, airports, and large businesses. In 1992 Vladimir Kumarin was the leader.

It was impossible to do business without their approval. My Dad and I got that approval through my acquaintance with Senya, a 25-year-old OCG lieutenant I had met a year earlier doing business in the Ukraine. Senya liked the fast-paced perilous work mafia involvement offered. He was a likeable chap, short and stocky, strong, always dressed impeccably in dark suits and expensive ties. He seldom used hand or facial gestures when he spoke; his portentous eyes relayed perfectly what he said, sometimes even before he uttered a word. My father agreed to let his organization use some of the office and storage space in return that we be left alone to run the business our way. But the director, Nicolai Pechenkin, also part "holder" and a man who had overseen the factory for many years, was approached by a Chechnya criminal group. They offered to pay him a good wad of cash if he would rent the factory to them so that they could store 3,000 tons of onions. Mr. Pechenkin, a tall, flabby man in his late 50s was in full agreement with us during bid negotiations. My dad had done all the legwork to finalize the deal, and Mr. Pechenkin seemed equally pleased. But the weary director fell into the category of people who couldn't resist the temptation to obtain fast money. Justifying the deal by the fact he had been director for ten years, he used it as leverage to undermine our plans.

Onions were a front for the Chechnya mafia's illegal weapons and drug racketeer. We did not find out about the deal until our next visit to the warehouse. The smell of rotten onions filled our noses before we even saw the containers of oozing vegetables stacked in rows all over our storehouse. The director refused to talk about it because he was unwilling to split what he had acquired through the deal. To remove the seepage would have cost us more money then we could afford.

I spoke to Senya about what happened, hoping the Tombovsky group might take care of the matter so that my dad

and I would not lose our business. But they were more inter-
ested in securing the huge Baltisky beer factory at the time, and
did not want to risk a fight with the Chechnya group over a *dead*
factory, especially since the Fortune Factory sat in Chechnya
mafia territory. Senya relayed this information to me and I knew
we had lost the factory. This was my dad's chance to accomplish
a workable business, doing what he was good at. He was so
excited the day he won the bid and this would wound him.

The next day after I spoke with my father, he received a
phone call from a frantic factory worker. The director had been
beaten in his apartment with a pipe the night before by two of
Senya's bulls. Senya, without the support of the OCG, had
ordered the attack on his own. Still, the Chechnya mafia had
claim of the complex and my father had to walk away.

M any officers and soldiers from the Afghanistan war ended
up at the military academy in Leningrad. While I was a
young medical cadet, I overheard some of those wounded
soldiers discussing huge drug smuggling operations taking place
out of Afghanistan into Russia. Boredom brought out loose
tongues. They talked about special pathways secured by the
Soviets to ship out the drugs, and they told about loads of Soviet
weapons being sold to the local pro-communist Afghan guerillas, and even to the Mujahadeen, who they were fighting
against. The selling of weaponry could easily be signed off and
explained as "lost" during battle.

Some of those hospitalized men had taken ill from the
Russian military chemical agents used by their own Soviet
Army against the Afghan rebels. Ignoring the treaty banning the

use of the chemical and biological agents that the Russian
military had created and perfected, the agents were being
secretly dispersed on a regular basis to build a database on their
efficiency and productivity. Such tests included chemical
agents—binary gasses, choking agents, nerve agents and the
latest Soviet military development group A-232 agents such as
novitchoke-5 (translated "newest") which are still a highly
classified military chemical in Russia. Some organic phosphates
were used in the mountains to draw rebels out of the caves.
Many of these agents were used during Russian/Chechen
conflicts in the Caucasian regions by the Russian military. (War
is a good place to test weapons, and I wouldn't be surprised if
Russia is using the war in Iraq as an opportunity to do the
same.)

The Afghan war began when the Soviet Communist Party
became nervous about losing power over the Afghani people.
They had worked hard to establish their pro-communist government inside that country in the 1970s. What could and should
have been a short war lagged on for ten years. Although the
Americans funded and created the Al Qaeda and supplied
Osama bin Laden with plenty of weapons to build an army that
would thwart Soviet soldiers, Russia had a powerful military.
But Russia was profiting well from that war. Opium covers about
60,000 acres of land in Afghanistan, which can produce 350
tons of heroin a year. High Russian military officials based in
Afghanistan transported hundreds of pounds of heroin through
Tajikistan using civil transport, prompting the Soviet Union to
increase border patrols. Weapons, drugs and precious stones
(lazuret was being mined and controlled by the Soviet military

in some Afghan locations) were smuggled in and out of Russia as a multi-million dollar industry that would create a giant foundation for a strong illegal black market in Russia. The rumors I heard during my days as a cadet have proven true today by organizations in Russia who are investigating the illegal and corrupt activities that took place within the Soviet Army by high-ranking commanders during the war.

Since the early 1990s, Russian news sources reveal about 150 Russian generals and admirals performed criminal activities, extracting about $10 billion from the Russian Federation. In comparison, between 1970 and 1980 there were 3,200 generals and admirals in the Soviet Army. Only 17 of those during that period were prosecuted for crimes. Of the 150 mentioned above, only a few were imprisoned; the rest were given amnesty by the Russian military courts—thus the reason corruption and the international black market flourishes today. For example, in 1992 General Lieutenant S.U. Beppaev, deputy chief commander of Russian ground forces in the Caucasian region, organized mass illegal sales transactions of Russian military armory to guerilla organizations in Chechnya. He was military chief commissioner in Dagistan when he was arraigned in 1998. General Major Gladeshev, chief commander of the Russian Ground Force division, was prosecuted in 1996 for his illegal escapades in 1993. He had organized the sale and transportation of mass military weapons, including artillery shells, propailed (anti-tank) grenades, and automatic rifles to the militia groups in the Adjaria Caucasian region without any directives or documents from upper echelon. His hearing was blocked by the military.

The international black market is an interwoven tapestry of hungry common folk, greedy military officials, power-hungry organized groups, and politically pressured governments. Destroying the core might be impossible. Even though the threat of large terrorist attacks looms over the world due to the continued and uncontrollable black market policies, politics and money rule the day. And wars can be part of this tapestry.

The first few months of working for the American government on counter-terrorism brought me humbly to my knees. I was disturbed to see reports and statistics on numerous terrorists and cells, their goals to destroy, their financial gains with which to do so, and the ease with which they could cross borders to bring about their deadly plans. Yet, I couldn't help but feel awe at the obvious proof that God had things in control. With the possibility of so much to go wrong, with the odds going against the U.S. as a nation, only a supernatural intervention could explain why the world has not self-destructed. How evident it is to see how God has shielded America, especially in light of the mass amounts of biological and nuclear weapons developed over the last 60 years.

In the natural mind there is much to fear. But when you see the whole picture, as I sometimes do at work, Godly respect replaces the fear. Yes, more terrorist attacks might take place, but God is still in control. He was in control the morning that first plane hit the World Trade Center in New York. We see loss of many lives and great turmoil over why He could allow so many to die. But the Christian walk is a walk of faith. And when trials like these appear out of nowhere, safety and assurance can come only through the exercising of our faith. God sees the big picture—we see "through a glass darkly." Our perspective is one-sided. We do not see into the spiritual realm now, limiting our perception and understanding. This is where faith must reside—inside us. Trusting God that He was and is in control is the right way to find solace in dark times. We cannot see the demons and angels fighting over our souls and over nations. We do not see those loved ones who have died, now happily in the presence of our Creator. We are locked in a place where pain and sadness prevail. And since we cannot see as those dear saints now see, we must believe God has a greater purpose.

This earth is a waiting room. The day will come when a door will open, and Christ will call out our name. On the morning of September 11, 2001, many doors opened; the Lord stood there calling them to Him. Although loved ones on earth saw an end to those who died, it was a beginning for them, a glorious new life where sorrow has no existence. Those people now with the Lord know why God allowed what He did, but many of us here on earth still do not understand. Rightly so, it was an ugly disaster. But faith can be our foundation of strength to deal with the loss. It might not give us answers now, but someday it will.

It is hard for people who have lost loved ones to see any good come from death. But let me put that pain into His viewpoint through the scripture in John 12, verse 24: *Except a corn of wheat fall into the ground and die, it abideth alone: but if it die, it bringeth forth much fruit.* God wants us to know that good can come out of tragedy. Sometimes death is necessary to bring forth additional fruit. And this is where faith comes in—because we might not know completely what good came out of that tragedy until we meet our loved ones again in glory.

Many times we do see fruit within the days, weeks, or years after a tragedy. For example, recently I saw a story on the news about a young college student who killed a Christian mother and her six-year-old daughter while he was drag racing his car. The husband, who lost his wife and only daughter, could not be consoled. For three years he sought revenge. He would not sleep until he saw the killer behind bars. But God had other plans for this heartbroken man who felt God betrayed him. The change began during the court proceedings as the widower watched the 19-year-old "killer" and his family tremble out of fear. It was then that the older man began to consider this kid's life and what imprisonment would do to that family. He asked his attorney to arrange a meeting with the young man.

The grieving husband and father did not expect any fruit would ever come from the loss of his family. But through that meeting the first bud popped forth. That college kid cried with deep remorse at what he had done, and the older man responded with great forgiveness. From there the fruit kept growing. The husband asked the judge to lighten the sentence. Instead of a possible 30-year sentence behind bars, the young man was required 500 hours of community service to speak about the dangers of car racing.

Today, both men, united through a tragedy, travel across America together as one heart, speaking to young people in schools and warning them of the dangers of selfish driving. The end result of this awful tragedy is something only God could have accomplished. A wife and child are gone, but not really. Their memory lives on through those students who hear the story. The husband grieves, but he knows he will see them again. Meanwhile, the student responsible for the deaths of a mother and daughter now saves lives.

The greatest fulfillment of John 12: 24 is through Christ's death for us on the cross. Christ died in a barbaric way, victim of the greatest terrorist plot ever. As Jesus' mother watched her Son nailed to that tree, she did not understand what good could come from it. Her heart broke, as did all who loved Him. The Father saw the bigger picture, the need to save lives through His son's sacrifice. Christ's death produced great fruit —eternal life in His presence for each of us. When we lose a loved one, remembering Christ's death is a comfort, because He left this earth too, left the waiting room and went into heaven—where He now greets all who are ready to walk through His open door. We received the greatest gift of salvation through that single *terrorist* act. God *is* in control, even when it seems He is not.

(A gentle reminder that loss is not easy. Jesus wept when His friend Lazarus died. Faith does not mean we squelch emotions. Grieving is part of the healing process. God gave us emotions, and when we are frail and broken, we should lean on Jesus and let those emotions have their way. Tears are a good coping mechanism.)

War is seldom caused by accident. If we look back in history, we find that wars usually occur for certain purposes of which the general public is not aware at the time. President Franklin D. Roosevelt said, "In politics, nothing happens by accident. If it happens, it was planned that way."

The Afghanistan war was political game between communism and capitalism. Neither the United States nor the Soviet

Union were concerned with winning or losing; both used war for political and financial gain. That same political ping pong game started much earlier in Vietnam in the 1960s and lasted ten years. Companies profited on both sides, thus the reason for a slow drawn-out paddling between Russia and America.

It is evident through the short time the American military was able to secure Afghanistan in 2001 after the September 11 terrorist attack, that the United States had planned a war with Afghanistan way before that World Trade Center assault. The takeover was too swift and too calculated. Anyone with common sense and the mindset to avoid being sideswiped by the media could not help but question the amazingly swift victory. Deputy Defense Secretary Paul Wolfowitz claimed in a television interview on November 18 that the U.S. military took only three weeks to plan the military onslaught. Wow! But evidence shows otherwise. Throughout the years prior to the 9/11 attack, the United States government had reason and purpose to overthrow Afghanistan. Careful study of America's interest in oil reveals it is most probable to surmise that if the 9/11 attack had not happened, the United States would have found another reason for that quick war. In 1991, after the defeat of Iraq in the Persian Gulf War, *Newsweek* magazine published an article reporting that the U.S. military was preparing an operation in Kazakhstan modeled on the Operation Desert Shield deployment in Saudi Arabia, Kuwait and Iraq. That news piece was titled, *"Operation Steppe Shield."*

The lifting of the Iron Curtain in 1991 provided the opportunity for American power to enter Central Asia, but the vast oil and gas reserves provided the motivation. Interesting to note is that in the past decade new oil reserves were discovered in the northeast Caspian (Kazakhstan) and in Turkmenistan, near the southeast Caspian. American oil companies and the U.S. government knew the Persian Gulf region was unstable, and saw the Caspian and Central Asia area as a substitute source for oil. U.S. troops began combined operations with U.S. Special Forces with Kazakhstan in 1997 and with Uzbekistan a year later. Their mission was to train to function in the mountain regions in the southern part of Kyrgyzstan, Tajikistan and northern Afghanistan. American officials did not want to employ the Russian pipeline system or use the route across Iran to the Persian Gulf to transport the oil and gas to the world market. Therefore, the U.S.-based Unocal oil company pushed the alternative route through Afghanistan hard and pursued negotiations with the Taliban regime. The bombing of U.S. embassies in Kenya and Tanzania by Osama bin Laden in 1998, caused the Clinton administration to launch cruise missile attacks on bin Laden's training camps in Eastern Afghanistan, ending discussions. It seems obvious through the meeting between Assistant Secretary of State Karl E. Inderfurth and State Department counter terrorism chief Michael Sheehan with Taliban's deputy foreign minister Abdul Jalil in Islamabad, Pakistan, that the U.S. was warming for war. Both American state officials warned Jalil that the United States would hold Afghanistan responsible for any future terrorist attacks by bin Laden.

The Clinton administration and Nawaz Sharif, then prime minister of Pakistan, decided on a joint covert operation to kill Osama bin Laden in 1999. (This tidbit was reported in the *Washington Post* on October 3, 2001.) But that operation was aborted on October 12, 1999 because of the overthrow of Sharif by a military coup headed by General Pervez Musharraf.

When President George Bush came to office, the British-based news source *Jane's International Security* reported on March 15, 2001 that the new American administration was laboring with India, Iran and Russia "in a concerted front against Afghanistan's Taliban regime."

From this small amount of documented information you are reading here, it is easy to see that wars usually are fought for reasons that involve business and financial profit ... such as the sale of oil. There is always a certain amount of racketeering involved in wars, and both sides will be guilty of this. So when a nation can make billions of dollars through the selling of drugs and weaponry—or oil—it is not difficult to understand how illegal activities flourish without too much interference.

After the fiasco with Senya and the onions in the warehouse, I steered clear of Senya as much as I could. He seemed as unrestrained as Nicolai and I didn't want to become part of his illegal hustle. But our paths crossed often at Hotel #1 where he would relay stories of the buying and selling of WMD material via black *Volgas* down dusty roads. He liked to brag about his job, confident that I knew better than to relay what he told me.

The last time I saw him was in July 1993, soon after I had dedicated my life to Christ. He was with his bulls inside the St. Petersburg Airport transporting illegal shipments to Germany. The OCG criminal group and most mafia organizations had V.I.P. entrances to the airplanes. This open arrangement with

Customs and the airlines is why Senya's group stood beside Customs so self-assured.

I was at the airport to greet my lovely new wife June, who was arriving from Seattle, of the United States of America. We had been married that previous May in St. Petersburg, and she had returned from America to spend a whole month with me and to help me finalize my immigration paperwork at the embassy. Because my bride was a U.S. citizen, I didn't tell Senya about my marriage. I didn't want her trailed or approached. But he spotted me and waved me over.

He was visibly upset, too upset to question me as to why I was there. His eyes were red-rimmed as he began talking in hushed tones.

"Igor, can you believe that Muslim mafia killed three of our guys? Three days ago five of their thugs forced their way into our office and shot them down with automatic rifles. We are retaliating next week … and believe me it will be a good one!" His eyes seethed, but he remained poised and polished, his right hand not far from the gun concealed under his arm.

We talked for a while longer before he apologized for not being able to give me a ride, and then he left. Years later Senya became headline news when he and part of the Tombov mafia were caught and prosecuted by the Russian Federation for mass killings and selling of illegal weapons. I do not doubt that if he is still alive he is probably out now and doing the same things.

Chapter Three

Weapons of Mass Deception

THE MIND BENDERS
SOWING SEEDS OF HATRED
MIND CONTROL (RUSSIA & AMERICA)
FAITH—WEAPON AGAINST BRAINWASHING

T he crooked seams in my gray uniform pants scratched my thighs, and the top two gold buttons on my crisp white shirt kept popping out of the too-big buttonholes. Yet I remained motionless alongside my classmates on stage, knowing that today would be the last time I would ever have to wear the itchy things again. I was 13 years of age, it was May 1978, and I was finally graduating out of the Young Pioneers. This meant I would soon become a member of the *Komsomol*, or young adult Communist Youth group—which required no uniforms.

My parents sat in the audience, looking as impatient as I felt. My teacher, a retired military colonel, continued his long chatter on the great ideals of communism. As he droned on, I felt as though the huge poster of Lenin hanging on the wall behind us was sitting on my shoulders.

"There is a teen organization in America called Boy Scouts that is using special agents to train children how to commit crimes, lie to their parents and become part of their evil capitalism," he recited. The dark circles under the colonel's bloodshot eyes matched his washed-out appearance. He leaned over the podium and raised his voice, while his right hand played tag with the creases zigzagging across his forehead. "Children born in the Soviet Union are the luckiest children in the world! Russia cares for us—they feed us, put us through college, and provide us with employment. Our wealthy enemy does not do this. Their rich leave the poor to die in the streets."

I sensed the colonel was not a happy man. His entire gloomy presence seemed to oppose the boisterous patriotic messages he constantly threw at us. With all the propaganda I had been privy to, I didn't dare question the unsettling feelings that often rose up inside me. I ultimately ignored any contradictions I might see or hear. It was safer and easier to follow the crowd. Going against the grain of communist society wasn't something a person wanted to chance. Too many dissidents already sat in prisons. The act of evaluating was not tolerated within our minds; reasoning was allowed only if it benefited the communist ideology. Our minds were the property of the state, and not until I became a Christian would I understand the full impact of how much of my mind the state had taken.

From the time Russian children entered daycare or preschool, they were taught about the "loving Grandfather Lenin." And once they were enrolled in school, all youngsters from the ages six to eight were enrolled into the *Octobrenok*, a patriotic organization meaning "Octobers." All young (Leninites) were required to wear a Lenin baby-face profile pin.

At eight years of age, the school kids graduated into another group called the Pioneers. Here they were initiated into the group with excursions to historical places exalting the revolution. My initiation took place at the Artillery Museum in Leningrad. Like the Boy Scouts, the Pioneers engaged in lots of activities, except our organization was mandatory and part of school curriculum. We trained ten hours a week in military exercise, often marching, one leg up, one leg down, in unison down the school halls while bellowing out our honorable communistic songs. The red scarves tied around our crisp white collars symbolized the blood of all the *so-called* Soviet heroes who had died fighting for communism.

One such hero that we sang about was Pavlik Morozov, a devout communist teenager who betrayed his own father for hiding grain from the communist authorities who wanted to confiscate it. The USSR honored Pavlik with a lifelike statue erected in the Krasnaya Presnya district in Moscow. He was eventually murdered by his own grandfather after his father died in the GULAG.

The Komsomol was for students between the ages of 14 and 25. It was a pre-military pro-communistic organization meaning "young communist." To ever hope to get ahead in the Soviet Union, or to become part of the communist party, students had to belong to the Komsomol. This group promoted the building of Russia's industrial complex by training the "future communists of tomorrow." Young men and women were sent to military campuses for actual defense training and to rural farmlands to learn about agriculture. We were required to wear a small pin of Lenin's face on our clothes, and we were issued special passports. We were also responsible to pay taxes to keep the passports updated.

"Are you ready to work and defend?" the sweating colonel shouted from the platform, in reference to "the enemy."

We stood and simultaneously tilted our arms to our foreheads and responded with a loud, "Always ready!"

The ceremony closed with the singing of Soviet Russia's national hymn. I was glad no one could read my thoughts, because my heart was not into the lyrics. Despite my lack of enthusiasm, that constant prattle of hate was already polluting my mind.

Propaganda was a huge force for mass mind control of populations in Soviet Russia. Through television movies and other media, people were kept abreast of the awful "atrocities of the west." Fed with hate, Russians bought into the communist brainwash because they were given a promise of being a superpower nation, another Roman Empire. Their patriotism blinded them from truth. As the United States rivaled them, Russia became jealous and hatred grew.

Even after the New Russian Federation came to power in 1991 there was not a change in the thinking of the majority of people toward America. Their blind patriotism had become possessive and obsessive, bred on lies and driven by greed. Russia has lost its superpower status; people now live in poverty; hopelessness grows like a cancer alongside corruption and crime. The current polls in Russia reveal about 60 percent of the people agree with the thinking behind the mass murders at the World Trade Center in 2001, simply because they have been programmed too well to hate the West. If a Russian leader comes along who can promise to give them back their super-power status, how easily another Stalin could rise to power, voted in by a majority landslide.

An example of the hatred sown inside the Russian population is best seen through the action of the Soviet army in 1945 after they took Berlin. Marshall Georgi Zhukov told the soldiers to do whatever they wanted in that city. For five days they plundered, raped women, and killed.

Edward Lemonov, a Russian leader of today's National Bolshevik Party, provides a glimpse of the tenacious power of communist mind control in his statement, "I never remember that I spoke with a pro-American position because, for a conservative Russian, anti-Americanism is as natural as love to the Motherland (Russia)... and in these feelings, the heart gets fed well."

Mikhail Suslov, the now-deceased Soviet ideologist who was influential in Nikita Khrushchev's demise and Brezhnev's rise to power, illuminates that hate mindset through a story told by his son-in-law. Inside Suslov's flat a giant map of the world hung on one wall with numerous little red flags on stickpins stuck into names of various cities from east to west and north to south. Often whenever the son-in-law would visit, Suslov's ritual would be to hold one of those tiny red flags in front of him, close his eyes, and jab it into the map. Wherever it landed, he would exclaim, "And here is where *we* are building socialism!" He was confident that the communist ideology was spreading, and his proof was on the map.

Altering the minds of the masses was Russia's way to take over the world and become the only superpower. No wonder the Soviet government spent millions of dollars to keep the communistic party alive in the U.S. for decades. Mind control must be understood as a serious threat to freedom. It is always the first weapon used to secure a socialist reign or dictatorship rule. Let's not forget how quickly Nazi Germany convinced the masses to embrace fascism.

Russian citizens did not stop hating Americans when the Iron Curtain was demolished. Mind-altering techniques are effective and not easy to unravel. Mind control is a vicious weapon and must be understood as such in order to fight its disturbing and deceiving influence. Mind control carries the great ability of governments, military, political, or terrorist groups to turn the minds of whole population, without its citizens having a clue as to what is going on.

In this time of brilliant technological advancements, people cannot be naive about the potential of mind control. A quick search under "mind control" on the Internet will reveal that even the American government is not in the ice age of mind control technologies of the masses. According to documents within the United Nations the United States has been working for some time with Russian scientists on a newly developed psychotronic weapon. The decade-long research on this computerized acoustic type mind control device is said to be capable of implanting thoughts into a person's mind without that person being aware of the source of the thought. Sound far-fetched? Not at all, these devices have already been tested against civilians during the Afghanistan conflict, and they are documented to be a positive approach in strengthening a nation's own military.

For example, mind control is a great resource to help soldiers who are fighting on the front lines handle fear. Is this the intention for developing such a weapon by Russia, a nation that believes in and has had an excellent history of implementing mind control techniques on the masses? Or is it being studied for a bigger purpose? It can be a dandy weapon to manipulate an entire army—or population.

Consider the recent "flash mob" fad, also called "smart mobs" or "swarming." These are ways of hitting out at the world by means of the technology of mobile communication (cell phones) and computing devices. Using a sophisticated text messaging network, people all over the world are allowing themselves to be led by the nose by a mysterious leader or leaders. This swarming behavior is affecting social, work, military and even political lives, and is especially popular with young people. It works through text messages sent by cell phones to numerous people, directing or instructing them to assemble at a certain place at a specific time. From there they might be told to participate in an action. The result is a sudden congregating of many people at a moment's notice. The group usually responds, without any idea who is sending the message or what is the purpose behind it.

For example, CBS news reported on the phenomena and showed a large assemblage flocking around a giant toy dinosaur inside a Toys R Us store. The entire group obeyed the text command to worship the dinosaur. The mob, seeming to enjoy the "game," waved their hands up and down before the toy beast in unison. As suddenly as they appeared, they disappeared.

This type of mass mind control is performed effortlessly because the person or persons sending the text messages remain incognito. The group thinks it is an innocent sport because they don't see who is communicating messages to them; thus assuming it is safe. They call this new craze a fun "mind game." But for what purpose would someone lead people around to do such seemingly ridiculous and pointless actions? A greater motive lies behind this control of masses than to play games with dinosaurs. What is worse, these swarms of people can be ordered to change direction at a second's notice and the police have very little control in knowing where the group is going or what it will do next.

Consider this: if 250 people are ordered to congregate in front of your house, this can be intimidating. But if those 250 people are told to bang on your windows, that comes close to terrorizing. Mob activity is by no means an innocent fad.

The U.S. military has been one of the earliest institutions to both fear and see the possibilities in swarming. David Ronfeldt and John Arquilla, authors of the book "Swarming and the Future of Conflict" (a research book put together for the National Defense Research Institute), declare that swarming is a deliberately structured, coordinated, strategic way to strike from any directions.

How easy this new type of mind control weapon can be used to coordinate terrorist attacks or mass murders. Howard Rheingold, author of *Smart Mobs: The Next Social Revolution*, and a man who promotes the craze, sees a profound shift in society through smart mobs. He believes the new technology using cell phones will prepare human talents to cooperate. He admits it is not all fun and games, and that this type of technology can be destructive. He believes some early adopters used swarming to coordinate terrorist attacks. I agree. Because of my experience in communist Russia, I believe this new fad is nothing short of a series of tests on how to control populations.

Mind control has most often been thought of in relation to cults or religious groups, where usually one leader has the uncanny ability to hypnotize, manipulate or emotionally pull people into an allegiance to his own singular views. Using the latest Star War technologies, such control broadens into a much wider scope. Mind control is as serious a threat as any nuclear or biological attack, and must be brought into the open and discussed. Bombs and disease can kill our bodies, but mind control steals our souls. It is the very weapon Satan will use to bring in one-world government and religion, and we must be prepared against this dangerous weapon of mass deception.

Mind control on the masses is not something new. We can see its evil basis back in Old Testament times. Remember the three godly men, Shadrach, Meshach and Abednego? They defied the mass worship of Nebuchadnezzar's huge golden image in Daniel Chapter 3, and were thrown into the fiery furnace. God understands the evils of this weapon against His people, and how it will be used in the last days. But He promises, through beautiful stories like this in scripture, that those people who will not bow down to idols, and who are willing to be followers of Him and not self-deified human beings or phony ideologists, will be safe. When we submit our hearts to Christ with a determination to follow His Word without compromise, persevering in the faith and keeping our sword and shield in hand, our minds will be protected against the invasion of mass mind control techniques. And like Shadrach, Meshach, and Abednego, Jesus will be standing with us in whatever "fires" are lapping at our feet.

The first few weeks as a new cadet in the Leningrad Military Medical Academy, in September 1982, had me pumped. Through my mother's connections with the two-star General Kolesnekov's wife Joana and a few other insiders, I passed all initial entrance exams. Things seemed to be going smoothly; I started to think that maybe this path for my life, though not what I wanted, might not be bad after all. Besides, I was now inside the most prestigious medical academy in Russia.

"You have been selected into the greatest and oldest military institution in the Motherland." That first statement by our classes' commanding officer, Lt. Colonel Koklushin, made us proud. "The best of the best military minds—generals, academicians, professors and great physicians—have all come through this place. From this day forward you will be honorable cadets trusted by the communist party and the Soviet military medical department. You are now called *children of the sun*. Make us proud!"

I felt pride at our first tours through the extensive campus. The impressive old buildings were well maintained, and each one had a history of its own. Nestled between the Neva River and the sprawling city sights of Leningrad, the numerous oak trees and land space inside the structure gave it a rural feel.

The excursion to the museum located within the Faculty of Biology and Parasitology excited me the most. Seeing the famous brains of two past military academicians was the moment I knew being a doctor could lead to some fascinating work. There, encased in formaldehyde, were the actual brains of two-star General Evgeny Pavlovsky, the father of military epidemiology and biology, and two-star General L.A. Orbeli, the famous physiologist.

"Dimitri," I exclaimed to my new friend, my face practically touching the glass that separated me from the brains, "I heard Lenin's brain is even bigger than this one!" I pointed to General Orbeli's brain. It was larger and in better shape.

"Well of course," Dimitri replied, his nose scrunched upward as he compared the two organs, "Lenin was our great leader. A smart man like that had to have big brains."

I was fascinated and honored, yet slightly appalled that renowned men were remembered by this kind of crude display. "You know, I don't think I would want my brains to end up under the same glass. After all they accomplished, this is their end."

Dimitri laughed and we moved on to the not-so-famous exhibit of human eyeballs.

Excitement and pride vanished quickly over the next month as commanders began to wear us down mentally with fierce Soviet mind-conditioning tactics. These methods were meant to break our spirits and keep us pinioned under communism—leaving us no room to entertain anything else but the communist ideal. The *politruks* were skilled in brainwashing. These specially trained commanders persuaded young minds by using constant repetition during lectures, both in groups and individually. Humiliation and punishment in front of fellow cadets kept us in line. Suggesting we snitch on our buddies during private meetings was meant to weaken friendships and cause mistrust.

Many cadets would not bow to these threats, and good friendships were formed despite the fear tactics. Friendship was what kept me sane. It was something I knew they couldn't take from me if I didn't let them.

One particular incident made me realize the depths the communist regime went to in order to become our god. My grandmother on my mom's side had given me a tin cross, and I had it around my neck when two of my buddies and I decided to chuck off our uniform shirts and sneak in some of the sun's rays during our three month practical training in the tank division. It was an unusually warm afternoon when we stretched out on the grass behind our barracks and closed our eyes.

The shadow in my face startled me into a forward sitting position, but the general's palm thrust me back down onto the grass. "What is this?" he yelled, his staunch face close to mine.

We had no idea that high officials from Moscow had arrived that day for their annual base inspection. The general stood up and a major, smelling of cigarettes and cheap cologne, knelt down beside me on one leg, his knee-high shiny boots squeaking as he did so. Reaching over, he tore off the cross and chain dangling from my bare chest. "This is not a Soviet medal!" he shouted.

My buddies jumped up to attention and faced the officials. "Comrade General!" they shouted. But I was pinned down by the commander's incensed look.

I yelled, "Guilty, Comrade General!"

"Yes you are!" the Soviet official replied, "All three of you in lockup, now!" he ordered.

Sitting in a cold dark cell with the rats for three days without our shirts and without blankets for warmth wasn't severe enough. They also shaved our heads and made us load cement slabs in and out of trucks all day long.

After that, one of my commanders, Commander Artmenyev, disliked me. He heard from the officials about my lack of loyalty to communism. Whenever our class was allowed to leave the university grounds and go into the city, he found excuses not to let me go, no matter how shiny my boots and belt were.

"You don't have it," he would growl in my face with a smirk, "You're too soft." It infuriated him even more that I aced all exams on the subjects of Marxism and Leninism because the colonel teaching my class knew my mother. Artmenyev did all he could to get at me.

Still, the seeds of communist ideology had long ago influenced my mind from the time I had been a Young Pioneer. It had ruled my life more than I understood. I accepted the order that excellence in job performance came before the feelings of human beings.

We were taught not to ask questions, but to work to protect our nation against the evils of capitalism. Revenge was our goal. We bought into the lies that life on the other side of the Iron Curtain had to be destroyed, at all costs, even if it meant risking our lives to do so.

Excessive mind-altering techniques generate feelings, and this is where many mind control victims get fooled. Effective mind control, through the use of habit, repetition, or fear, will always produce emotions. The goal behind these "taught" feelings is to become real and consistent within a person's expressive makeup. A person will then let go of the normal compassionate emotions felt for other people and instead respond with what the mind has been trained to believe.

When I relocated to the United States, as a new believer, those learned feelings inside me began to surface over and over. Out of nowhere, intense feelings of disdain towards Americans would pop up, and I found myself reacting to those feelings with critical remarks. I couldn't understand this. I liked the sincerity and honesty of Americans, their freedom, and I adored my American wife. But, I had endured 20-some years of brainwashing.

The constant barrage of anti-American propaganda had done a mind-bending job in my head. I didn't know what real compassion and love was. I had become a self-centered and uncaring person. All of this was affecting my relationship with my wife and my Lord. I had to fight back.

Feelings borne out of mind control can be understood in light of something as simple as a mother singing every day to a small child near an open window. With her melody comes the sweet smell of ripe apples wafting in through the open nursery window, the soft feeling of her silky skin and the glow of her loving eyes. As the child grows, every time that same song is heard, it triggers a memory, which evokes an emotion of sweet smelling apples and mother's lanolin-soft skin. That simple repetitive act forms a habit, which in turn arouses feelings that become difficult to separate.

To properly obey God, I had to combat habitual feelings that I had grown to accept as being part of me. They were not part of me; they were developed and bred out of lies; they reared up in opposition to the truth. In order to get back my own mind and undo the lifelong lies that I had been taught to believe, I had to understand mind control, and acknowledge that my mind had been altered, that I had been victim to the techniques which the communist government had used on me and the masses.

I had to be diligent to know God's words in order to undo the programming that had invaded my mind. By His grace I learned to pause when those habits would surface, recognizing that they were not truth, and that they went against my will and my desire to be like Christ. I fought those feelings with scripture verse after scripture verse, careful that I did not let my guard down.

Mind control is used to increase control over individuals through a variety of techniques, such as excessive repetition of routine activities, intense humiliation, fear tactics or sleep deprivation. It takes place when a person's attitudes, beliefs, and personality are shaped, without the person's knowledge or consent. Stifled and lifeless emotions will emerge, as they did with me. That is why terrorists can kill children and women without a blink of an eye. They are programmed to obey, and their response is easy because they no longer have feelings of right and wrong with which to fight, no conscience to tackle. Hate becomes a justified motivator. They become something similar to a zombie, although they will sometimes show and feel great emotion for their cause.

Repetition played a major part in the USSR's process of brainwashing. My father worked in an industrial top-secret pro-military factory making models for submarines. Every day before work, at nine in the morning, his boss would give a five-minute speech on the greatness of Marx and Lenin. And once a month Dad and his co-workers were required to participate in tedious two-hour communist lectures. Employees had to be attentive, because if they were asked a question and could not answer, they were publicly humiliated and shooed off by the party. In response to these speeches, employees were expected to bring in five converts to communism; if they didn't they would be reprimanded.

A political manager was hired to make sure that employees were fed plenty of propaganda. Men like this were specifically appointed to work their brainwash in schools, colleges, work places and the military. They were paid well by the Kremlin with such gifts as free flats, summer cottages, cars, vacations, and food coupons. To obtain this kind of luxurious position meant securing good connections in high places.

During communist holidays, workers had to take part in demonstrations. My dad would volunteer to carry the heavy flagpole in the parade so he could earn ten rubles. He did this for six hours in the cold weather, keeping warm off the bottle of vodka he kept hidden in his pants pocket.

Another way that Russia controlled minds was by applying deprivation and humiliation techniques. The government did this by belittling those who had an education or intelligence and rewarding those who didn't. My father had a degree as a technical engineer, but he accepted factory work instead, because he was paid 150 rubles a month more then an engineer's salary. Educated people with college degrees made a lot less then factory workers, and this is where Soviet Russia squashed the minds and stole the heart.

After resigning from the army in 1991, I could not afford to live on a physician's wage because a doctor made less then 40 rubles a month, less than a taxicab driver. My father's college education didn't feed his family, and he had no choice but to let go of his interests. Pilfering people's intelligence, motivation and talents smashed confidence and opportunity, bending wills into controlled submission. Stripping a population of inspiration and enthusiasm by taking away their dreams is an effective way to control the masses.

Fear is a great tool for those who want to employ effective mind bending. Today's successful ploys by terrorist groups—to steal or develop weapons of mass destruction—involve recruiting people who are willing to deliver or plant such a device. Convincing people to take high risks or be willing to kill themselves can be accomplished through the use of fear tactics. Muslim terrorists are brainwashed from birth to believe that dying for Allah and participating in the Holy War will give them a special place in heaven; they are willing to die for this religious cause because they think they are doing the will of Allah.

There are also people, particularly women, who are not Muslim and come from either Russia, Dagastan, or Georgia, who are captured and trained to be suicide bombers against their will by the use of forceful mind-twisting methods.

Terrorist groups work hard to properly execute their agenda and strengthen their political (or religious) statements and goals.

They do whatever it takes to get willing subjects. Certain camps are designed particularly for women, ages 11 to 25, because women can be easier targets for mind control, especially those who have psychological problems. Such vulnerable subjects are trained to be "shahids," which is the Muslim term meaning "martyr." To do this, the women are put through a severe abusive ritual. For weeks they are raped, beaten, and doped up with drugs, such as cocaine or heroin. Hallucinatory drugs are also administered. After the women are completely broken, they are taught how to use explosives. When they are ready to go on a mission, they work in pairs so that if one woman fails to activate the device, the other one will do it. They are trained to die, and they are never allowed to return alive.

Movies and television can be a huge tool for mind control of the masses; it is a good way to numb the emotions against acts of violence. It sets the right tone for any future event of aggression, preparing viewers to accept violence as normal, or just to be passive about it. The daily intake of smut desensitizes audiences not to care.

Consider what happened in a busy park in Seattle, Washington about seven years ago. A young woman was raped in broad daylight in the midst of a small crowd, all of whom stood around watching the crime. Not one person answered her pleas for help, giving the rapist a "go" sign to finish off his victim.

Didn't those people feel anger at the woman's demise? Surely they could have at least thrown rocks at the man. Had their emotions been stripped away from them and they did not even know it? I would say so! This is a prime example of what television can produce.

A healthy and sound mind is ready to respond either physically or emotionally to inappropriate behavior. We see this in Jesus when He upturned the moneychangers in the temple. His indignation for transgression caused Him to respond both physically and emotionally.

Without even realizing it, a constant diet of Hollywood movies is altering people's minds to be rebellious, hateful, prejudiced, critical and emotionless. Audiences see so many images of people murdered in one day, that if another holocaust were to happen, those people would join in and cheer the killings with no consideration for humanity. Then everyone becomes a terrorist, making terrorism a potentially worldwide epidemic. People who do nothing about an act of aggression against innocent folks are just as guilty as the ones doing the act.

One shouldn't be too surprised at the reason the entire German population closed their eyes to the imprisonment and slaughter of the Jews. Adolph Hitler had a grand ability to seduce crowds, even over the radio. The people were like the crowd sanctioning the rapist without feeling much about it. Hitler's fierce methods of propaganda deceived millions, not only by using fear methods, but also by using keen rhetoric in his speeches. He played on their nationalistic patriotism. That is why he rose to power. He was a man who spoke from the heart, which caused a surplus of emotions from his listeners and created a tight unity among the German nation. His dogma of inborn racial superiority, "white's are supreme," provided his followers with a positive view of life and made them feel they were moving forward towards a goal. He solidified his strong charismatic rhetoric with presentations. He used fear tactics to make sure the audience knew who the chief commander was. One of the ways he did this was to taunt his spectators to jeer what he was saying. Once he had lured them to participate in his mind game, he would order his soldiers to go down and make an example of what happens to those who reject the supreme leader.

Hitler also used symbols as part of his mind-bending techniques—the eagle or iron cross. He had them displayed on walls, podiums, and flags throughout his regime. Symbols, like the image of soldiers standing behind him at his rallies, helped to invoke power. Wherever Hitler was, his symbols followed. In time, the symbols themselves were enough to demand submission.

When a government or political or religious figure can strip people of their feelings, make them numb to violence, truth and compassion towards another person, then they are able to wield great power. One of the reasons Americans remain a compassionate people as a whole is because they have had free choice up until now. My mom, who now lives with my dad here in the States, told me that one of the things that touched her heart deeply was seeing the giving hearts of the American people after the 9/11 attack. She was amazed to see thousands and thousands of U.S. citizens standing in line to donate blood.

Compassion is important towards innocent people of all races. Even as I write this book, thousands of civilians have been killed in the Iraq War. Because Saddam Hussein was a terrorist dictator does not mean every Iraqi citizen followed in his footsteps. Many were forced to live under his dictatorship against their will. We should not allow our contempt for one dictator to make us to become callous towards human life. Empathy for other humans should never grow cold in a believer's heart. We must be careful that political propaganda and patriotism do not become idols unto themselves, becoming greater than Christ's will for our lives, or undoing His biblical commandment to "love your enemies."

The news media are huge weapons for mind control and great feeders for propaganda. Look how easily the American population was drawn into the Y2K deception before the year 2000 rolled around. Millions were sucked into the foolish notion that as soon as midnight struck on January 2000, computer terminals might crash, causing immediate famines, droughts, and disasters. People made millions off that scam. My wife and I laughed at the nonsense of everyone running around hoarding food and water, and the millions of dollars spent to "Y2K-proof" computers. We didn't worry. We had faith in Microsoft.

On January 1, our outdated computer turned right on over to the year 2000 without any glitches whatsoever. If the majority of the entire United States population (sad to say, including quite a number of Christians), was so easily duped by this yarn, what else will they buy into, if they haven't done so already?

It might sound incredible to some people who never miss the world news at six o'clock, to learn that American news is filtered and programmed to sway people's minds. It is no wonder that most countries get our news before we do. Just open onto the Internet and visit other nations' news Web sites. In a few weeks you will discover a disturbing pattern: much of the news, especially news concerning America, will not be broadcast on

American news stations until at least two or three days later. By the time it is shown on ABC, CBS, NBC, or CNN, the same news information is often changed, watered down, twisted, or missing important facts. It wouldn't be hard to deceive viewers with a piece of news footage that has been "sliced and diced."

It is ironic that the same day as I am writing this, CBS News presented viewers with a grand distorted example of a "slice and dice" news piece in their two-part segment titled, "The Dark Side of Home Schooling." The news special focused mainly on the North Carolina murders of two teenagers by their 14-year-old brother, who subsequently killed himself too. The kids were supposedly home schooled. After the reporter highlighted a few other isolated cases of abuse, CBS concluded that home schooling was "out of control," and then implied that more legal regulations were needed on home schooling parents. The entire news investigation left viewers to believe that home schooling equaled child abuse.

The biased report left out the important facts that social services had contacted the North Carolina family 11 times before the murders and had even removed the children from the home at one point. Also missing from the segment was the fact that this family did not comply with North Carolina's home school laws. They were not typical parents. They were breaking the law from many angles. Obviously a tougher and highly governed social service could not prevent the tragedy. How would stricter regulations on home schoolers make a difference? Today there are over 1.7 million home schooled children in the United States. Compared to a nationwide average, these kids do very well.

The scheme behind this piece of propaganda is to encourage further state and federal government regulations against American citizens, another push to violate constitutional laws by distorting facts and getting viewers to accept the changes as "necessary" because "home schooling causes child abuse." This piece could have also been aired to benefit the public schools. The more home schoolers, the fewer government funds received by the schools.

The news story opened a door for innocent and good home schooling parents to become sudden suspects, possibly turned in to social services by brainwashed neighbors who fell for the CBS special. Let me soberly remind the reader of Karl Marx's proclamation that "the co-relation of a parent and child is disgusting." Home schooling, one of the most beautiful freedoms in this nation, promotes a strong and secure family unit, something socialism and communism hates.

The average person would not be bulldozed if they would take the time to research what they are hearing instead of eating everything handed to them on a platter. We should read the labels before we swallow the food, so we know what we are eating. Because of the strong visual presentations through television shows and sitcoms and the Internet, all governments these days are in an advantageous position to persuade the population without people knowing it.

From past workable methods and today's new technologies, mind control of the masses is easy in today's society. Look how quickly Hitler persuaded an entire nation to his evil ways. Fortunately, he didn't have the use of television, computers or mobile phones.

Discerning between right and wrong is not always easy, but those who seek the truth will find the answer. It is imperative that people analyze what's going on around them. In this time of great compromise, where "darkness" is now considered as "light," where what was once considered sin, is no longer sinful, Christians need to stay true to their biblical heritage. America contains many Christians, but sin abounds on every corner, and idols are easily creeping inside homes and churches. Society is changing, and we must be careful not to follow a change that contradicts the Bible. We must be willing to stand for the truth, no matter how many people may disagree.

Millions closed their eyes to Hitler's murders, and similar numbers hailed Stalin despite the evil atrocities he ordered against his own people. Following a multitude that hails one man or ideology can often be a dangerous choice. Jesus warns more than once in Matthew 24 to "let no man deceive us." Our admiration for a leader, pastor, or public figure should never replace our allegiance to our Lord.

History reveals there are few perfect leaders. And seldom does a man make it to the top of the political rung without selling some of his soul. Any head of a government is up against heavy peer pressure, and most will be persuaded by the opinion of the polls.

If polls show 70 percent in favor of removing the phrase, "In God We Trust" from new currency, only a leader completely surrendered to Christ will be able to remain steadfast in an unwillingness to bow to those numbers. Unfortunately, in today's political arena the world has yet to see a leader in any country willing to make a 100 percent commitment to the one true God, as did King Josiah, mentioned in II Kings Chapters 22 and 23. He did not give a hoot at what his congress thought; he tore down *all* the idols and burned them. After the high priest had discovered the Law of Moses during the repair of the temple, King Josiah rent his clothes and repented of the evil his nation had succumbed to. He drove out the fortunetellers and those that dealt with sorcery, and he caused the people to once again follow the true word of God.

Because of King Josiah's commitment to follow the law and not the polls, scripture says of him in Kings Chapter 23, verse 25, *And like unto him was there no king before him, that turned to the Lord with all his heart, and with all his soul, and with all his might, according to all the law of Moses; neither after him arose there any like him.* This stands true today. Because King Josiah humbled himself to the Lord, God held back Israel's judgment until after Josiah's reign. This is a Godly leader. A true believer, no matter what position, will never compromise the Gospel of Jesus Christ.

Thinking as an individual takes courage. Not allowing oneself to be bamboozled by other people's opinions and re-marks is not always easy, but extremely necessary in order to retain spiritual insight.

Anti-Christian regimes know that faith can protect a free will and a sound mind. That is why Lenin feared religious belief. Religion was not an opposition to his communist ideol-ogy; locking up a church door was effective enough, but faith rooted in the heart spread like wildfire, and that worried him. How could he get a society to worship him if they loved God more? That is why he called them "believers" and strove hard to stop those who preached the true Gospel of Jesus Christ. Religion is never a threat, but relationship is. Lenin knew that people's minds founded in faith and dedicated to Christ Jesus would be hard to conquer.

"Being of a sound mind" means not worrying about what others think of us. The fear of others is a dangerous open door for controlling minds. We see this happen in scripture when the Jewish crowd, people who had followed Jesus previously and knew He did nothing deserving of death, allowed the fear of the Pharisees to manipulate and persuade them to go along with their shouts to "crucify him." Cult leaders like to prey on people who are people pleasers. They know how easily they can get that kind of individual to do their bidding.

Mind control is a great terror weapon bludgeoning today's churches, and this chapter only touches on it briefly, though it deserves the attention of an entire book. Phony religious leaders use similar tactics to control assemblages within churches, as did Hitler and Stalin.

The worst mistake a Christian can make is in believing that all churches are safe zones. Not so. In Soviet Russia the government used churches to validate their constitution's "freedom of religion," using pastors hired by the KGB as a guise to fool the people. True believers were beaten and imprisoned, and few citizens were made aware of this.

The numerous false doctrines spreading across the world, and the extra-biblical, esoteric experiences that are introduced with these "new" revelations are a great preparatory tool for mass mind manipulation. This kind of seduction works well because feelings are involved. Forming an anti-christ government cannot be accomplished without mind control, and the church is the first to be targeted.

This is why I oppose the "slain in the spirit" act, which some churches promote as something supernatural by God, but which is a practice not supported by scripture. The action involves individuals or groups of individuals passing out and falling backward while being prayed for, usually during an emotional and demonstrative church service—a complete contrast to the theme of the scriptures that exhort us to maintain a sound, reasoning mind. In comparison to God's Word, we see men and women of God falling down face forward in worship, which means they are not on their backs, and they are always cognizant. In I Corinthians 14, verse 25 the Apostle Paul backs up this scriptural truth: *And thus are the secrets of his heart made manifest; and so falling down on his face he will worship God, and report that God is in you of a truth.* To me, going backward and passing out is a mockery and shows great disrespect to the holiness of God. If any of us were to meet the Queen of England, I doubt we would fall on our backs and pass out in front of her throne. Just because thousands are doing something, doesn't make it right.

If we yield our minds toward grandiose feelings and supernatural extravaganzas without testing the origin, we are in grave danger of deception. How vital it is that we maintain our ability to reason and think and discern. Keeping our minds in an active state of reasoning and thought, making sure to question and compare everything in light of scripture, will guarantee our safety.

In Acts Chapter 17, verse 11, the men of Berea searched the scriptures daily to see whether what Paul was preaching was true. Because they questioned what they heard, the scripture says that they were "nobler" than those people in Thessalonica. What a compliment! They used their own minds. They used logic and made sure what they heard was in line with God's will and Word.

As Ephesians 6 commands, we must put on the *whole armor of God*. This means using God's weapons and our free will to discern between good and evil. The Apostle Paul confirms God's heart on such matters when he warns Christians to "test the spirits to see if they be of God" in I John chapter 4, verse 1. He knew that many false prophets (and, we can add, terrorist groups, cults, and occultists) would be going out into the world and fooling good people.

Without guarding our minds and our salvation, we jeopardize the very freedom we now have. It is no wonder Paul brings the sobering warning to work out our own salvation with fear and trembling (Philippians 2:12).

Mind control does not take place only in terrorist camps or religious cults; it can happen within our own living rooms. These are serious days we live in.

Aligning our lives on the side of truth by studying the Word of God, keeping our faith high, praying without stopping, guarding our salvation, and guarding our freedom to reason are the best ways to deter anyone from altering the precious free minds God gave us. You may also try turning off the TV.

M ethodical and constant suppression to rob soldiers of their "self" during my service in the academy sometimes meant throwing them in military prison for a week or two. The pressure intensified with each passing month. Harsh treatment of soldiers was common, in fact between 15- and 17,000 soldiers died in the Soviet Army each year during the 1970s and the 1980s under a "natural" cause classification. The biggest recorded suicide rate by officers in the Soviet Army (and in the New Russian Federation today) came from the same unit I was assigned to—Strategic Rocket Forces.

Some soldiers were unable to cope with the mental demands and ended up in the military mental ward. One afternoon I heard knocking outside my room, followed by screams. I hurried out to the corridor with my comrade Batya, and saw Tkachenko, a fellow cadet, thrashing on the floor, his wrists bound by cuffs, his head oozing blood. All his fingers were busted from having beat them against the wall. He continued hammering his head onto the ground while the two officers, standing beside him, looked bored.

"His future is the mental ward," Batya whispered.

I stood there watching until an ambulance pulled up to our barracks and took Tkachenko away. I never saw him again.

Getting away from military stress seemed impossible, except for the cadets who were fortunate enough to get married. They were allowed to live off the base with their spouses. First year soldiers were only 17 years of age, but that didn't stop them from marrying—they would do anything to get out of the barracks—even if it meant marrying the ugliest girl in town. One young cadet I bunked with married a schoolteacher who was 22 years older than he was, to gain a little freedom. He was a happier man after that, not because he loved his wife, but because he had his own flat.

The idea of marriage was never far from my mind, but I was too shy around the ladies to convince any of them to marry me.

Two years later, in 1984, when my Mother pestered me to meet Lena, the well-known General Kolesnekov's stepdaughter, getting off the base was not the only persuasion I had in agreeing to see her.

Chapter Four
First Fruits of Radiation

The young men were hard to look at. The skin on their arms and faces looked puffy red and wet, like Saran wrap. Some had lost their teeth and moaned from the ulcers lining their mouth, throat and esophagus; the heavy layer of white fungus inside their mouths gave off a pungent smell similar to rotten flesh. Most of the patients couldn't talk.

"Igor, it is terrible, isn't it?" my mother-in-law Joana, whispered to me as she noticed the surprise in my eyes. She moved to the next patient and picked up his chart. The young blond navy officer in the bed managed a half grin for the head nurse. She leaned down and patted his shoulder and exclaimed, "Your looking handsome, son, don't let these burns spoil your day. Your eyes are women catchers!" The tall starched white cap, sterile dress and shoes did not detract from my mother-in-law's infectious charm. Somehow her self-assured and vibrant presence broke through stiff formalities and eased the worries of the irradiated patients.

The nuclear accident happened in August 1985 while I was still adjusting to married life with Lena. We had gotten married the year before, so I was now off the base in a small rented flat, greatly relieved to be away from those drafty barracks. I was enjoying a rare quiet dinner with my wife when her mother telephoned me with the news of a "classified" nuclear mishap up at Chazma Bay Naval Station, not too far from Vladivostock. Joana informed me that the irradiated victims were being sent to her ward at the Naval Hospital Therapy Clinic under a secret operation. She asked if I wanted to observe firsthand the effects of radiation on the human body. I agreed, knowing that her job as chief nurse would help me avoid the rat-race of red tape.

A Soviet Victor class K-431 submarine, which runs on nuclear fuel and has two reactors, was in port and docked for maintenance when the explosion occurred. The active zone of the nuclear reactor was being replaced because of an improper seal on its containment. A huge crane, positioned on a floating platform in the water, was being used to lift off the outer lid of the reactor just at the time a military torpedo boat sped by, developing waves underneath the crane's platform and causing the machine to shift. Both outer and inner lids came up out of the reactor at a technologically unsafe level, self-activating a chain reaction inside the reactor core and causing a devastating thermal explosion which ruptured both the submarine's aft bulkhead and the pressure hull. The core was blown out of the reactor, and the roof of the refueling hut was thrown 82 yards away. Fission products from the reactor flew into the sea.

Ten sailors were killed at the initial blast, and the responders and port employees who rushed to the scene instantly became contaminated, some of them receiving a radiation dose dozens of times higher than lethal doses. Thirty percent of the seaport's submarine plant became contaminated. Dunay, a city close by, was fortunate; a natural hilly landscape shielded it from the approaching cloud, but the radioactive plume contaminated one mile of surrounding forest.

The KGB instantly classified the operation and forced all responders, witnesses, and relatives of the dead seamen to sign documents verifying that they would remain tight-lipped about what they saw. Because the clean-up process was quickly performed in sync with the hush-up of the accident, sailors and port employees worked on the mess uninformed and barehanded.

The few dozen sailors with severe burns and acute radiation syndrome (ARS) had been moved to my academy to be treated at the prestigious Military Navy Hospital Therapy Faculty, where my mother-in-law worked. The academy stretched for miles and housed numerous military clinics, hospitals and research facilities. That was my first experience studying radiation burns and ARS, and I was taken aback at its effects on the human body.

"Are they allowing their relatives to visit?" I whispered to Joana, noticing there were no civilians in the ward.

"No."

I nodded and moved beside her to the next victim. He was older, in his late 40s, and looked scared.

"This one has ARS, third level," Joana stated. She showed me his report and pointed to the word "gastrointestinal," meaning he had less than a few weeks to live.

Acute radiation syndrome is sometimes known as radiation toxicity or radiation sickness and is caused by irradiation of most of the body by a high dose of penetrating radiation, usually in a matter of minutes, and in some cases up to 30 days after exposure. ARS is brought on when the dose is external, irradiating most of the body, weaving through the internal organs, and in some cases accompanied by skin damage. At the onset, the illness will include nausea, weakness, intense vomiting, headaches, fever, abdominal discomfort, and reddening of skin. One to two weeks later, patients will develop watery and hemorrhagic diarrhea. In the final stages, patients become violently ill. Mucous membranes become ulcerated, swollen and dry; in some cases, depending on exposure rates on the skin, dry or wet desquamations appear with future secondary infections. Breathing and swallowing are difficult and painful, and in many cases the patients can be fed only parenterally. The number of red and white blood cells and platelets in the bone marrow will fail dramatically, a first lab sign of acute radiation illness development. Patients have a difficult time fighting this kind of infection while retaining the natural clotting activity of the blood. Death occurs usually after two to 12 weeks following exposure as a result of generalized infection (sepsis) and internal hemorrhaging. Recovery is possible, depending on the dose of radiation, with correct medical treatment.

The sailors who tried to take care of the reactor problem with their bare hands landed in the burn center and faced numerous skin grafts, although in most cases grafting was futile. Gangrenous hands and fingers had to be amputated. The frail sailors and responders who did manage to get out of bed and take short walks down the corridors reminded me of the dazed drunks I often saw stumbling down the busy streets of Leningrad.

A month later I heard that the sailors and workers who died at the Chazma Bay incident had been buried in unidentified cemeteries; relatives were not privy to their whereabouts. To confiscate the contaminated one mile of asphalt, 3600 miles of soil and sand, 350 tons of construction material, and 760 tons of metals, the Soviet government built four deep trenches nearby and used the place as a radioactive waste cemetery.

Joana's position at the Leningrad Military Medical Academy came about through her marriage to General Anatoly Kolesnekov. She knew everyone, had powerful connections, and a huge pull in the affairs of the academy. Joana reminded me of a race car's engine. Her constant, confident, outgoing, and gracious personality was unbeatable. I knew no one else who could outshine her exuberance. Partly Jewish (but never mentioned), her prominent nose seemed to lure onlookers straight down its base to her energetic green eyes.

She was an attractive nursing student when she had married Lena's birth father, Antone, an engineer in the military in the early 1960s in Siberia. Lena, her first and only child, was born in 1966. Four years later Antone was sent to Swidnica, Poland, to work for the military transportation department. That is where Joana met the general.

Anatoly Kolesnekov, a reserved man with a potato face, was in his mid-40s, and the youngest general in the Soviet Army. Despite his age, he had built a formidable reputation in Poland, especially during the uprising in Pozna when he refused Polish workers bread and freedom from the Soviet rule. And so it was, his forceful presence and esteemed position caught Joana's attention, and she wasted no time flirting with him.

The general's wife was dying from cancer when their affair began. After his wife passed on, the general proposed. Joana accepted, divorced her first husband, and married Anatoly. Lena was five years old at the time. The general's daughter Maria was 17, and his son Nicolai, aged 25, was an officer in the army. He would later become a professor of linguistic and Arabic languages and go on to work for the military counterintelligence department in Moscow under four-star General Sorokin. Lena would seldom see her real father after this; the general's children would not accept Joana because they despised her relationship with their father at the crucial time their mother lay dying. Yet Joana remained loyal to his children and treated them with the same respect she showed her own daughter.

After leaving Poland in the 1970s, General Kolesnekov became chief of command over the Siberian region, which housed a million-size army with numerous divisions. His charge included overseeing all nuclear and strategic complexes and WMD stockpile areas. He accumulated his own personal helicopter and multiple vacation cottages all over the country, where he often met for secret parties with high officials. He was also the chief consultant at the Leningrad Military Academy, on the general staff. Because of his successful involvement in the many operations in pro-Soviet countries—Czechoslovakia, Poland, Mongolia, Romania, Hungary, and East Germany—he was one of a few in the USSR who received the highest awards and medals for honorable military interventions, organizations, and takeovers.

Joana stayed married to the general, but took lots of boyfriends while he was away on assignment or vacationing. He knew this, and didn't make much about it because he too liked an array of women. Their marriage became one of convenience. Both had become powerful figures in their jobs, and they used one another to maintain the tight control they held in high places.

I had met General Kolesnekov on my first date with Lena in her home. It took some coaxing on my mother's part to get me to set up the date, and after I did, my mother supplied me with a bouquet of flowers to impress the family. It was with reluctance that I took the over-sized floral arrangement and headed to Nevsky Prospect. The general's spacious apartment, nestled between the floors of other grand flats belonging to high officials, was nicely furnished with impressive high ceilings. I had preferred to spend my few hours of freedom with my buddies at the bars, but once Joana opened the door and introduced me to her daughter, I quickly lost my edge. Lena was nicer looking than I had anticipated.

General Kolesnekov was shorter than I expected, but his arrogant presence made up for his size. He barely said a word to me, except for a muttered, "Come in, cadet." He did not shake my hand, and left the room as fast as he entered. I called after his back, "Yes, Comrade General." Looking around, I quickly got it that there was no such thing as an equal communist system. My parents could only dream of owning a flat so big.

As the weeks passed and I came by to see Lena on a regular basis, Kolesnekov began to warm up to me, and actually take care of me. I noticed that my commander at the academy stopped harassing me and allowed me to take my off-the-base breaks without the usual flack. He started allowing me extra excursions off campus as well. Late nights with Lena got me the privilege of personal escorts back to the base in military se-dans—orders of the general.

Whenever I was kept from an important family event or could not get released for a date with Lena by my commanding officers, Joana would override Commander Koklushin's author-ity and go straight to the general's close friend, Chief of Acad-emy, General Colonel Ivanov. This action irritated Koklushin and caused the other officers and commanders to tiptoe around me.

Joana, "godmother" to everyone around her, worked at the Harvard-like academy of the whole Russia, hiring whom she wanted, making deals with those who needed medicine (she was also in charge of pharmaceutical department), and arranging hospital care for certain ill friends, despite the fact the navy hospital was off-limits to civilians. Through her many kind favors, she built a large network of people that she knew would repay her at a later date if she needed a favor. The trade-offs were well worth her time. If Lena and I wanted to go to the opera, we talked to Joana, because she had connections to get us front row tickets. She had connections in Moscow and Poland if we needed something there. She could get people jobs or money, medical drugs or healthcare. She was a tank, never hesitating in strength or character to get what she wanted.

I used Joana's influences to build up my own network of "friends" and make my life easier inside the academy. Most of the cadets in the academy came from prominent families, but the lower-rank commanders generally came from the regular army, a harsh service where family prominence is not common. For this reason, the commanders despised our position. If a sergeant or officer disliked you it could mean a miserable time. One time my commander's wife was sick and needed medicine that could be found only in Bulgaria. Joana made a few calls and got me the drugs. After this I had clout with the commander and he treated me well. With some of these officials on my side, I was insured extra peace against the gutsy bullies who wanted to "get" me because of my position and connections. I had to be wise and discreet to keep the ball in my park, yet, all in all, having the general and Joana on my side provided me with status power protection—and links to some classified information I shouldn't have known about.

Joana threw great parties. Once everyone drank a bottle or two of the finest vodka, generals and high commanders often bragged about their service during classified operations. Colonel Vasileve, chief of the special operations of the Group of Soviet Force in Poland, blabbed on many occasions on the Soviet activities in Vietnam. That is how I learned about the 200 specially trained officers who were sent in during the war to

divert the U.S. forces and assassinate their high commanders.
They had hidden in the jungles of Vietnam for months, targeting
and blowing up U.S. military and air bases. Out of the 200,
Vasileve was only one of 12 who returned.

I also learned that during small conflicts in parts of the
world, such as Libya, Syria, Latin America and Cambodia,
biological and chemical weapons were tested on civilians in
those countries. Tests were successful because of infiltrators—
KGB associates who married native-born women and became
citizens. All political assassinations and changes of regimes in
countries in Africa, Asia, Europe and Latin America were
supported and sponsored by the USSR in an effort to persuade
those countries to accept a communist and socialist lifestyle.

Many KGB agents led double lives and had a few wives both
in the Soviet Union and in politically unstable capitalist nations, having close contacts with the country's main political
parties and even working for CIA as double agents. Many times
they never returned and those men were classified as "lost in
operation." Their families in Russia were given pensions from
the government, but in reality the agent lived somewhere else,
such as in Israel or Chile.

General Maniylov, chief KGB official over the Leningrad
region, spoke about Liteynay 6, a secret building with tinted
windows, security cameras, and underground flooring, where
citizens who were considered dissidents were snatched away at
night and harbored, never to be seen again. I also heard about
past executions that took place 50 miles outside the city for
political prisoners and the mass graves still protected by high
walls to keep investigators out. I learned more about missiles

hidden from U.S. satellites, aggressive actions on bio-research, and the updated policies that would ensure Russia becoming the nuclear superpower of the world.

One hundred years ago a handful of scientists started the steamroller that became the tyranny (and the promise) of the Atomic Age. These curious men and women explored the nature and performance of atoms, initiating paths of research which changed our understanding of the building blocks of matter. Their discoveries paved the way for development of new methods and tools with which to explore our genesis and the way our bodies function, both in sickness and in health. Little did those pioneers know just how much their discoveries would change our lives and affect our world—for both good and bad—in modern medicine and in modern science.

If we were to go back to science class 101 we would remember that the building blocks of matter are *elements*. The smallest particle of an element that still preserves the identity of that element is the *atom*. All atoms of a given element are identical to one another, but differ from the atoms of other elements. If we were to flip through some history books we would see that the Ancient Greeks first predicted the existence of the atom around 500 BC and named the predicted particle "atomos" which means "indivisible."

In 1803, a scientist named John Dalton paved the way for modern acceptance of the atom by proposing a systematic set of hypotheses to describe it. But scientists of his day considered the atom to be simply an inferior player in chemical reactions, a boring positively charged "glob" that contained scattered electrons. Then a series of brilliant discoveries by four scientists—Becquerel, a French physicist, Marie Curie and her husband, Pierre, and Ernest Rutherford—challenged that premise at the end of the 19th century, and opened the door to the atomic science of the 20th century. Often working together, they helped release the genie of the atom.

Antoine Becquerel was familiar with the work of X-ray founder Wilhelm Conrad Roentgen, whose discovery was the first to start the scientific ball rolling on December 22, 1895. Roentgen photographed his wife's hand while she placed it in the path of X-rays, which Roentgen created by beaming an electron ray energy source onto a cathode tube, and got the image of her skeleton, still showing the ring on her finger. Roentgen's discovery of these "mysterious" rays capable of producing an image on a photographic plate caught the attention of Becquerel. (Today Wilhelm Roentgen's name is remembered by the radiological term "roentgen" which is defined as a measurement of radiation in the air.)

In March 1896, as Becquerel was studying the related phenomena of fluorescence and phosphorescence, he made a remarkable discovery. He found that while the phenomena of fluorescence and phosphorescence had many similarities to each other and to X-rays, they also had significant differences. While fluorescence and X-rays stopped when the initiating energy source was halted, phosphorescence continued to emit rays some time after the initiating energy source was removed. However, in all three cases, the energy was derived initially from an outside source. Then during a time of overcast weather, Becquerel found he couldn't use the sun as an initiating energy source for his experiments, so he placed his wrapped photographic plates in a darkened drawer, along with some crystals containing uranium. Much to his delight, he saw that the plates did not require the presence of an initiating energy source; the plates were exposed during storage by invisible emanations from the uranium. The crystals emitted rays on their own! The stage was set for the next three scientists.

Working in Becquerel's lab, Marie Curie and her husband Pierre, began what became a life long study of radioactivity. Becquerel had already noted that uranium emanations could turn air into a conductor of electricity. Using sensitive instruments invented by Pierre and his brother, Pierre and Marie Curie measured the ability of emanations from various elements to induce conductivity. On February 17, 1898, the Curies tested an ore of uranium, pitchblende, for its ability to turn air into a conductor of electricity. The Curies discovered that the pitchblende produced a current 300 times stronger than that produced by pure uranium.

Although they tested and recalibrated their instruments, they still found the same perplexing results. The Curies reasoned that a very active unknown substance in addition to the uranium must exist within the pitchblende.

In a document explaining the hypothesized element (which they named *polonium* after Marie's native Poland), they introduced the term: *radioactive*. The Curies were able to extract enough polonium and another radioactive element, radium, to establish the chemical properties of these elements.

Marie Curie continued working alone after her husband's death and established the first quantitative standards by which the rate of radioactive release of charged particles from elements could be measured and compared. She also found that there was a decrease in the rate of radioactive releases over time, and that this decrease could be calculated and predicted. Her greatest and most unique achievement was realizing that radiation is an atomic property of matter rather than a separate independent release.

Marie died in 1934 of leukemia, more than likely brought on by extensive exposure to the high levels of radiation during her studies. Today's radiation term *curie* is named after Marie and is classified as a unit used to measure radioactivity.

Not until Ernest Rutherford stepped forward in 1911 in the research was the structure of the atom understood. Rutherford conducted a series of experiments in which he bombarded a piece of gold foil with positively charged (alpha) particles emitted by radioactive material. Most of the particles passed through the foil undisturbed, suggesting that the foil was made up mostly of empty space rather than of a sheet of solid atoms. Some alpha particles, however, "bounced back," indicating the presence of solid matter.

Rutherford's work showed that atomic particles consisted primarily of empty space surrounding a well-defined central core called a nucleus.

Rutherford laid the basis for the tenacity of atomic structure. In addition to defining the planetary model of the atom, he showed that over time the radioactive elements undergo a process of decay. Rutherford—using experiments many labeled "splitting the atom"—was able to artificially transmute one element into another, which in turn unleashed the incredible power of the atom which would eventually be harnessed for both constructive and destructive purposes.

Scientists can now create radioactive forms of common elements called *isotopes*. Each isotope has a fixed rate of decay which can be characterized by its half-life, or the length of time that it takes half of the radioactive atoms in a sample to decay. Because each isotope decays at a unique and predictable rate, different isotopes can be used for a variety of purposes. For instance, isotopes play an important role in modern medicine because they can be ingested and traced in their path through the body, revealing biochemical and metabolic processes with accuracy. These isotropic "tracers" are presently used for practical diagnosis of disease as well as in research.

Radiation is a two-sided coin. On the one side it is useful in both medicine and anthropological/archaeological studies. On the other side, the same materials can be used to destroy human lives. How detrimental those materials would end up being wouldn't be known until almost 40 years later.

Albert Einstein wrote to President Franklin D. Roosevelt on August 2, 1939, right before the beginning of World War II, that Nazi Germany was working to purify Uranium-235 to create an atomic bomb. This information prompted the United States Government to form the Manhattan Project, a project that involved fast research and production that would produce a feasible atomic bomb. Between 1939 and 1945 more than $2 billion dollars was spent on the Manhattan Project. Leading scientists were brought together to come up with the formulas for refining uranium and putting together a working bomb. They did well. On July 16, 1945 at 5:29 a.m. at Los Alamos, New

Mexico, the finished bomb was detonated for a test performance. The white to orange blaze that flashed across the morning sky ushered in the Atomic Age.

The words of the witnesses on that frightful day substantiated how the discovery of radiation could ultimately bring about man's own demise. One witness said he felt that the equilibrium in nature had been upset—as if humankind had become a threat to the world it inhabited. J. Robert Oppenheimer, the top man in charge of the project, though overjoyed about the success of it, understood the severe reality of its effects on the future. He quoted a remembered line from The Bhagavad-Gita, "I am become Death, the destroyer of worlds." Ken Bainbridge, the test director, replied to Oppenheimer, "Now we're all sons of bitches."

Several participants wanted to take back the atomic beast they had created and signed petitions to stop it, but their protests were useless. The beast was designed for destruction, as was proven on August 6, 1945, when a uranium bomb, nicknamed "Little Boy," was dropped on Hiroshima, Japan, killing 66,000 people and injuring 69,000 others with its 16-kiloton atomic explosion. Four days later on August 9, Nagasaki received a 23-kiloton plutonium bomb nicknamed "Fat Man," killing 80,000 citizens and injuring over 25,000.

Ecclesiastes 1:18 summed up that first nuclear bomb test day best: *For in much wisdom is much grief: and he that increaseth knowledge increaseth sorrow.* In this fallen world where magnificent developments of weapons of mass destruction exist, it would be unrealistic to suggest that these destructive weapons would someday go away and cease to be. Despite well-meaning advocates who fight to end nuclear production and clear the world of such weapons, power hungry nations never allow it. Looking at history, we learn that there has never been a time when people lived peaceably together.

According to scripture, there never will be until Christ returns to claim His Kingdom. Yes, Satan will use the peace ploy as a con to bring in his one world rule, but it will be short-lived. I Thessalonians 5 verse, 3 says: *For when they shall say, Peace and safety, then sudden destruction cometh upon them.* Men and women who lust for power and control do so contrary to God's will. They work under the same mentality of Satan and his demons when they opted to rebel against their Creator and become like "The Most High."

The book of Revelation speaks of "the great wrath" coming upon all humankind in the last days before Christ's return. This will be a time like no other on earth; evil will come to full power and there will be hellish wars and complete destruction. The creation of the nuclear bomb continues to flourish under today's advanced technology, while scripture lets us know that final judgment will someday come by mankind's own hands.

The mere explosion from an atomic bomb is deadly enough, but its destructive influence through radiation fallout continues to poison and kill long after the blast. With all the radiological discoveries came the huge responsibility and worry that in dealing with this very potent tool, accidents could happen. The worry was justified.

The 1985 Chazma Bay accident is one recent example that illustrates the potency and destruction of radiation. But there have been other accidents even earlier. A large part of the South Ural population (in Russia) had been exposed to radiation because of four big accidents starting from 1949: the Mayak Plutonium Production Complex (1,828 affected persons), the contamination of the Techa River by nuclear waste between 1949 and 1956 (124,000 affected persons), the Kitty accident of nuclear fallout after an explosion of a container filled with nuclear waste in 1957 (272,000 affected persons), and the radioactive contamination of large areas after a whirlwind at Lake Karachai in 1967 (42,000 affected people).

In the late 1960s, Palomares, Spain got hit with the radiation beast after the U.S. Strategic Air Command (SAC) conducted Operation Chrome Dome, which, in the interest of national defense, required the Air Force to fly aircraft carrying nuclear weapons around the world 24 hours a day. On January 16, 1966, two B-52 airplanes, each carrying four thermonuclear weapons containing 239 Pu (plutonium) flew to the southern borders of the former Soviet Union.

On their return trip to the United States, one collided in mid-air with a KC-135 tanker aircraft during a refueling operation over Spain. Fire erupted on the planes and the B-52 broke apart and scattered all four nuclear weapons over Palomares. Two weapons landed safely and were recovered, one in the water and the other on the beach near Palomares.

But the third and fourth weapons burst. One hit the low mountains west of the town, and the fourth struck agricultural land to the east. Both explosives burned, causing some of the plutonium inside to also burn and spread plutonium contamination throughout the area.

Because of partial chemical burning of the fissile material, a cloud formation, dispersed by a 35-mph wind, contaminated 1.4 miles of farmland with plutonium. Wind changes contaminated another 650 acres of land.

An agreement between the United States and Spain called for removing the top four inches of soil in contaminated areas, which ended up being 1,100 miles of soil. The decontamination procedure required 747 people and eight weeks of labor, and resulted in filling 4,879 metal 55-gallon drums. Some soil with surface contamination levels was mixed with petroleum oil, plowed under to a depth of eight inches, and then covered over with another layer of topsoil.

All of the indigenous population's croplands were destroyed after the Air Force contracted 140 trucks to move 3,400 truck-loads of replacement soil from a dry riverbed. The soil with high levels of contamination, together with other contaminated materials, were transferred to the United States for burial.

The Spanish government, concerned about public perception and panic, prohibited the U.S. Air Force cleanup crews from wearing anti-contamination suits or full face masks. Only uniforms, hats, and surgical gloves with tape over the openings between gloves and clothing were permitted. This resulted in internal contamination of some service members, who were monitored by urinalysis for plutonium content. Counter to U.S. recommendations, civilians were not restricted in their movements in or around the area. In the hilly, rocky area surrounding the impact site of the fourth weapon, it proved impossible to reach the initial cleanup standards set by the Spanish Government. Therefore, the limits for this area were adjusted to meet the conditions, with the agreement that the area would not be used for agriculture. Where the soil could not be removed, workers soaked it with water to bury the contamination. Although the local population was warned that the area was contaminated, the area was never restricted by local authorities. Spanish citizens eventually began to farm some of the land.

Six years after the incident, follow-up studies found that there was little change in the community and in exposed persons. Of the 714 people examined through 1988, 124 had urine concentrations of plutonium greater than the minimum detection limits.

There have been other radiation accidents between Palomares and Chazma Bay, but the biggest and most lethal accident would happen at a nuclear plant in Chernobyl in 1986. That accident would rattle the confidence of the entire world, raising a sharp reminder of how destructive radiation can be.

The first time my parents met the general he was dressed in full uniform, and I suspected he purposely did so to intimidate them. But after we all drank a few shots of cognac, everyone relaxed, and the general seemed to enjoy my family's company. It was evident that night that my parents and Joana had already decided my fate. Not one of them had asked me if I wanted to marry Lena; they only asked what day I thought would be best for the wedding. Being a participant in the general's life clouded my senses, and I let myself be seduced by it. My swollen head helped me lose some close friends. Later, by the time I "floated back to earth" and realized my stupidity, I found solace in maintaining close friendships.

I married Lena in May 1984, at the age of 19, despite the part of me that fought it. She bored easily and liked constant change; she was a social butterfly. I preferred the opposite. Even so, I was committed to make the marriage work.

I was working many night shifts when I began to hear rumors of my wife's affairs. I became depressed, not only at Lena's actions but because both sets of parents were making all the decisions for us. It seemed as if I had no control in my own marriage or my career. Worse, I hated myself for lacking the guts to do anything about it; my marriage into a prestigious family was too great a shield to give up. So I settled for being a pawn on the general's game board, moved only by his hand. I had made a trade-off—and now it had me strung up like a puppet on a string.

Chapter Five

The Horrors of the Red Zone

C ommander Koklushin spread his booted legs and rested his fists on his hips while our unit lined up in formation outside the barrack rooms. It was nine at night and emergency meetings like this seldom happened unless we were facing reprimand. I wondered what trouble we were in this time, and swallowed, waiting, as Koklushin pulled a switchblade out of his pocket, opened it, and lazily started cleaning his fingernails with the sharp tip. It was April 29, 1986; the cool spring night air that filled the corridor, along with our commander's silence, made us quiver.

"I bet this is about Alex," I whispered at Dimitri, remembering the hashish his relatives in Azerbaijan sent him earlier that week. The foolish cadet had smoked it the night before with his comrades. The sour smell permeating our rooms probably gave him away.

Our commander, a good-looking man with a square jaw and thick brows, turned, faced the young men, inhaled until his chest rose, and spoke without emotion. "Something happened in the Ukraine at the Chernobyl Nuclear plant. There was a mishap in one of the reactors. This caused a radiation leak."

No one reacted. He went on. "Military divisions are working there now. Our academy's facility is organizing teams of responders to help in the area. Our best physicians, nurses, and lab technicians will be in this group, which means your unit will lose some instructors. Until they return, you will cooperate with the substitute instructors and give them full attention. This is classified information and the civilian population does not know about this. You are entrusted by the highest officials to safeguard this information."

Koklushin saluted and dismissed us.

On April 26, 1986, at 1:23 a.m., less than a year after the Chazma Bay tragedy, the Soviet Union faced a worse disaster—one that would shake the entire world by irradiating 2.2 million people.

On that day, before the sun broke through the dusky skies, pipes began to swell and crack under the pressure of an overheated reactor located inside the Chernobyl Nuclear Plant. The plant was the main energy source for the Ukraine and the Belarus regions. Four hundred workers, working in split shifts, were employed at the large nuclear complex and lived eight miles southeast in the nearby port city of Chernobyl, which had

a population of 12,000 people. The hard working townsfolk
employed at the plant made better salaries then the ship build-
ers nearby, but all the people shared common interests. After
work they enjoyed meeting for dinner, taking their children to
the park, or going out together for a movie at the only theatre in
town. The city contained two colleges, four schools, one hospital, and a library. Ten miles north of the town's nuclear plant,
49,000 people resided in the city of Pripyat and another 90,000
folks occupied the obscure surrounding villages. A dense forest
nestled close to the cities. Kiev, the capital of Ukraine, was 80
miles away.

The Chernobyl Nuclear Plant sits near the Pripyat River at
the northwest end of a cooling pond, an artificial body of water
of 13 square miles that was constructed to provide cooling water
for the plant reactors. During normal operation, the plant
discharged warm water counterclockwise around the pond,
taking in cool water near the north end.

When the reactor overheated, workers tried to cool the
reactor too quickly, causing two rapid explosions to rock the
area and spew an atmospheric release of one million Ci (curie, a
unit used to measure radioactivity in the air) radioisotopes from
the core of the reactor. A prolonged release of large quantities of
radioactive substance flew into the atmosphere and spread
throughout the northern hemisphere, across Europe. Radioactivity transported by the multiple plumes from Chernobyl was also
measured in Canada, Japan and the United States. Only the
southern hemisphere remained free of contamination. Meteoro-
logical conditions and wind regimes during the period of release
contributed to the spread. Belarus, Ukraine, and partial areas of

Russia suffered serious radiological, health and socio-economic consequences. Although the radiological impact did not reach the entire globe, public awareness of the dangers of nuclear energy slapped the world in the face.

The number 4 reactor of the Chernobyl nuclear power plant was to be shutdown for routine maintenance the evening before the accident. But the test was carried out without proper communication among the team in charge of the test and the employees in charge of the operation and safety of the reactor. This lack of co-ordination and awareness between the plant's staff led the operators to take actions which deviated from established safety procedures. Their actions were compounded by the significant drawbacks in the reactor's design, which made the plant potentially unstable and easily susceptible to loss of control in the event of operational errors. The combination of these factors provoked a sudden and unmanageable power surge, which resulted in vicious explosions and almost total destruction of the reactor.

The two explosions sent fuel, core components, and structural items into the air and produced a shower of hot and highly radioactive debris, exposing the destroyed core to the atmosphere. Radiation contaminated the sky as the plume of smoke, radioactive fission products and debris rose from the core 1,000 yards into the air. The heavier debris in the cloud was deposited close to the site; lighter components, including fission products and all noble gas inventories, were blown by the prevailing wind to the northwest of the plant.

The remaining Unit 4 building was ravaged by fires, giving rise to pillars of steam and dust. Fires also broke out on the adjacent turbine hall roof and in storages that held diesel fuel and inflammable materials.

The alarm sounded at 1:23 a.m. in the plant's fire station. A dozen firemen rushed to the scene of Reactor 4. After accessing the situation, they set the alarm code to "extreme emergency," requesting help from every fire station within 100 miles. Three other fire crews, each with a little over a half-dozen men, arrived within ten minutes, but it would be two hours before reinforcements arrived from Kiev. The first fire crew went up to the roof, while the other responders tackled the fires inside the building. They worked feverishly in a thick, smoky and poisonous environment, all the time receiving severe radiation exposure. By 5:00 a.m. they thought they had tamed the beast; yet it was still alive, spewing deathly doses of contamination into the air.

A dramatic orange-blue haze illuminated the darkness around the entire reactor area, showing evidence of radioactivity in the sky. Citizens living close by were edgy at the lack of information given on television news reports as to what happened and what was being done. Some people, out of fear, started hosing down the radiation dust from their homes and cars.

Although the fires were put out, the firemen still had to contend with the graphite fire. (Once the graphite mixed with oxygen after the blast, a chemical fire erupted.) There is little expertise on fighting graphite fires, since it cannot be extinguished by water. There was a fear that any attempt to put it out might disperse more radionuclides, perhaps by steam production, or provoke a criticality excursion in the nuclear fuel.

By the time the firemen from Kiev arrived, the first crews were so weak from radiation sickness that they could not climb down the ladders, and had to be carried down by the relief crews and transported to hospitals, where the majority died of acute radiation sickness in less than a month.

Three months later our facility, the Military Field Therapy Faculty, began to take in and treat irradiated responders who had worked in the Red Zone of the Chernobyl cleanup. For clinical practice, our class had the opportunity to work hands-on, treating and studying the effects of irradiated patients.

One young soldier from the chemical battalion division, Vasily Shevcov, had the worse case. He had responded at the onset of the disaster and remained working at the radiated site for two months. His diagnosis was neuro-circulatory dystonia, an intermediate condition between acute radiation syndrome (ARS) and chronic radiation illness (CRI). The difference between both illnesses is that ARS develops from receiving high doses of radiation in a short time and CRI is developed from receiving small doses into the body over a longer period of time. CRI, unlike ARS, will cause neurological problems such as involuntary muscle twitching and vessel spasm which lead to blood pressure problems and loss of concentration.

Vasily was one of 7,000 military soldiers who worked on the roof of Building B and Unit 3 at the Chernobyl nuclear plant. Those workers came to be known as the "biological robots," because machines and electronic equipment were inoperable around them due to the strong gamma-neutron radiation field.

During my break I noticed Vasily hanging around the

restroom smoking. "Look," I said, walking up beside him, "doctor's orders are that you curb that smoking..." I didn't finish. My eyes fell to his bandaged hands. He had developed gangrene and recently lost six fingers. His weary eyes sank into the dark circles around them. He had lost his hair, and looked thinner than the week before. He already had numerous skin grafts on his chest area. I didn't say any more. He was bad enough; why keep him from what he enjoyed? I helped him light up another cigarette.

From that day we formed a bond. I made a point to see him each day and he talked a lot about his work in Chernobyl. Our conversations seemed to lift his spirits.

"They won't let my parents see me, you know," Vasily said as I checked his blood pressure. "They don't know about these yet." He lifted his wrapped hands. "I am tired from the grafts. They might as well skin me."

I knew that every time Vasily was sent across town to the burn center at the Military Navy Hospital Therapy Faculty to treat his radiation burns, he faced a painful process. If patients became resistant to morphine during the process of bandage change and necrotic tissue replacement, they had to be strapped to the operating table. Plastic tubes placed between their teeth kept them from biting their tongues when the pain became unbearable. In those times it was best if they lost consciousness because it was easier on the health professionals to proceed with surgical manipulations.

I felt badly for Vasily. It was his first year in service and, of course, the newer soldiers worked the most dangerous areas at the nuclear plant. The constant contact work by hand with highly radioactive material is why he lost fingers and had skin grafts on his chest and shoulders area. It would be a long recovery process for him, and I doubted he would ever have children. I was glad he didn't bring up that subject.

Vasily slowly moved into a seated position on the bed. "You know," he said, "we were sent into Chernobyl completely unprepared."

"What do you mean, unprepared?" I asked the private. I replaced his chart at the footboard and sat on the stool beside his bed.

"No one informed us of the dangerous radiation levels or the risks we were taking," Vasily said softly. "We figured it out though. My unit did not want to go on the roofs and inside the facility. They pushed us to go. A handful of soldiers refused to eat for days in protest. Those guys were arrested. I never smoked before in my life before all this. Or drank. Now I drink shaving cologne."

He trembled as he spoke. I was well aware of his addictions, but worried more about his state of mind. He had lost his appetite and hardly slept. I feared his depression would weaken his immune system from fighting infection. "So they never had you decontaminate?" I asked him.

"We barely had breaks. I learned later that if they would have just told us to tape shut the openings of our outerwear most of us would not be as sick."

"No personal dosimeters?"

"What's that?" Vasily asked.

I shook my head. These guys had been sheep led to sure slaughter. I answered, "A dosimeter is a tool used to measure radiation doses. It lets you know when levels are too high for your body, so you know when to leave the area."

"No, maybe some guys had those, but not my unit. They were not concerned about us at all, Igor. It is hard to deal with this, you know."

I wasn't surprised. I knew well enough the military's take on caring for their own. I patted his knee and left him alone.

The saddest thing indeed about the Chernobyl nuclear accident was the unprepared response immediately following the blast. Firemen responded bravely and showed dedication to their profession, but they were unprepared for a disaster of that enormity. Their lack of preparation and training would eventually cost most of them their lives. Only a few of them carried a personal dosimeter to measure the doses. Those who did check the gauge pooh-poohed the readings as faulty instead of realizing the needle flies back to zero when there is an overexposure level. Every employee had a personal dosimeter, but no one could find the keys used to unlock the stainless steel lockers where most of them were stored. Few respirators were used. Gauze surgical masks were available, but the firemen opted not to use them. They were working in a radioactive Red Zone, yet their response was handled as if they were simply fighting a house fire. One fireman removed his helmet because he felt hot; another used his bare hands to handle radioactive material, and one fireman who sat in the radioactive dust received third degree radiation burns to his buttocks. Even after they were relieved from duty, they did not remove the radioactive fallout from their bodies. This caused severe radiation damage to the skin, and eventually became the source for secondary infection.

Worse than the lack of safety preparation during the response, Russian officials did not want to take responsibility for the possibility of dangerous radioisotopes filtering into the yards of surrounding communities. It seemed no one wanted to be the bearer of dreadful tidings in case the Kremlin wanted someone's "head" for incompetence. That was the reason the civil defense chief of the Chernobyl plant, Sergey S. Vorobyev, waited two hours before calling his superiors in the Kiev region. And when he did, Vorobyev diminished the peril of the disaster by minimizing the details and size of the incident. Afterward Vorobyev opened the underground shelter facility (built under the plant in the event of such a disaster) to operate his command post. But he told none of the remaining 268 employees to evacuate and join him underground. They continued working and showed up at the plant the next day, never told of the high levels of radiation emitting from the core of blown Reactor Number 4. The blast was equivalent to over 40 tons of TNT and the roof of Reactor 4 was completely gone, yet no one dared question their superiors. Vorobyev put the secretary of the communist party in charge (a man who knew absolutely nothing about radiation), to make dose reports. However, the secretary compromised the reports going to Moscow, making the documents show reasonable levels of radiation instead of the actual dangerous levels that were contaminating large regions.

KGB officials stopped phone calls from going out to some republics and blocked radio signals to prevent the story from becoming international. Because of the deception, no immediate evacuation took place for the thousands of civilians living nearby. It wasn't until Sweden started picking up abnormal radiation levels that the incident was forced into international news. Four whole days after the explosion, the officials in Kiev were finally given the accurate details of the incident.

Within hours after the explosion, the Soviet Civil Defense began sending civilian survey teams outside the plant to test the level of radiation. Because these men were non-military, the teams did not have the proper calibrated monitoring instruments and know-how to get accurate radiation level readings. Because superiors hushed up the details of the explosion, the firemen fighting the fires were not forewarned of possible radiation exposure. A handful of scientists sent to the destroyed Unit 4 to assess the situation also kept mum about possible radiation leakage into the air. The first symptoms of acute radiation syndrome on firemen began surfacing 15 minutes after the explosion. In the villages nearby, a half-mile from the nuclear core, people started finding pieces of the core's graphite strewn across streets and yards. The chunks of graphite were so contaminated that if someone stood beside one piece for an hour they contracted a 50 percent chance of dying.

Meanwhile, the first measures taken to control fire and the radionuclides releases consisted of dumping neutron-absorbing compounds and fire-control material into the reactor crater. Helicopters hovered over the gaping Number 4 reactor and dropped 5000 tons of lead, sand, clay and other absorbents. But the lead evaporated into a secondary poisonous cloud and contaminated all the territory around the nuclear plant with lead poisoning covering a radius of several miles. A total of 213 children would later be tested in that region with a concentration of lead in their blood hundreds of times higher then normal.

The first responders faced other serious problems. They feared all the water at the bottom of the cooling pool under the reactor might turn into steam and emit more radiation. And they were worried about seasonal rainfalls that would carry contamination into cities. Within the next days, responders worked hard to build a dam to prevent any seasonal floods from going towards the Pripyat River, and they blocked sewage, hoping to stop the city's water from becoming contaminated. Frustration built as responders, with no idea how the reactor might behave, waited for permission to proceed from their "slow-as-molasses" superiors.

Ten hours after the reactor blew, the military and National Guard entered the scene at the plant, making up 80 percent of responders. The mishap became a classified operation. For ten days after the explosion one million Ci radioisotopes were released every day, bringing a grand total release of over 40 million Ci.

On the early evening of the 26th, one full day after the reactor blew, evacuation orders were given to surrounding cities. It was not until the following day that 1,200 or so public buses and 200 trucks rolled into Pripyat to evacuate the residents. Two trains were also readied at the Yanov Train Station. Yet another eight hours passed before law enforcement officials let the people board the trains and vehicles.

The 47,000 people who were evacuated, including 17,000 children and 80 non-walking civilians, were driven out of the city through the less contaminated back roads. Another 1,500 evacuees left by trains. On the borders of the zone, responders set up gas stations as deactivation points for decontamination of transport vehicles and people. Bleach solutions were used to wash vehicles; showers and changes of clothing were used for some of the public.

By the 28th, the third day, the radiological background exceeded normal levels by 40 times, including roads, vehicles, and animals. The surrounding forest was heavily contaminated, and overworked responders thought that cutting and burning the foliage might kill the contamination. They were wrong. Instead, the burning trees released radioactive smoke and caused another secondary contamination. Discovering their mistake, they hastily put out the fire and cut the trees into small pieces and stored them in special containers, which were than placed underground and topped with a thousand tons of concrete. This job was difficult and took months to complete. One of the dangerous radioisotopes released into the air was cesium 137. The Belarus forest was contaminated with cesium over 1,600,000 acres of forest. This is 27.9 percent of the Belarus territory. Not only was the water in the river and ponds contaminated, but 7,000 underground wells in the Gomelsky region of the Ukraine could not be used for drinking water. The responders could not rest; they also had wells to dry up.

The second evacuation started on May 2 for everyone living within a 17-mile radius zone, covering the Ukraine and the Belarus Republic. A total of more than 100,000 persons and farm animals were evacuated during the first few weeks following the accident. Decontamination procedures performed by military personnel included the washing of buildings, cleaning residential areas, removing contaminated soil, cleaning roads and decontaminating water supplies.

Today, in the Ukraine alone, three million people live in contaminated zones. One attempt was made by the administration to reduce thyroid doses of stable iodine to block radioactive uptake by the thyroid (Me92). Its success is doubtful. People who refused to leave their homes during evacuation were compensated and offered yearly medical examinations by the government, based on their annual doses. The residents in the less contaminated areas were provided with medical monitoring. By November 1986, 80 percent of evacuatees were allowed to return for their personal items; the remaining 20 percent lost their items to over-contamination.

Twenty-eight people died of acute radiation syndrome (ARS) within a month following the Chernobyl incident; 22 of these were reactor operators, technicians, and engineers who tried to insert control rods or open valves by hand. Others who died were the first firemen who were on the roof for the first three hours after the accident. In the first few days of the disaster over 2,300 children were hospitalized in local clinics with development of ARS. Later, over half of them developed thyroid adenomas and acute leukemia. Many of these kids died.

The responders continued to clean up the site for a few years, and continued to receive moderate doses of radiation. Out of 600,000 of those responders, tens of thousands eventually died from the chronic radiation illnesses. The military pilots who dropped materials inside the reactor's hole to stop the fire received serious doses. The last pilot died in Seattle, Washington from acute leukemia in 1998. The scientists and responders working in the Red Zone with improper protection developed complications in their respiratory tracts in the form of chronic bronchitis, bronchial asthma, pulmonary fibrosis, and some lung cancer.

United Nations General Secretary Kofy Annan reported that at least seven million people were affected by this catastrophe; three million would need continued treatment, and the men involved in the response would need constant monitoring.

We live in a nuclear age that offers no certainty as to when or where another incident—terrorist act, act of war, or accident— —might occur, only that it will most likely occur again. We can be sure the odds of another disaster are stacked against us. Learning from the disasters of Chazma Bay and Chernobyl is extremely necessary for safe and correct response in the future. Nations need to be prepared to handle all and any large-scale WMD event.

Proper training and education to the general population, as well as to responders, on the subject of correct response and recovery is vital for panic control and smooth evacuation and response of the population.

The Chernobyl disaster wouldn't leave me alone. I was forced to face up to the reality of what that mishap was costing people.

"Igor!" The stocking-footed cadet stuck his head inside the barracks where I was visiting and studying with my friends for our final exam on military toxicology. "Come here," he said, motioning me to get up. I had lots of formulas to memorize and the interruption into my concentration annoyed me. But the look on his face told me it was urgent, so I slid off the bed and followed him out of the room. "The phone in the hall—it's your mom."

"Thanks," I muttered. The young cadet paddled back to his warm room and I headed for the hall corridor.

My mother knew better then to interrupt my study period, so I knew something was wrong. I scurried past two more rooms where other students were lounging with open books and quickly grabbed the black phone on the hallway table.

"Mom, what's up?" I asked.

"Your Uncle Nickolai went back to Krasnoyarsk today," Mom said, sounding worried. "He's going to Chernobyl."

The Chernobyl incident, which had happened two months earlier, was still a huge concern on everyone's mind. Our family was especially concerned when Uncle Nickolai volunteered to help clean up the mess. My parents, my grandmother, and Nickolai's wife, my aunt, had tried to convince him not to go, but their words were wasted arguments. Thousands of civilian volunteers and military responders, dubbed the "liquidators," were moving toward Chernobyl to help clean up the biggest nuclear accident of modern civilization, and he wanted to be part of it. He seemed oblivious to the idea he could die from radiation sickness.

Nickolai Popov was married to my mother's sister, Vera, and was the owner of a pig farm and the captain of one of the local fire departments in the Krasnoyarsk Region, Siberia. I always loved him because he was a jolly man and treated me well. When I was a child, for every summer vacation my parents would take me on the four-day train ride to Siberia where we

would visit my grandma and stay with Aunt Vera and Uncle
Nickolai. My uncle's half-acre pig farm never included a dull
moment. I loved racing and riding the fat pigs during the day. At
night, on my trips to the outhouse, I chased the cat-size rats
around the pigpen. My appearance never stayed quite as clean
during those trips out into the country, and my mother would
complain. But skinny Uncle Nickolai would pat his out-of-place
posh belly and pipe up in my defense, saying, "Let him be,
Albina. A good farmer gets dirty. It is hard work taking care of
animals!"

Aunt Vera, a hefty kind woman with an attractive face,
served us plenty of food using the fresh vegetables out of her
garden and the leftover meats she brought home from the
hospital's kitchen where she worked as head chef. She cooked
double portions for me and let me sneak down and play in the
dark underground pantry where she stored all her homemade
canned and marinated foods.

I tried to calm my mother on the phone, but I knew Uncle
Nickolai was headstrong and nothing that any of us could say
would change his mind. He had told Aunt Vera, "I am forty-
eight years old; I will live to be eighty, but before I do I will own
a car. They are paying me to do this; how can I refuse? It is just
for a few months."

I hung up the phone with Mom feeling uneasy. I knew how
serious the Chernobyl task was, and I remembered all too well
the Chazma Bay patients I observed with my mother-in-law last
year. I also worried for my uncle because this disaster made that
submarine nuclear accident pale in comparison. I understood
the dangers that ionizing radiation and the levels of hazard

exposed to the thousands of responders who would be working around the plant, not to mention the folks living nearby.

With all that was transpiring within my family, it seemed ironic to me that Uncle Nickolai and Aunt Vera also lived about 25 miles from Krasnoyarsk 26, where the Devyatka area (large classified nuclear warhead production facility) was located. Condemned prisoners worked at Devyatka to dig natural uranium from the mountain for the development of nuclear warheads. Since the criminals were sentenced to die for their crime, the Soviet officials had no concern that the convicts were handling live radioactive material.

The area was known for its purifying process of uranium. Oddly enough, the land used to belong to my mother's parents before the revolution. My grandfather had owned three villages with thousands of acres of property before it was taken from him by the communist regime in the 1920s.

One of the towns taken from my grandparents was called Balchuck, a place my grandmother loved deeply. She remained there, although she no longer owned her property, until the day she died.

The Devyatka area housed large nuclear reactors that were cooled down by the adjoining Yenisey River. Pipes were built inside the river to flow into the midst of the reactors and back out again into the water. A huge hydro station, similar to Hoover Dam but three times bigger, was built miles away. It was used to increase the speed of the river flow ten times, to flush radioactive waste that was secretly being dumped into the water. An increase of the water flow was needed to move the contaminated materials along the bottom of the river. The last time I had been to that river, as a teenager, the water was a weird black color, and no form of life could be found in it.

Living near the uranium mountain didn't harm my uncle, but his job as "liquidator" for the Chernobyl clean up sure did. Three months after my uncle finished working at the Chernobyl plant, he returned to his home. Right after he elatedly bought his car, he developed radiation illness. He lost energy, lost concentration and memory, lost weight, lost coordination of his muscles, had severe headaches, and gained pains in the bones of his legs. He found refuge in his vodka and died a few years later in 1991 from leukemia, a form of blood cancer, in the same hospital where his wife worked as chef.

While I was dealing with my own personal woes (parent pressure, the rigors of the communist military, and an unfaithful wife), emergency responders like my Uncle Nickolai and Vasily, fighting the world's biggest nuclear disaster, were being swallowed up, much like Jonah was swallowed by his whale. Others were fighting both nuclear disasters and the entire Soviet regime in those years of 1985 and 1986. Ways to combat such disasters will always result in unnecessary fatalities whenever there is a totalitarian government at the helm of the boat. The storm came, and the ones who had to fight the raging winds were thrown overboard by the numerous officers and captains through delays, lack of instruction, and improper tools.

Any type of WMD event cannot be dealt with properly if people are afraid of their government or the government refuses to be up front about the ordeal. Covering up facts during the crucial moments of the Chernobyl explosion led to lost lives of responders and radiation contamination of surrounding regions. The fact that the government worried more about their political reputation abroad than the welfare of the millions of people from radiation exposure bears truth to the fact that a nation void of God will never put human life ahead of political agenda.

One of Christ's greatest commandments, one of which He said there was none greater, was this: *Thou shalt love thy neighbor as thyself.* When God is removed from government and forced out of people's hearts, then this love that moves people to react with compassion toward one another becomes lost, and stale, and "self" dominates the heart instead, leaving no room for anyone or anything else.

Emergency responders usually choose their profession because they do carry inside themselves an inner spark of compassion and concern for their neighbor. Saving lives is a job that takes more than mere strength. There is no greater job, no profession more honorable than being willing to risk one's own life to save another human being. It is a profession built on this greatest of Christ's command.

Thus, shouldn't these people be trained adequately to face the risks involved while saving lives? Absolutely yes! They need to be prepared to work as one unit to minimizes mistakes and fatalities. Being stuck in the belly of a whale will not accomplish anything during a disaster. Having the essential means to do what is necessary for proper response will keep the whales at bay, and eliminate confusion and unnecessary loss of lives.

A nation that is willing to spend the money to equip emergency responders for WMD disasters will be able to turn an uncontrollable situation into a controllable one, and fewer people will die. Despite the fact superiors did not relay vital information to the responders during the Chernobyl incident, the responders reacted with what they did have, working hard to stop the disaster and risking their lives to do so. Had they been informed and trained for such an incident with proper procedures and equipment, I believe half of the people who died would still be alive.

The USSR kept their military up to par in WMD preparation. When it came to civilian issues, such as the Chernobyl Nuclear Plant accident, no money was ever delivered to update proper equipment or training. How sad this is when we see almost one third of the world's atmosphere contaminated by the worst nuclear disaster known to date. It won't be until the year 2016 that the actual number of people affected by the lingering effects of ionizing radiation will truly be known.

Every responder that is facing a terrible plane or car accident, fire, nuclear explosion, flood, or a biological outbreak understands that they are responding to the call, knowing they face the possibility of dying. There is a God-given faith that buoys them to go beyond their natural feats, and it is supernatural.

The many firemen and emergency responders who died trying to save people in the 9/11 disaster in New York did not turn around and go back home when they saw the fire and smoke. They faced the storm; they walked on the water, knowing that whether they lived or died, they were doing the right thing, doing what was pleasing to God, and doing what any caring individual would do. They loved their neighbors as much as

they loved themselves, and died proving that God's love is still
real and alive in our dysfunctional world.

In the Gospels we are told about the time Jesus slept in the
boat while a storm raged on, filling the boat with water. The
disciples were scared because they feared the boat would sink
or be swept away by the torrential winds. They woke Jesus and
said, *Master, carest thou not that we perish?* Jesus responded
and rebuked the seas by saying, *Peace, be still.* Immediately the
wind stopped and a great calm replaced the maddening tempest.

Christ had slept while the ship lunged back and forth under
the power of the storm, not once concerned about His life or his
disciple's lives, because He knew their lives were in good
hands. His Father was in control of that storm, and no matter
how much the waves bellowed and the lightening roared, His
Father was at the helm of that ship. Jesus had complete faith
and trust in His Father. And this is the same faith that God
desires each of us to exercise too. A faith that is strong and sure
during the most awful hurricanes that suddenly come out of the
blue and knock us over; a faith that will still our hearts. We
can't predict when another disaster or war might happen, when
a plane will crash, or when a child will drown, but God promises
that no matter what "red zone" we might face, He is in control.
And this is the comfort that we must rely on, and take into our
heart— *Peace, be still.*

The day I took my military oath in 1982 (second right).

My mother Albina and I. She had great expectations for me (left).

At the Red Village Military Training Facilities near Leningrad in 1982 (right).

Taking a break from medical studies in 1983, with friend Dimitri Tonkope (right).

That's me as Chief Officer for the Medical Unit in Jawor, Poland in 1989 (left).

Soviet medical officers in training at the academy in 1985 (below).

The Leningrad Military Medical Academy where I trained (bottom).

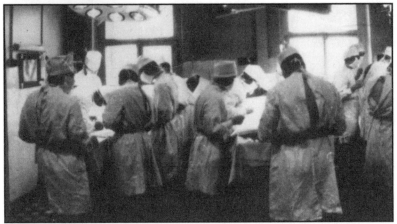

I am inside this outfit during my training with the chemical analyzer VPXR (military field chemical intelligence monitoring equipment). This suit provides protection as we responded to "enemy attack" (left).

The Military Field Therapy Clinic/Facility where I studied radiation-related illnesses, including Chernobyl military victims.

My graduation day at
the Leningrad Military
Medical Academy, 1988
(above).

Post-military days outside
Hotel #1 with my medical
students. I am standing
next to Dr. Irina Baktina,
college director, in the
front row (left).

June and me
(next to bus
door) with
Christian Airline
Personnel
Missionary
Outreach
group in St.
Petersburg,
1993 (right).

My great grandparents, Isaac and Mary Shafhid, who were trapped and burned in the synagogue by the German army in 1941 (above left). My grandfather, Mendel, about the age of 18. He died in World War II (at right).

My father, Vladimir, (left) and my mother, Albina (below), now living in the U.S.

That's me helping June do mission work in St. Petersburg in 1993 (left).

Two of the greatest moments in my life. Above, I am receiving water baptism in 1993 at the Technical University in St. Petersburg, with members of Calvary Chapel. At right, I am shown on the day that June and I were married, May 15, 1993, in St. Petersburg, Russia.

Chapter Six
"Nuclear Winter"

TRAINING AT RED VILLAGE
EPICENTER OF A NUCLEAR BLAST
UNPREPAREDNESS WILL BE DEADLY

The ground underneath my feet rippled before I heard the sound, and I knew it had happened. Within seconds a muddy-gray billowy stem soared up from the earth like a tornado, giving birth to a spectacular red-hot fireball at the top. The mushroom cloud shot up 1,600 feet into the air with a deafening blast. The loud noise, the shaking earth, and the gloomy overcast sky provided an ominous setting.

Leonyd pinched me in the back and yelled, "It's time."

I nodded at my tall friend and wanted to move, but the incredible sight had me mesmerized. Although the entire military crew knew the exercise was not using an actual nuclear device, the large drums of gasoline and explosions they had used imitated a real nuclear explosion well enough. The power of the blast made me feel proud and excited, yet at the same time edgy and nervous. I knew if this had been a real device, we would not have been standing there staring at it, but rather face down, covering our eyes, and fearing for our lives.

Leonyd grabbed my arm and broke through my distraction. "We have one hour, Igor. Come on!"

I turned away, and we high-tailed it back to our designated area. The test device had been detonated at six o'clock that dreary morning on July 16, 1986, just a few months after the Chernobyl mishap. We had 60 minutes to erect our portable clinics and don our protective wear before the *cloud* came.

We were in a place called Red Village; a military training compound located 40 minutes away from my military academy in Leningrad. The gated site, a classified training ground for military medical cadets and other military chemical and re-search institutions, sat on a hill amid the forest and open fields, away from the townsfolk and overlooking the outskirts of Leningrad. The area housed a full service battalion to maintain the post and guard it against intruders. No one could get inside without proper documentation.

Military field exercises were arduous, and usually took place in the summertime, sometimes before summer break. They always simulated a "West" attack, with nuclear warfare being the most probable scenario. Our unit consisted of about 100 men, all training on proper WMD response. Training exercises often lasted two days and dealt only with military battlefield evacuation of soldiers, never scenarios involving civilians. Even though it was summer, these drills were referred to as "nuclear winter."

That day my division was training on mass casualty warfare in the event of an enemy strike, and how to organize the evacuation process of victims from the battlefield and contaminated zones after a nuclear/chemical impact. Along with the *nuclear* detonation, a combined *chemical* release made the day even more difficult; our post had to deal with multiple tasks and circumstances. For instance, we had known there was a possibility of a chemical attack. Only after the surveillance teams detected the presence of a nerve agent (simulated) in the contaminated areas did we start opening the stockpiles of antidotes.

I had been up at the crack of dawn with my unit, not sure when the device would be activated. Our orders were to be ready. We threw on our army fatigues and left the bunks without hope of getting much of a breakfast. At the time of detonation, we were to secure our area (the Field Medical Point), put up our medical tents, get into protective wear and began treating *contaminated* patients.

We had to deal with various issues concerning external contamination of the soil and air with both radiation and chemical agents. Thus our drills had to be within a strict time frame, especially because of concerns about the change of humidity factors and the possibility of rain. Military helicopters, tanks, flatbed transports and other heavy-duty vehicles had been arranged at different locations; it was the job of the military medics to deliver the *victims* to our area. Because helicopters could not land near our camp for fear the blades would blow the potentially contaminated dust into our tents, my unit was also in charge of making sure the medics delivered the victims to their appropriate location.

The exercise was huge, simulating multiple casualties. My unit was to expect about 200 victims—both real people and Rescue Randys (dummies)—to proceed though the 14-hour ordeal. Majors and colonels watched us closely, recording every move. Everything had to be done in great detail. During a real WMD attack, one mistake could cost us our lives, as well as unnecessary spread of contamination. The Soviet military treated those exercises as if the event were the real thing. We were expected to act accordingly.

During live nuclear activation exercises, similar to the 40-kiloton device that was dropped September 14, 1954 at the Totskoye Test Site in the Southern Ural Region, 45,000 soldiers and officers, 600 tanks, 500 artillery guns, 600 heavy-duty military transports, 320 airplanes, and 6,000 different sorts of machinery were used. Soldiers were supplied with plenty of chemical and radiological instruments to monitor radiation levels on specific areas, themselves, and stockpiles of protective gear and gas masks (PPE). They started practicing 45 days before detonation and dug 236 miles of trenches and 500 special underground facilities.

Our response to these exercises, whether real or feigned, had to be perfect. We were not allowed mistakes. That is why the Soviet Army often did not inform us whether or not they were going to be using real chemical agents during exercises. The commanders did not want us getting lazy and removing our masks. Despite the fact the agent was diluted, the chemical was strong enough to hospitalize soldiers that compromised orders. This deceit was common practice, even in earlier exercises. At the Totskoye nuclear test in 1954, three bombs were dropped, but only one was genuine. Battalions were told all three devices were real, so they would respond at the highest efficiency level.

In those days of Soviet rule, soldiers trained in unacceptable levels of radiation exposure rates—up to 25 R/hour (roentgen per hour, the measurement of radiation in the air). In comparison, today's dose limits for U.S. responders during training or actual events on a radiological incident cannot exceed 5 rem/year. The USSR did not stop exercises for responder casualties then, and neither does the New Russian Federation today. In most cases accidents in exercises involving tank divisions, air support and thousands and thousands of military personnel using real armories and ammunition are hard to avoid.

A real scenario demands clinics and decontamination units to be up and running within a certain time frame. Our unit was in charge of four field medical processing tents, or "clinics." These clinics were where we would treat the wounded and contaminated victims. Weeks prior to the exercise, on our pre-training days, we were forced to polish our set-up technique and get the tents erected and ready for medical service within an hour. If we failed to meet that deadline, we had to take the entire tent down and start over.

Rainy days were used to replicate contaminated rainfall with radioisotopes from the original cloud or radioactive fallout; leaky tents were unacceptable. We spent most of our time putting tents up and taking them down all day long on those wet pre-training days.

Eight of us cadets grabbed one end of the long canvas roll and another eight grabbed the other side. We undid the fasteners and unfolded the tent on the ground. We each had a specific job to do, and we would put the tent together as though we were circus performers facing a delicate and dangerous high-wire performance without the use of a net. With precision skill and speed we erected the padded, multi-layer skeleton into place.

"I got the shovels," I hollered through the drowning noise of artillery and air strikes. I tossed a shovel to the cadet next to me. We had to make sure the tent exterior walls were secured into the ground to prevent contamination from seeping underneath the canvas.

I looked up at the sky. It was overcast, and I expected rain to fall within a few hours. I remembered how many times we had to pull down our tent during pre-training after rain leaked inside. I didn't want our unit to fail that day. "Dig deeper in the ground; we need to make sure this rain stays outside!" My back ached, and I felt dizzy from moving so fast on an empty stomach, but there was no time to think about my woes.

Thirty minutes had passed by the time the exterior was secure, leaving about 20 minutes before we had to don our protective wear. Once inside the tent, a few of the fellows went straight to fixing the negative pressure spaces, pipes, and engines into the right location for proper room pressure, along with the multi-filter systems for radiological and chemical protection. Leonyd and I inserted the inside walls to form our few rooms. Two other guys prepared the floors with plastic and rubber layers

We then set up the portable surgical tables (covering them with rubber sheets), portable anesthesiology equipment, surgical instruments, oxygen tanks, small field X-ray machines, antiseptics and deactivation solutions, and antidote/antitoxin kits. Everyone was responsible to remember exactly where every instrument and antidote was placed.

Each small clinic held three field operating rooms, which were set up to perform lifesaving thoracic and abdominal interventions, as well as deal with all possible trauma injuries. Three patients could be in surgery at once in one tent. The rest of the victims, wearing masks for protection, were laid on stretchers in waiting areas inside and outside the clinics.

Engines ran inside to keep negative air pressure filtering any type of biological or chemical agents in aerosol form and, in some instances with certain filters, radioactive dust. Most challenging was keeping the contaminated rooms decontaminated, which was strenuous both physically and mentally. After each patient, the designated rooms had to be cleaned. We did this by deactivating hazardous fluids from all used instruments and using a portable apparatus filled with disinfectant to create steam. Once the condensation settled, the negative pressure inside the tent was used to draw out the water. Big dry pads were then used to wipe down the equipment. From there we constantly swabbed surfaces to check contamination levels to make sure there was no secondary release of chemical agents, especially off-gassing from victim's contaminated skin and wounds.

The most complicated surgery to perform was abdominal intervention. If we had to stop any type of internal hemorrhaging, we had to proceed even with the presence of radioactive contamination on victims, or we could lose the patient. Performing surgeries while wearing protective gear was not a pleasant task. The gray-toned rubber suits (worn only for chemical and biological release) and full-faced gas masks were bulky and heavy. I felt as if I were stuck in an overheated coffin-sized sauna. Sometimes, depending on the agent, we had to wear the "elephant-nose" mask with the charcoal filters. Although they gave us 100 percent protection, they made breathing difficult, and caused quick dehydration. Often guys in my unit who forgot to take breaks for water, collapsed, and lost consciousness. Today the Russian army uses newer advanced masks that allow soldiers to drink with their masks on.

While our unit was busy, other groups were in charge of assembling the two decontamination stations, each containing multiple showerheads for cleansing victims and military personnel. Those tents, resembling long 1,000-square-foot submarines, must be up first and operational before we could proceed with our duties properly. Entrances, located at each side of the tent, were protected by numerous layers of soft zip doors. Trenches were dug around the external part of the tent and lined with heavy plastic, then filled with an awful smelling concentrated bleach solution to catch the contaminated water drainage from the showers.

The submarine tents used plastic walls inside for separating the walking victims from the patients on stretchers. The decontamination process went the length of the tent, from one side to the other. On the side of the walking patients, which held about 20 people at once, numerous large showerheads shot out disinfectant solution from all angles at high pressure.

After each long shift, the doctors were allowed breaks. To do so we had to visit the "decon" station. First we entered the submarine and went through a disinfectant shower with suits on.

Then we proceeded to another section, where we removed the drenched body suit. Before we removed our masks, we swabbed the skin and any areas that might collect agents, like the armpits or around the neck. If we were contaminated, we had to go through a thorough wipe down. If not, we inhaled, quickly removed our masks (careful not to breathe during this process just in case some agents were still present in the air or lodged in the corners of the mask), and wiped down our faces with pads soaked in a disinfectant solution before moving into the next shower section.

We preferred to have enough equipment so that we did not have to "doff" with the victims. Once we were dry, we were able to relax in the special small "break" tents nearby to catch a smoke and eat some snacks.

The side with the stretcher victims was set up differently. Medics either sprayed the patients themselves or placed the stretchers on a long slow-moving roller that delivered the victims through a series of pressurized mini-showers. Contamination levels were tested before and at the end of showering. If victims from either side were still contaminated, they had to be moved into the casualty collection point area in the big tent and go through a rigid sweating technique for hours (covered with plastic bags to sweat out remaining radioisotopes from pores).

The big tent, called the Military Field Hospital, accommodated about 120 patients, usually in double layer beds. It was the most important tent, since it functioned as the base of the entire procedure. It was made to withstand hot zone temperatures; victims could be stationed inside for days without risk of internal contamination.

Setup time was five hours for the skeleton of the 7,000-square-foot hospital. Each tent was complete with multiple entries, surgical rooms (designated as either "clean" or "contaminated " depending on presence of external contamination), a pharmacy, stockpile rooms, refrigerator storage for blood, and a full laboratory.

Throughout the training at Red Village, special survey and mobile teams were responsible for developing radioactive scenarios. Prognosis was based on intelligence gathered: modeling of contamination area, explosion, the size of the hot zone, level of destruction, field dosimetry, and physical dosimetry of irradiated victims inside the contaminated area. Clear pictures of the potential of radioactive fallout and radioactive footprint (radioactive fallout settled on the ground) are beneficial for a proper response to a nuclear attack. It also helps to know what geographical area and regions have been affected by the blast.

The survey team's job was vital to let army forces know what areas were safe and when they could start moving toward the hot zone. They constantly moved before the troops, using dosimeters to check air for levels of radiation. If levels started to rise, they redirected the company. Geographical information, the direction and speed of the wind, humidity factor, and the time of day, provided critical information for proper response.

Those surveys were documented on maps, along with what kind of device was used, how big it was, if it was activated in water, in air, or on land, as well as the date and time of activation, figured to the second. The maps were marked with different colors to identify the level of radiated zones in order to help responders and medics know how to process victims.

In the event of an actual nuclear attack, when there is enough time to know about the approaching missile and where it might hit, cities and towns should be divided into zones. During Russian nuclear exercises, all civilians in the cities were part of the drill and instructed to do a certain thing according to their zone location. The general radius was 35 miles, including all zones.

The first zone was the "no go" zone, the area five miles from the epicenter. This first zone meant complete evacuation of all civilians, animals, and anything that could be moved.

The second zone was a five- to seven-mile radius, where everyone was told to hide behind hills or in trenches for at least three hours before activation. Ten minutes before the blast they were instructed to lie face down, headed away from the blast.

The third zone was the area seven to nine miles in radius. An hour before the detonation, the population in this third zone was told to move out of the buildings; ten minutes before detonation they were told to lie down in the same position as the second zone group.

The fourth zone was a nine- to 35-mile radius. Because of the concern for potential contamination following the radioactive fallout, this area of population was instructed to go inside their houses two hours before detonation, close windows and doors, and wait to see if there was to be an evacuation process.

In a real nuclear explosion, massive fires can be expected. Anything left in the target area will be destroyed and melted into the ground. Trees will be uprooted by the shock wave, and the area close to the epicenter might look as if it had been hit by an ice storm—from the melted soil or sand. The air blast is enough to suck things up into a column, or the mushroom stem, over six miles high, and the blast will shift the ground area. For example, the three-feet-deep trenches dug by soldiers might end up three inches in depth afterward.

While I was setting up my tent a few miles away, the troops stationed close to *ground zero* had the difficult job of collecting the wounded. Multiple numbers of medics were rushed to the scene, as well as specially organized rescue and survey teams, to monitor the areas with ground contamination as well as chemical agent concentrations.

Working close to the epicenter of the blast was risky. Although the blast was not made of actual radioactive nuclear materials, the Soviet army planted dozens of either square or round 270-pound lead containers with multi-window openers in the area to release radiation. Each one held up to 500-900 Ci sources; like cobalt 60 source. The source inside the square container with the one-sided window developed a 90-degree angle exposure of intense gamma waves; the round sources were more dangerous because they popped up and radiated at a 360-degree angle. Many soldiers ended up irradiated with mild doses.

The soldiers rushed around gathering the *wounded*, using trucks or fast, maneuverable flatbed amphibious vehicles (small sanitary machines with two seats that travel over water or land). Those machines hauled five victims at a time on the back. Both Rescue Randys and live soldiers were used to simulate the wounded; each one was tagged to show different wounds or contaminated surfaces. They were then transported to our area either by ground or helicopters.

"They're here!" yelled Amyir, the shortest cadet in our unit, as he scrambled into our tent. The padded suit on his small skinny stature made him look like a plump space creature. I couldn't help but grin looking at him.

The day was long and stressful and humor was essential to lighten our burden before we faced the first onslaught of victims. I leaned close to Amyir so he could hear me through the masks. "Gotcha," I shouted back, "Bring in those aliens from planet bimbo and let's study these specimens!"

The main factors of a nuclear detonation are 1) shock wave, 2) thermal impulse, 3) penetrating radiation, 4) radioactive contamination of large areas (development of radioactive fallout and radioactive footprint), and 5) electromagnetic impulse.

Different nuclear devices can be used— thermonuclear, hydrogen bomb, or neutron device. Each device causes different effects on territory, buildings, and people. Since I trained on thermonuclear devices, I will discuss these.

SHOCK WAVE

A shock wave happens usually after any type of explosion. But after a nuclear blast, the wave is extreme. Immediately after detonation, the air is pressurized so high in the core of the blast (epicenter) that it moves out from the center with great speed, at 360 degrees, faster than the speed of sound. The speed of the shock wave is based on the air pressure at the front of the shock wave. Its speed slows as it travels farther from the center.

In the first two seconds, the shock wave might travel 3,300 feet; in five seconds it can go 1.25 miles; in eight seconds it will move 1.87 miles. If the device is detonated on the ground, one shock wave develops. The shock wave then births powerful micro-tornadoes that move at 200 miles per hour and can suck up vehicles, building pieces, and people. If the device is activated in the air, it produces one wave, but a different type. The same applies for a device detonated in water. If it is an underground device, it can cause serious underground damage to water and sewage pipes.

Based on concentration of material in front of the shock wave—and on its speed—Russian Civil Defense and their military have specific training based on that speed and what to do the first few seconds after detonation. The one thing that a person should never do at activation is run around looking for a shielding object. This would be futile; the wave is too fast and too strong.

THERMAL IMPULSE

The next factor to consider after the blast is the thermal impulse. Thermal impulse is a large amount of ionizing energy that includes ultra violet and infrared waves and forms within the fireball area in the middle of the explosion. It produces intense light, and a new sun is formed, which can be seen for miles if it is megaton activation.

In the first second after detonation inside that thermal impulse, the brightness is two to four times greater than the light of the sun. Looking directly at the fireball would cause blindness. At night the brightness is even worse because of the contrast to the dark. At the time of a blast, energy changes into thermal energy and heats up all material that is close by, which causes the materials to catch fire and melt down. Temperatures could soar over 1,000 watts per cubic centimeter area. This heat would vaporize within seconds any person who is close to the core of the blast.

Thermo burns are no different than burns from boiling water; but keep in mind the closer a person is to the center, the worse the burn. If the atmosphere is clear, the fireball would be more stable and spread farther. If a 20-kiloton device were detonated, people in a 2.7-mile radius could receive first-degree burns. Closer than that, they could develop third-degree burns. By comparison, a one-megaton device, would cause first-degree burns on victims as far away as 22 miles.

The positive news on nuclear weapons is that terrorist extremist groups usually don't have the means or capabilities to use the powerful megaton devices. These large nuclear devices each have their own special code and, without knowing them, activation is impossible. Terrorists might possibly be able to get hold of the smaller devices, under 20-kilotons, and activate them—and they are powerful enough. One 20-kiloton device is equal to 20,000 tons of TNT. The bomb dropped on Nagasaki equaled a 23-kiloton device, and over 80,000 people died instantly.

What is worrisome, however, is that even the smaller devices could give off dangerous levels of radiation. The penetrating radiation would be much more serious than the shock waves or thermal impulse on the smaller device; terrorists would be more than satisfied that the explosion would cause extensive radiation damage.

PENETRATING RADIATION

Penetrating radiation is the third factor of a nuclear explosion. It is based on the invisible activity of gamma waves and neutrons which come from the zone of detonation. Gamma-neutron ionizing radiation is the form of first radioactive impulse that could travel, if a megaton device, over 100 miles from the hot Red Zone. (With an underwater detonation, the earth shields the gamma neutron impulse from going as far.) Keep in mind radioactive contamination could be lethal for mass populations.

RADIOACTIVE FALLOUT

Another factor is the radioactive contamination from radioactive fallout. The mushroom cloud contains a lot of different radioisotopes, which are hazardous for people and environment—soil, water, and animals. The presence of radioisotopes in the cloud could cause external and internal contamination of people for miles, depending on the size of the device. The good news is that in the event of a 20-kiloton detonation, the level of radiation drops down reasonably fast in affected areas in the first hours after detonation. Not until 24 hours has passed would the activity of radioisotopes drop a few thousand times more, allowing responders to safely proceed towards ground zero with their rescue mission.

ELECTROMAGNETIC IMPULSE

Electromagnetic impulse is the last factor or effect that could develop after a reasonably sized detonation. It is a powerful gamma wave field which could destroy electrical machinery, equipment, and electronic types of computers in a short time.

This is a big problem for responders if vehicle engines fail to run and some communication is interrupted. In some cases this electromagnetic impulse could go as far as 7.46 miles. Everything close to ground zero would be temporarily or permanently destroyed. In large devices that might be activated during a war, these impulses could travel hundreds of miles, burning large antennas and cables and destroying in-ground cables and communications.

The first group of tagged "pretend" wounded victims brought into my tent was comprised of young soldiers from the local tank division. Rain had started to fall a half-hour earlier, and the *casualties* were muddy and wet, making the difficult task messy. We worked fast to perform our duties—identify the injuries, the zone they had come from, and their levels of contamination.

"This one is hemorrhaging," Amyir said. "He goes to room three."

"Open fracture," I called out. "Get him to room two."

"Ruptured spleen," Leonyd added, "room one."

We each took our places with the other doctors in the operating rooms and proceeded with the drill. Meanwhile the medics and responders looking for and bringing us patients were working hard to keep pace with their instruction. Their job was exhausting and psychologically demanding, and I knew that an actual nuclear attack by the "enemy" would not go as smoothly.

I stopped what I was doing when Leonyd grabbed my elbow. He pointed at the side of my protective gear on my suit and showed me a rip in my elbow area. Without thinking twice, I pulled out a small medical packet called IP-1 from the work satchel hanging over my shoulder. I removed a soft capsule with a thick short needle, as well as a few packets of chemically soaked pads. I glanced at Leonyd and he grimaced at me. I wiped over my thigh area with the pad and automatically plunged the painfully thick spike into my leg, straight through my suit, injecting the saline solution. After the removal of the needle, Leonyd placed round sticky patches over the holed areas.

Following procedures, I left my station and went into the decontamination "submarine." This standard procedure had to be done by any trainee if incidents like this occurred. Of course, I did not show any symptoms of nerve agent because that day they used a simulated chemical. If it had been a real chemical release, the syringe would have been filled with 6 mg. of atropine, the standard antidote against nerve agents. My leg throbbed, but I ignored it when I returned to the job at hand.

Without a good civil defense program, a nation is left defenseless against a WMD attack. Communist Russia kept Civil Defense a number one priority; civilians had a place to go in the event of an enemy strike. Underground concrete facilities called *mini-cities*, were built underneath the bigger cities, connected via subways and supplied with stockpiles of food, beds, and generators for electricity. Schools, colleges, and workplaces constantly practiced evacuation drills. The Soviets calculated that if they had a ten-minute warning before an explosion, the Civil Defense program would decrease the effects of WMD on civilians from 85 to 7 percent.

In comparison, the United States population at this time is left defenseless against a WMD assault. Its defense program consists of tracking approaching missiles and trying to counter an attack with its own missiles. If any country were to deliver a massive attack using multiple warheads, some cities would be hit and civilians would die because they had no place to dodge the bomb. (Russia has the capability to kill half of the U.S. population in a short period of time. In fact, during the cold war, calculated plans were to send many missiles to hit certain areas of the United States where fault lines were prominent. The goal was to put several states under water). Even with an hour's notice, the population could not outrun the destruction above ground. It took Russia trillions of dollars and decades to build its underground facilities. Until America is willing to do the same for this nation, it will not outlive any concentrated attack with nuclear weapons.

The chance of survival is limited even more without proper training for responders. Immediate emergency reconstructive work must be applied inside each zone area for proper response to a nuclear, chemical, or biological attack. The reality of the situation is that responders would be dealing with an enormous emotional and destructive situation.

If it were a nuclear attack, complete or partial destruction of areas would result, along with total or partial thermal fires. There would be serious issues with complete or partial contamination of atmosphere and soil, as well as potential flooding from damaged waters pipe.

The main focus for responders is to work as a unified team, each responder unit stationed at specific areas for specific jobs.

Communication and backup are important to maintain some level of order during chaos; hearing from survey teams is vital in order to collect accurate information for safe response. Constant and complete coordination is essential.

Development of clean pathways inside contaminated areas is necessary for backup responder units that would be dispatched into the area, making it possible for workers to get air to victims trapped under debris. Operation cannot be stopped, and so it is important that these new responders get to the appropriate zones.

One concern for responders is using volunteers. While volunteers have big wonderful hearts to help, their lack of knowledge on proper response could delay the rescue process and possibly make more work for responders, especially if the volunteers become victims themselves. There should be response groups used specifically to organize volunteers in order to diminish problems.

Organization of mass evacuation and equipment operations must be done in a short time without overly traumatizing operators or responders. Safety issues would be difficult to comply with; in some cases, it would be a constant compromise of safety matters based on the immediate situation to save lives. Psychological effects would be dramatic—on responders as well as the wounded. Responders can feel overwhelmed at bloodshed and might end up forsaking their training techniques to save lives. Sometimes compromising safety cannot be helped, but without maintaining that unity with their team members, the rescue procedure could be hindered. It is a traumatizing task, and wisdom needs to overrule fear.

There will be plenty more Stalins and Hitlers and terrorists entering our world, men who want to dominate—and WMD will only thrive under their direction. The cold fact is this: nuclear weapons, built as offensive warfare, never as defensive weapons, have not diminished in production over the last 20 years, but instead have grown into a monstrous global threat to all humankind.

The hydrogen bombs used to destroy Hiroshima and Nagasaki were measured in kilotons; today's bombs are measured in megatons. A one-megaton bomb contains the explosive power to wipe out 80 Hiroshimas. With this kind of lethal weapon there would be no survivors.

From reading portions of scripture in the book of Revelation, it seems reasonable to say that what John saw on the island of Patmos might have been a vision of nuclear exchange. He described it the best he could since he had no understanding of advanced technological weaponry. His mere mind probably could not fathom how a holocaust of that magnitude set before him in vision could be anything other then supernatural. Mortal men, to him, did not hold the capabilities to destroy the earth. And as recently as 70 years ago, not one person in the world believed so either.

Reading the book of Revelation seems incomprehensible, unless we view the destruction as a supernatural display from the hand of God Himself. But now, the nuclear age has made John's vision explicable as a possible humanly contrived annihilation. It is still possible that God can use supernatural intervention to judge the evil on the earth, since scripture states God did so in freeing the children of Israel from Egypt. I believe that

nuclear exchange will be occurring in the last days, even if
supernatural judgment is also occurring. When the nations fight
against the antichrist army, they won't be reverting to outdated
sabers and cannons. Nuclear, biological, and chemical warfare
are the advanced weapons of this age, and it would not seem
plausible that these weapons would be ignored during the great
tribulation time.

Could this be why Jesus said in Matthew 24, verse 21, *For
then shall be great tribulation, such as was not since the beginning of the world to this time, no, nor ever shall be.* Could it be
that He knew that end time technology would produce weapons
never before used, arsenal capable of destroying the earth? I
believe so. Revelation Chapter 8 seems to clearly back up the
possibility that God will remove His restraining hand on humankind and let them destroy themselves with their own great
inventions. We read of the poisoning of the oceans, the burning
up of the grass and the trees, and the sun scorching people with
great heat.

Verses 8 and 9 could describe a nuclear explosion in the
water: *And the second angel sounded, and as it were a great
mountain burning with fire was cast into the sea: and the third
part of the sea became blood; and the third part of the creatures
which were in the sea, and had life, died; and the third part of
the ships were destroyed.* Verse 10 also implies a nuclear device,
causing radioactive fallout to make the waters bitter. *And the
third angel sounded, and there fell a great star from heaven,
burning as it were a lamp, and it fell upon the third part of the
rivers, and upon the fountains of waters; and the name of the star
is called Wormwood: and the third part of the waters became*

wormwood; and many men died of the waters, because they were made bitter.

Revelation 6, verse 14 states: *And the heaven departed as a scroll when it is rolled together; and every mountain and island were moved out of their places.* During a nuclear blast, the atmosphere does roll back on itself from the tremendous rush of air caused by the thermal impulse.

Revelation explains the horrible plagues that will afflict mankind, the widespread wars and famines, and the atmosphere that will become so polluted it will reduce visibility by one-third (moon and sun darkened). Even if God is using His own super-natural plagues, human-created WMDs alone could cause the entire global carnage on the earth described by John.

I believe it is safe to say that currently, in this present moment, Satan's goal is not to prompt nations into a global war using WMD, simply because he does not want to destroy the world. Rather he wants to usurp God and gain complete control over it. During Christ's temptation in the wilderness, it is inter-esting to note that the devil's persuasions all evolved around getting Jesus to worship him. This is his goal for God's people as well—and the whole world.

We should never become complacent. There are enough WMDs developed now to destroy this world, but Satan has not yet succeeded in his mission. There is unfinished business between him and God, and he plans on taking as many onto his side as he can.

How can he effectively get humankind to bow before him? Force and bullying hasn't worked too well in the past, but he knows his most ingenious plan will work, and he has been perfecting it and bringing it to completion for hundreds of years. Deceptive love, false promises of peace, and mind control are his greatest tools in this plan. How does he accomplish this deception? By fooling people, of course, into thinking they can live in a good and peaceful world without wars or famine or terrorism. His devoted followers have pushed his deceptive agenda by participating in elite societies, clubs and orders—all of these different groups united secretly to bring about this socialistic new world order.

Christians should be knowledgeable about current events and those whose objective it is to form a one-world government and religion. It is not something we should dismiss as a silly conspiracy notion. The Bible is clear that this is what Satan will do; there is plenty of biblical history (Tower of Babel, for instance) and recent history (Napoleon and Hitler) to prove his desires are to gain world dominion. With that knowledge we should be keeping watch on world news and know who the players are (who our enemy really is) in this ever-evolving sinister plot that spans generations.

I don't have time to delve into the history of this subject, but your own research will turn up enough facts to shed some insight on who was and is behind forming a one-world government and how it is being worked into our world today. It shouldn't be difficult. Over the last 14 years the idea of a New World Order has been blatantly introduced and promoted by high-level politicians through speeches and magazine articles. A conditioning of the masses is now underway for acceptance of the idea, and few seem to blink an eye over its open presentation into the world.

When Satan's real mask is removed at the end of time, then he will be exposed for what he is, the father of lies. Many nations will become confused and start fighting against him during the Battle of Armageddon. Satan's evil that prompted humankind to develop the WMD will come in handy for him to destroy God's creation. He knows that an ungodly nation that harbors nuclear/biological/chemical weapons, such as Russia, China, and North Korea, are excellent candidates for using this weaponry as a "power" to horsewhip other nations under their submission. I remember all too well in the Soviet army how I reveled in the fact that my country had so much power over all the other nations. Let us not be naïve; those thoughts are still alive in the Russian Federation. That is why the Russian military recently started refreshing its new generation of ICBMs (Intercontinental Ballistic Missiles), which have been lying in stockpiles for years, and have been placing them inside strategic controlled areas. Those that fight to do away with weapons of mass destruction will not succeed, because no one nation will give up its place for power—and the Day of Wrath will come, and nuclear war will be inevitable.

Cling to a great promise from our Lord for the righteous who endure faithful to the end: *For God hath not appointed us to wrath, but to obtain salvation by our Lord Jesus Christ, who died for us, that, whether we wake or sleep, we should live together with him.* (I Thessalonians 5: 9-10).

We finished the day at the Red Village exercise with good results. Most of our victims who were processed and treated inside the medical points *survived*. In a real scenario with contaminated mass casualty and multiple trauma victims, survival of wounded is based on intensity and quality of medical support given patients in a timely manner. If the process of immediate treatment slowed down for any reason (loss of doctors during the blast or lack of equipment), the level of expectant victims dramatically rises.

For our exercise we had plenty of qualified medical professionals to take care of the few hundred patients coming into our clinics. But in a real WMD scenario, not hundreds, but thousands of wounded and contaminated victims would become overwhelming to doctors. They would be fortunate to save 70 percent. Many fatalities lying in stretchers outside the medical tents would end up as corpses by the end of the day because they would never have reached the operating table.

From our drill, we lost only two percent of the 200 *casualties*, based on multi-trauma conditions and cranial injuries. No one was lost from intoxication of nerve agents. We finished at eight in the evening with our last patient, decontaminated the tents, and headed back to the base, exhausted and famished.

Chapter Seven
The Silent Wars

SMALLPOX AND ANCIENT AZTECS
CRUISE SHIP AND QUARANTINE
CLINIC DUTY IN POLAND
VACCINES AND HOPE

L ena and I bundled up in heavy coats, boots, and fur hats, while Joana went downstairs to the hotel lobby to inquire about our driver. We had arrived in Moscow the day before by train and didn't expect to see so much snow by morning. My mother-in-law returned, poked her head inside the door and said, "Let's go."

We had traveled all the way from brisk Leningrad that icy February day in 1987 to arctic Moscow to discuss my future with General Sorokin, but it was my mother-in-law, not me, who was going to have the private meeting with him. Our driver, a sergeant major, met us at the lobby door and, with a grunt, introduced himself as Vladimir. He didn't say another word as he led us out back to a black Volga. The car's dark tinted windows were in keeping with the discretion of our trip.

Although Vladimir ran red lights and slowed down for no one, police officers saluted as we passed.

I spoke up and asked, "Why are the police officers saluting us?"

Joana threw me a look, but Vladimir replied, "They know this car belongs to the Ministry of Defense. The more zeros on the license plate, the higher the rank. We have three zeros in front."

After about an hour, the driver turned the limo into a shabby brick-walled entrance. I was surprised as to why we were coming to such a place until he passed through the gate and turned the corner. A magnificent hotel sat in the middle of the parking lot. The inside of the grand building looked more like a tropical jungle with its exotic décor of tall palm trees, fruit baskets filled with coconuts and bananas, and bamboo furniture. It was an odd contrast to the icy weather outside.

Joana caught my expression and laughed. "This is one of the internal KGB hotels, Igor. This is where we stay tonight."

After we freshened up in our fabulous room, Joana changed into evening wear and bid us goodbye. She was on her way to meet with General Sorokin. Meanwhile Lena and I had a dinner date with Morechenko, her stepfather's cousin, a popular man I had not yet met. I had heard much about him because he worked as Leonid Brezhnev's personal interpreter for Fidel Castro for many years and, because of that position, shared friendships with both leaders.

Vladimir drove us to the elegant palace-like apartment and Morechenko greeted us at the door dressed in a KGB service uniform.

"Welcome, friends!" he exclaimed, holding out a bottle of champagne. The balding man led us to his living room and we sat down on a golden couch. The walls of his apartment were covered with classy oil paintings.

"I have something to celebrate. Not only your arrival, but…" he pointed to the military insignia on his shoulder, "my promotion. What a life. Yesterday I was a civilian and today they put a uniform on me and make me a major!"

"You became a major in one day?" I blurted out. "It will take me 15 years to reach that level."

"Well, you know this business," Morechenko dismissed my words with a wave of his hand and grinned. "By the way, your father-in-law was the youngest colonel in the Soviet army in his day—but surely he deserved it. My new boss, who happens to be the son-in-law of Brezhnev, is already major general, and he is barely 40 years old."

After dinner the new major brought out two photo albums. There were many pictures of him standing close to Brezhnev and Castro. A few pictures of Brezhnev and Castro standing in laboratory facilities caught my eye.

"Were these taken in Cuba?" I asked.

"Of course, in Havana," Morechenko said. "These special facilities need material and proper training. Cuba can get material from the U.S. or Russia, but proper training comes only from places where you come from. We coordinate and support biological research programs in Cuba. You should know this."

I did know about so-called exchange programs between the Soviet Union military and the Cuban military. At the medical academy we had a Faculty Number 5 ward, which was dedicated specifically to train foreign military medical professionals, including Cubans.

"Remember, Igor," he added, "Cuba is within walking distance of the United States. After the Cuban crisis we had to terminate our nuclear program there. So we came up with something that cannot be easily seen by satellites." He smiled again and changed the subject.

We met up with Joana around midnight and she gave me a big hug and confirmed that my future was secured—my next post would be in Poland.

It was November 8, 1519 when Hernando Cortes hid in the marshes with a group of his soldiers, and watched the Aztec Indian priest perform another violent human sacrifice on the top steps of the pyramid temple. A crowd of naked warriors, their faces painted in dull colors, cheered as the priest raised the still beating bloody heart mass into the air. Sickened at the sight of the barbaric sacrifices to their Aztec gods, combined with his desire to see them convert to Christianity, the tall Spaniard leader impatiently ordered his 600 men to raid the 150,000 native forces in the snake infested, but flourishing, agricultural city of Tenochtitlan.

In the early 1500s Tenochtitlan, a capital city that now lies in ruins under the present Mexico City, was a prosperous civilization of grand palaces and defense-structured canal ways. The Aztecs had developed intricate irrigation systems for their crops and gardens. If it weren't for the human sacrifices performed regularly, one would think the city was quite an advanced and sophisticated society for that time.

Cortes snatched the Aztec King Montezuma and took most of the city, then left command in the hands of his officer in charge, Pedro de Alvarado. But on June 20, 1520, when de Alvarado began treating the Indians harshly, they revolted. Cortes returned to Tenochtitlan to face the uprising. Although the Aztec's king was killed, his numerous agile warriors out-numbered Cortes and his men, who were forced to pull back and escape.

Before sailing away, Cortes gave orders to leave behind the body of a Spanish soldier who had died from a strange illness. The dead man was covered with a myriad of tiny pustules. Within a few weeks one-fourth of the Tenochtitlan population died as the deadly pathogens continued to spread to the coun-tryside.

Meanwhile Hernando Cortes regrouped his forces and returned to Tenochtitlan, unaware that the thriving population had been practically reduced to a ghost town. The weakened Aztec army could not fight the Spanish soldiers, and Cortes quickly closed off the body-strewn city. Was Cortes' decision to leave behind the diseased body a calculated strategy of *biologi-cal warfare*? We will never know for sure, but we do know his decision to leave the contagious man behind won him the city and altered history, allowing Spanish Mexico to become what it is today.

Smallpox had been around long before the Aztecs. Ancient manuscripts, found in 3730 to 3710 BC during the reign of Egyptian Pharaoh Cezerka Amenofisa I, tell of a disease that left small pus-filled boils on skin. Visible pustules found on the mummified body of Egyptian Pharaoh Ramses V in 1157 BC

suggests he died from smallpox. The disease was so dreadful
that in those times in the East, people worshipped the "pestilence" gods in hopes that they would refrain from sending
further punishment upon them.

India's medical text, written in 400 AD, described smallpox
symptoms perfectly: red, yellow and white pustules accompanied by burning pain. In 578 AD the Abyssinian Army attacked
Mecca to destroy the Kaaba Shrine. The book of Koran de-
scribes the attack and surprisingly mentions evidence of smallpox with the statement, "God sent birds to shower the Abyssinian army with stones that produced pustules and sores that
spread like a pestilence."

In 581 AD smallpox spread across northern Italy to southern
France and followed the spread of the Islamic religion through
North Africa and Spain. In 1000 AD a large epidemic was
recorded from Japan to North Africa, and crusaders also spread
the disease in Europe.

In 1633 smallpox struck the Native Americans who lived in
Plymouth colony in Massachusetts. The situation was called the
"finger of God" because, as one Bostonian wrote, "The Indians
begun to be quarrelsome concerning the bounds of land they
had sold to the English. But God ended the controversy by
sending the smallpox amongst the Indians at Saugust, who were
before that time exceeding numerous. Whole towns of them
were swept away and some of them not so much as one soul
escaped destruction."

The dreaded disease reached the Huron tribe north of Lake
Ontario in 1635. It was spread by the Portuguese into Brazil,
killing 44,000 Indians in 1660. The governor of Canada, in

1679, recorded that smallpox desolated the Indians to such a degree that they thought no longer of wars, but only of bewailing the dead for whom there was already an immense number.

More recently, in Asian countries in 1971, more than 20,000 patients were recorded with smallpox. In the same year Africa reported more than 26,000 cases. In October 1977, the last case of naturally acquired smallpox occurred in the Merca District of Somalia, and in May 1980 the World Health Assembly certified the world free of naturally occurring smallpox. Unfortunately this certification offers a false security, because the smallpox strain is alive and well today in countries whose goal is to develop and use this pathogen as a weapon of warfare.

Fast-forward to the present and ask: what would happen in today's cities if there were a biological release of smallpox by terrorists? Imagine hypothetically that some evil doers release a device full of genetically modified pulmonary plague (with insertion of the complete copy of variola major virus, better known as smallpox) into a crowded dance hall on a 2000-passenger cruise ship headed for New York City. There was no vaccine back in 1520; neither is this pathogen on the cruise ship preventable by vaccines. How would a modern city hold up to such a scourge in comparison to ancient Tenochtitlan? I wish I could say that advanced medical technology has made the probability of epidemics extinct, but this is not the case.

As I write, evil scientists are developing new viruses containing strains of plague, smallpox, Ebola, and Marburg. Marburg fever gets its name from the town in Germany where it broke out in 1967, and shares its symptoms with Ebola. The disease was spread from African green monkeys brought to

Germany for experimentation. It is an incurable disease with symptoms that include headache, nausea, toxic shock, hemorrhaging eyes, bruising, and thinning and blood seepage through skin. No matter how many vaccines medical scientists can develop to counter these newly modified diseases, a deadlier pathogen can be created and perfected to outperform and outrun any new vaccine. This is why today's world is susceptible to the same mass epidemics that the Aztecs confronted hundreds of years ago.

Back to the hypothetical cruise liner: Two-thirds of the vacationers are infected, but will not show symptoms for another two or three days after they leave the ship. The passengers that remain in New York probably could infect at least ten other bystanders. The sick people who end up in hospitals infect everyone they are in contact with. The folks who left the ship and did not stay in New York City spread the disease to other U.S. and European cities.

Everyone on the cruise ship who had not been treated on time with preventive antibiotics and who inhaled a pathogen would die from plague—which would be the majority of those who were sick. By the time the disease is identified as plague, almost everyone aboard that ship would be showing symptoms.

Antibiotic prophylactic treatment is only effective if started 12 hours before initial symptoms appear. Those who are given strong doses of antibiotics to slow down the plague would only become more susceptible to the aggressive smallpox virus that would be ready to rear up out of hiding. In a natural outbreak of smallpox, over 30 percent of the people infected who are not vaccinated against smallpox would not make it because there is limited treatment for the disease. In the hypothetical case of the cruise ship, the percentage numbers would be much higher.

Doctors, concerned at the number of patients arriving at the hospital showing symptoms of severe migraine headaches, harsh coughing and bloody sputum, might misdiagnose the disease as flu, until they do X-rays and start suspecting some other pulmonary disease. Once doctors draw lab tests, they would discover a few days later that the culprit is pulmonary plague. By the time they contact the Center for Disease Control (CDC), almost everyone in contact with patients will be infected. Realizing the death rate of pulmonary plague without treatment is 100 percent, doctors would quickly administer heavy doses of antibiotics to themselves and to the secondary infected medical professionals treating the infectious patients. The aggressive disease on the people from the ship moves quickly through the lungs and multiplies inside lymph nodes, spreading to other organs through peripheral blood circulation. Overnight they fall into a stupor and are vomiting, their pupils dilated and their pulse rate rapid. With raspy breathing, cherry-stained cheeks, and dry, white-coated tongues, hallucinations wreak havoc on their mental state. Within four days the victims are dead.

Doctors have no idea that this disease is genetically engineered and that smallpox is hiding behind the plague germ ready to emerge. After 12 days, the variola major virus suddenly pops up in the secondary infected people who are being treated with antibiotics for pulmonary plague, or who are recovering from the disease. Medical professionals are baffled and again call the CDC. But the infectious pathogen is not contained. The plague/smallpox epidemic spreads throughout New York City,

infecting almost 200,000 in the first few weeks just from plague.
From the smallpox virus alone, because there are no vaccina-
tions or correct quarantine measures, at least 40,000 people die
in the first 20 days; and ten days later millions are infected.
Panic spreads the disease to other states as people flee the city.
Within a few months, hundreds of thousands would be dead.

Today there is no known vaccination in the United States for
pulmonary plague or bubonic plague. (This type of plague is
transmitted through rodents and insects; pulmonary plague is
transmitted through the respiratory system.) Most people are not
vaccinated against smallpox. The first thing the CDC would do
in the event of such an epidemic is to administer mass amounts
of antibiotics to the mass population for prevention. But if the
epidemic is brought into a city through bio-warfare, and the
disease is genetically engineered with two different bacterial
and virile pathogens, this action by the CDC would be futile.

The cruise ship scenario is an ugly reality to what silent
wars can produce. It is hard to fight an invisible enemy.
Stopping the bio-attack is the best solution, but, if a bio-weapon
is used and successfully dispersed, many people will die,
especially if the microorganism is genetically modified.

Genetic engineering is formally known as recombinant DNA
technology. It allows scientists to plug genes, combine segments
of DNA from one type of organism with the gene of another
organism. This means that the goals of genetic engineering and
biological warfare are to develop genetically modified organisms
with properties different from the original. The outcome would
be a strain more resistant to antibiotics or completely resistant,

more toxic, possibly undetectable, and more stable in the
environment. They might be more virulent, impossible to treat,
and easier to handle by ... whoever is using them.

To contract any kind of disease, a person must first be
exposed to it, and then must be susceptible to the microorganism. Contagious diseases, such as plague or smallpox, can have
direct and indirect modes of spreading. *Direct spread* means
being in close proximity to the affected person. Sneezing or
coughing will produce droplets with a spread of five- or ten-
micron particles holding live pathogens, and will infect someone
nine yards away. *Indirect modes of spread* are through aerosol
particles, one- to five-micron in size. The danger of the indirect
mode is that the release of the pathogen through a dispersal
device (if it is a professional weaponized agent) not only results
in an almost 100 percent infection rate, but the microorganism
will have a long "hang time" in the air, allowing for potential
secondary release hours and days after it is first dispersed.
Aerosol release can then be spread by direct methods, from one
person to another or from contaminated clothing.

Quarantine is the main way to control epidemics if there is
no existing vaccine against the spreading disease. For hospitals,
emergency training on quarantine procedures is a must. Hospital preparation and quarantine are addressed in Chapter 9. It is
evident that any nation not prepared for epidemics will fight a
losing battle.

Individuals can minimize the death rate by using common
sense, and this is the greatest tool needed to save lives. The first
thing a family should do in the event of an outbreak of any sort
is to stay home, isolate themselves from the public, and not

leave under any circumstance until the epidemic is controlled. Cities can prepare by having emergency plans set up in advance so that each neighborhood knows what to expect. Television and radio contact should play an important role so that families are updated and can follow useful instruction. By breaking down the city into sections, food and medicine can be delivered in safe bundles to homes by workers wearing the appropriate protective gear; this would keep the spread at bay. All of these measures, though seemingly extreme, are the only ways to slow down and contain the spread of the virus or bacteria.

With new diseases like SARS (Severe Acute Respiratory Syndrome), a virus which has a questionable and suspicious origin, and other aggressive new strains of influenza going around (Vietnam and Thailand have just reported a deadly bird flu that is a virus worse then SARS), every parent and adult should use common sense and initiate a family quarantine when they are sick or have sick children. The last few years the average death toll from influenza in the U.S. per year was between 20,000 and 30,000 people. Some of these folks, including children, would still be alive today if people reacted and responded to viruses and their spread more seriously.

A reasonable plan of quarantine within each household can save lives and control epidemics. Parents should stay informed on what diseases are going around and be familiar with diagnosing simple flu-like symptoms of a sick child: fever, sore throat, swollen glands, or a hoarse constant coughing coming from the respiratory tract. No one wants to be sick, and if everyone practiced safe quarantine now with the treatable viruses, it would be that much easier for people to respond correctly in the event of an actual fatal outbreak. It is too bad that doctors seldom make house calls in America today; it would help eliminate unnecessary spread between patients and people who are sitting inside a busy waiting room at the doctor's office.

What about vaccines? Where did they originate and are they the answer to fighting bio-terrorism? During the Russian epidemics between the 17th and 19th centuries, every year a half million people became infected and at least one-third of them died. In Siberia whole regions died from smallpox. The Russians fervently tried to find a way to battle the spread. They came up with their first variolation technique, which involves scrubbing the skin and rubbing in virile material from infected patients. While in the sauna, they would whip and massage themselves with dry tree branches which had been infected from the pustules on smallpox victims.

Before the 18th century, the first vaccination houses were opened in Moscow and St. Petersburg, and inoculation was performed by variolation. After the Empress Katerina II and her son allowed themselves to be inoculated with smallpox, others followed suit.

In 1801 needle vaccinations became popular. After the Velensky Institute of Vaccine in St. Petersburg opened in 1808, a serious drop of smallpox cases occurred.

In 1763 during the French and Indian war, Lord Jeffrey Amherst, the British commander in chief, used blankets that had covered smallpox victims as a form of inoculation by placing them directly on healthy people.

But the first variolation transfer of smallpox as inoculums into susceptible individuals took place in China. The Sung

Dynasty records practices of variolation between 960 and 1280 AD. They ground up dry scraps from the skin of smallpox victims and used the powder as a nose inhalant to protect the healthy person. About the same time, Turkey and Persia found a way to remove the liquid from smallpox pustules with a needle, drop that liquid onto the skin and rub it into the broken skin.

English physician Edward Genner came up with the greatest results on variolation in 1796. As a village doctor, he observed that milkmaids were seldom getting human smallpox. And if they did contract the disease, they did not develop disfiguring scars. He did note, however, that they were susceptible to the less infectious cowpox from the cows. Doctor Genner decided to experiment, feeling sure that cowpox and human smallpox might somehow work against each other. He removed the cowpox fluid from the infected pustules of a milkmaid and variolated the cowpox fluid into the skin of a young boy. After cowpox pustules developed on the boy, Genner variolated the human smallpox onto his skin. The boy healed completely and never developed smallpox. Two years later the same experiment took place on another patient, except the material used for variolation came from the infected pustules on the cow's teats. This was when Doctor Genner came up with the term "vaccine," named after "vacca," which means cow.

In the 18th century, the Prussian army did inoculations every seven years by using the scrubbing technique. They had 800,000 troops; because of the inoculation, only 8,360 became infected, and less than 300 died. In comparison, the French did not believe in repeat variolation; as a result over 280,000 people got infected and 23,000 died of smallpox.

Vaccinations are an important part of the fight against epidemics, but only if they are administered on a repeated basis. For every vaccine, the human immune system has a different "shelf life" against different diseases. That is why Soviet Russia kept up on vaccinations every year or so. The down side is that repeated vaccinations can cause dangerous side affects that might not show up until years later. There are always risks involved with vaccinations, and the quality of the vaccination should be a concern.

The best way to give the immune system the advanced memory against future contact with disease is by using live pathogens in weak concentrations. Using vaccines as a protection against bio warfare is only part of the answer and shouldn't become an illusion for protection. Vaccines cannot protect anyone from all of the genetically modified agents out there today. With a natural outbreak of smallpox, where people are vaccinated on time in mass numbers and the sick are isolated quickly, the outbreak can be contained.

A simultaneous multi-location outbreak of a disease can reduce the effectiveness of any public health system and spread like wildfire, with no way to control it. Vaccines are not the answer here; only severe quarantine on the population. Especially if smallpox is released into the air, there is no way to know what outside areas are contaminated. Underground facilities designed with filter ventilation systems are the safest way to protect populations from aerosol release, but the United States does not have these facilities. Russia and other nations know this, which is why they are developing many vaccine-proof agents. Only an underground bunker with a good filtering system and stocked with personal protective equipment will give complete physical protection.

Disease is nothing new. If we view the history of it in scripture, we see that God is the author of its origin, which He allowed because of man's fallen condition. He most certainly is in control of it. God first introduced the contagious leprosy to Moses in Exodus Chapter 4, verse 6: *And the Lord said furthermore unto him, put now thine hand into thy bosom. And he put his hand into his bosom: and when he took it out, behold, his hand was leprous as snow.*

In Exodus 9: 9 to 11 God sends boils upon Egyptian humans and beasts under Pharaoh's rule to get him to release the Hebrew slaves. He threatens more plague in 9:13 to 16 when Pharaoh refuses to heed God's words: *And the Lord said unto Moses, rise up early in the morning, and stand before Pharaoh, and say unto him, thus saith the Lord God of the Hebrews, let my people go that they may serve me. For I will at this time send all my plagues upon thine heart, and upon thy servants, and upon they people; that thou mayest know that there is none like me in all the earth. For now I will stretch out my hand, that I may smite thee and thy people with pestilence; and thou shalt be cut off from the earth. And in very deed for this cause have I raised thee up, for to shew in thee my power; and that my name may be declared throughout all the earth.*

Historically, God is the Chief Physician of all diseases, including all the bio-weapons developed today. He understands disease and the importance of quarantine. This is why He instructed Moses and Aaron about the plague of leprosy in Leviticus, Chapter 13. He tells them what signs to look for to determine how infected they are and what to do with the person who is contaminated or "unclean." A person who had signs of being leprous, which included skin discoloration and bald spots, then was quarantined for a week. After a week, the priest checked on the patient again. If that person looked better, they had to wait another week. If after that week they worsened, then they had to be isolated and taken to a leper camp.

In Chapter 15 of the same book, the Lord instructs on the contamination of infectious sexual discharges and how to deal with them. Verse 5 says: *And whosoever toucheth his bed shall wash his clothes and bathe himself in water, and be unclean until the even.* God commanded quarantine on certain diseases back then, and it is a medical solution that stands true today in modern times, especially in light of the development of new bio-weapons. If there are no vaccines available, strict quarantine is the only way to control the spread of disease.

Plague is mentioned often throughout the Bible in the Old Testament, and God used the disease to judge rebellion. This is why I believe God has thus far supernaturally held back nations that develop bio-weapons from using them against other countries. With all the diseases out there today, especially the metric tons of stockpiles full of weaponized biological pathogens in the Russian Federation alone (not including other nations such as China, North Korea, Israel, or India that have secret bio-weapon programs), we can see that God is indeed in control of all diseases. (China's actual biological programs are mostly unknown, but the country is rumored to have technically sophisticated bio-weapons programs.) There are enough bio-weapons sitting in warehouses and institutes in Russia alone to kill the entire population many times over. It is disturbing that Russia has not been forced to diminish or destroy its huge bio arsenals. Nations, especially America, seem asleep regarding this most frightening matter. Therefore it is no light miracle that epidemics have not surfaced and killed off mass populations of late. God is the only explanation for the restraint.

God used plague to judge Pharaoh's evil heart and to convince Pharaoh to release His people out of slavery. Exodus 11: 1 and 5 states: *And the Lord said unto Moses, Yet will I bring one plague more upon Pharaoh, and upon Egypt; afterwards he will let you go hence: when he shall let you go, he shall surely thrust you out hence altogether... And all the firstborn in the land of Egypt shall die, from the firstborn of Pharaoh that sitteth upon his throne, even unto the firstborn of the maidservant that is behind the mill; and all the firstborn of beasts.*

God used plague to judge the Philistines back in 1320 BC when they stole the Ark of the Covenant. We see what happened in I Samuel 5. Verse 6 says, *But the hand of the Lord was heavy upon them of Ashdod, and He destroyed them, and smote them with emerods, even Ashdod and the coasts thereof. Emerods* are boils or tumors, and a clear symptom of plague.

God even used disease to judge His own people when they criticized His ambassador Moses. In the book of Numbers, Chapter 16, verse 45 God says: *Get you up from among this congregation, that I may consume them as in a moment.* Immediately Moses and Aaron fell on their faces (take note of the power of prayer here) to convince God not to destroy the Israelites. Moses quickly commands Aaron to make atonement for the people, which he does. In verses 47 and 48 we read: *And Aaron*

took as Moses commanded, and ran into the midst of the congre-
gation; and, behold, the plague was begun among the people:
and he put on incense, and made an atonement for the people.
And he stood between the dead and the living; and the plague
was stayed. The plague is stayed, but not before 14,700 people
are dead (verse 49). Probably no more then 15 minutes passed
by the time Aaron went to the altar, grabbed the incense, and
ran into the throng. Even with today's advanced technology to
mutate pathogens into deadly weapons, no one has been able to
develop a biological microorganism that moves this fast. As a
doctor, I recognize that God is most definitely ruler of all disease and we should not think that any human has the wisdom to
outwit God.

The comforting fact about this biblical story is how Moses
and Aaron persuaded God's hand even during judgment. He
heard their prayers and showed mercy. This is a beautiful
moment of Moses representing Jesus standing in the stead for
us, interceding on our behalf. Our prayers are powerful, and we
must continue to pray for this nation and all nations, asking God
to mercifully keep His Son Jesus standing between all bio-
weaponry and His people.

The first pandemic of plague happened in the Byzantine
Empire during the reign of Justinian I, in 541 AD. One hundred
million European people died, including 40 percent of the
population of Constantinople. The second pandemic of plague,
called the Black Death, started in 1346 AD in South Ukraine at
Caffa, a modern city of Feodosiya on the Black Sea. During the
importing of marmot fur (a type of rodent) from Asia, hungry
fleas carrying the plague bacillus buried themselves inside the

fur bundles. The fleas found their food source by biting humans and spreading the plague disease from the ships into the city. In 1347 Venice declared that no one could leave a ship for "quarantagiorni," which means "40 days of quarantine" because 17,000 people died in 18 months.

By 1348 plague entered Britain at Weymouth. Between 1346 and 1352, a total of 24 million people died. Another 20 million died before the end of the 14th century. In 1664 the plague returned to Great Britain and killed 70,000 people. The outbreak in China in 1860 reached Hong Kong by 1894, and spread by steamships to San Francisco in 1900. In the United States, the last urban plague epidemic occurred in Los Angeles between 1924 and 1925. Even so, the World Health Organization reports 1,000 to 3,000 cases of plague every year.

And so it was, in 1988, a year after Joana's talk with General Sorokin, and after I graduated and finished my internship, that I was transferred to Jawor, Poland. There I served as officer and chief of the medical clinic over four battalions. I had my own pharmaceutical department, and I was responsible for ambulatory service, epidemiological control, as well as overseeing stockpiles of antidotes and antitoxins for the whole military base. My clinic's station held 30 beds.

The base was located inside an 18th century fortress secured by a half-mile long, 15-foot high, brick wall. It was rumored that this was where Napoleon's army had been stationed, as well as German soldiers in WWII. Inside were housed the Military Engineering Center for special projects and the Ministry of Internal Affairs department. One thousand or more soldiers and officers served inside. Two secure entrance points guaranteed no one could enter or leave without proper documentation. It was not an ideal place for privates because they were not allowed to leave the stockade at all during off-hours. But the officers, like me, were fortunate in that we had free access inside and outside those looming old walls.

During my station in Poland, we had a few outbreaks of dysentery, and later virile meningocephalitis, a tick-borne disease that causes neurological problems and fluid in the spinal cord. The meningocephalitis episode was a rather uncommon outbreak to catch in our fortress, and I found it questionable. Even more questionable was the Polish Secret Service that suddenly showed up to camp outside our compound. Our military officials then ordered us to transport all semi-conscious patients from the base to the main hospital in big freezer food trucks instead of the usual ambulances.

The higher echelons worried about intentional biological releases, so I had to keep a careful eye on each outbreak and report to headquarters anything suspicious. I suspected there was a presence of bio-weapons in Polish territory by the Soviets because of the types and style of vaccinations I was performing on certain select privates, officers, KGB, and civilian employees of the Ministry of Internal Affairs. I also suspected an overconcern of the base's antidote and antitoxin stockpile by the KGB and the two top military epidemiologists from the central medical command.

Annual vaccinations were performed in mass numbers against anthrax, TB, and influenza, but the isolated vaccinations I gave to those working in "special projects" were not known to me. Despite my close relations with the chief medical officer, Colonel Shevchenko, commander over Poland, and Colonel Leshev, chief therapist of Soviet forces, nobody would tell me what type of vaccination I was administering.

On typical vaccinations, such as that for anthrax, the pressurized pistol I used to shoot into the arm muscle contained the name of the vaccine and its exposure date. But the selective vaccinations given outside the scope of the entire battalion never had markings. For these cases, I was never called back to check patients' arms for skin reaction afterwards, as was always my task for routine vaccinations. I knew that they were checked later by other professionals, and it wasn't my job to know who or why.

My own first horrible experience with the anti-plague vaccination occurred at the age of five in 1970. Russia showed serious intentions of developing bio-weapons because of the great risk of contracting plague, while it considered contracting malaria or the Korean Hemorrhagic fever as no threats at all. The plague vaccine used on the population gave only partial immunity and had an unstable immunological response. It was made with a dead vaccine called *colle vaccinia* and was good only against bubonic plague. Immunity developed within one week and was good for six months.

A kind nurse administered the anti-plague vaccine to me by first scrubbing my forearm in three triangular parts with a sharp tool and afterward applying one drop of vaccination liquid on each bloody scrape. Once she did this, she made eight small cuts over each of those three areas. Using a non-absorbing pad, she rubbed the areas well and then waited 15 minutes before letting me leave the room. "If he gets sore, don't worry," she told my parents. "Just give him some hot tea and some aspirin."

Overnight my arm became swollen, red and itchy, and my lymph nodes were enlarged and sore. After three days of a continued high temperature and distressed arm, my parents took me back to the doctor, who said I was having a bad reaction to the vaccine and not to worry. Weeks passed and I was not getting better. I experienced profuse sweating at night, and my arm looked like a fried sausage. Necrosis developed and made for a huge painful ulcer that exposed my flesh down to the bone.

I later found out that my vaccine was from the EV strain, named after the small boy who died of bubonic plague in 1926 on the Island of Madagascar, a small nation off the East coast of Africa. The vaccine was developed and cultured from his swollen lymph nodes. I received 300 million of those live microbes in a volume of .2 milligrams.

Obviously those anti-plague vaccinations were given not only out of fear that the U.S. might hit Russian soil with bio-weapons, but because the Soviet government was developing huge bio-arsenals and knew accidental biological releases were possible. (Such was the anthrax accident in 1979 in Sverdlovsk, a city that stored and produced biological agents. Dozens of innocent citizens died due to a lack of proper maintenance by employees inside that bio facility.)

The STI vaccine against anthrax, dispensed in the 1960s and the 1970s, was administered as "an influenza vaccine" during my school days. A scrubbing technique was not used; instead, students were injected with live anthrax under the scapula (side of back) with a long needle for deep inoculation. It

was the worst time for my classmates and me. We would stand in
line half dressed, dreading what was to come. And since they
said the vaccine was good only for 12 months, we knew what to
expect every school year.

Vaccinations were performed because Soviet Russia had
developed a prime strategic bio-weapon of sporulated anthrax
which, when dispersed into the air in an aerosol form, enters the
respiratory tract and develops one of the deadliest forms of
diseases called inhalational anthrax. No anti-toxins are available to thwart this disease. The Soviet army stopped the vaccinations for military personnel for a short time in the late 1970s
and resumed them in 1987.

The secretive inoculations and the busloads of soldiers who
left our Polish base every day to work near the airports doing
"special projects," left me with no doubt that facilities were
being maintained for stockpiling bio-weapons and chemicals in
preparation for war.

Lena stayed in Leningrad to finish college and wouldn't
arrive at my base in Poland until June, six months from the time
I first arrived. I kept my mind off what she might be doing
without me by busying myself making a profit on the Polish
black market. Because of my relationship with the general, I
had connections inside the Russian border and at the train
stations. Whatever I had shipped to Poland from Russia was
never opened for inspection. (The military armory that was later
removed from Poland when the Soviet military pulled out was
sold on the black market in the same manner.)

I sold television sets, refrigerators, and black caviar to
Polish civilians. But my most profitable "business" was selling

them gasoline. This was big business for many officers. Siphoning gas out of military vehicles—ambulances and jeeps—brought a hefty profit. Polish gas was expensive. We gave them good deals and got extra cash in our pockets. Many high ranking officers, especially the gutsy ones, managed to drive entire tank loads of gasoline out of the fortress and sell the thick liquid on the black market. They made enough to buy themselves Mercedes Benz cars. KGB officers and employees of the Ministry of Internal Affairs were involved in larger scams, such things as trafficking diamonds between Russia and Poland.

One brisk November day I asked my head medic and best friend on the base if he wanted to help me sell the 40 jars of black caviar my mother-in-law had sent me. "Come on, Alexander," I pleaded, "I made the sale, we just have to meet the guy and get the money,"

"Nah, Doc," Alexander replied, amused and shaking his blond head, "I think Valyera should go; he is gifted in sales."

Valyera, our usual ambulance driver, was restocking the linen cabinet as we talked. He shouted out, "I will go!" A short guy, he was tough and had a track record for selling the most gasoline among those with a private's rank. I trusted him.

"Okay, come on, Valyera," I said. "Let's go make a little money. I have a buyer to meet in Swidnica. I'll give you ten percent."

Swidnica, the same city where my in-laws became engaged, was where the main military headquarters was located. It was a 40-mile drive from my base. The meeting place was to be in front of the *Commandentera with Galptvacta,* the temporary Soviet military prison.

Normally I didn't wear my uniform outside the base because our superiors were concerned about the rampant tales of Satanic groups trying to kidnap military men. A few privates had disappeared without a trace already. Because we had only 45 minutes to get there and didn't want to be late, we didn't change clothes.

"Count your money!" Alexander joked as we left the building with coats in hand.

We had arrived around three in the afternoon and parked the ambulance vehicle in the sprawling parking lot adjacent to the prison. The Polish fellow I had arranged the deal with arrived in a small beat up car and shut off the engine a few parking spaces down. Valyera remained inside the ambulance while I got out and walked to the other car with my box of caviar in hand. My connection, a medium built man in his 20s, met me. We shook hands. I didn't like what he said. "Let's finish this deal over there behind that old building; there are too many of your military guys around." He was pointing to a dilapidated structure at the far side of the lot.

"No," I replied, "I have the caviar right here. Let's swap and get out of here. Show me the money," I demanded.

The guy held out a wad of rolled bills, plainly making it hard for me to view the money. I grabbed the roll out of his hand and he bent down and picked up the box of caviar. I was about to say, "Hold on, I need to count this money," when I was interrupted by some shouts. I looked around and saw four thugs banging on the driver's window of my ambulance, taunting Valyera with shiny steel knives. I was wearing my uniform and knew that getting into a fight would not be wise, and getting murdered worse. I didn't wait to see what would happen next. I ran, hopped into the passenger side and yelled, "Go, Valyera!" My driver gunned the engine and tore us out of there.

Alexander was right to stay behind. The other guy got my caviar, and Valyera and I made out with three dollars and a long roll of paper. That was one deal Alexander wouldn't let us forget for a long time, but it didn't stop me from taking other dangerous risks.

I had become hardened to the numerous beatings I witnessed over the years of my service. I remember driving to the clinic one day and finding a group of privates standing around jeering and kicking someone on the ground. When they saw me they hurried off, leaving behind a soldier with a knife protruding from his belly. I wanted to laugh. I was fed up at that soldier for playing this game again; it was the third time he had stabbed himself. He knew where to put the knife so he wouldn't injure his internal organs, so deep was his desire to get out of the army. He lay there bleeding, and I thought the whole thing funny. I ignored him, walked into the clinic and told Alexander to deal with him. I simply didn't care anymore.

Even worse, I had contracted the most contagious disease of all, complacency. I disregarded my wife's interest in my best buddy when she finally arrived later that year, and ignored Alexander's interest in her. It would take more than a vaccination to cure me of a callous heart.

B io-warfare can be carried out either through the use of a strategic method or a tactical method. Strategic warfare is implemented during international wars with the support of cruise missiles. In these instances biological agents would be dropped in large populated areas as bomblets, or released as aerosol off aircraft. Targets would be predominately civilian population and not military forces. The goal would be to gain control of the population or shift government powers by completely incapacitating the populace and completely ruining the nation's economy.

Disease can boomerang to the attacker if the population is not isolated (another iron curtain), or enough distance isn't maintained between them and their target. For instance, if Russia attacked Europe or the Asian theater, the spread could make its way back to Russia and start an epidemic there. Distance from Russia to the United States would be workable. If an aggressive country is confident that ballistic missiles filled with biological agents do not possess danger to their own nation, they could move forward and probably use missiles with the most virile and contagious agents (smallpox, plague, and Marburg).

Using the strategic method requires a severe and fatal victory; otherwise the nation attacking with bio-agents will face a harsh nuclear retaliation, bringing on the start of WWIII. In a tactical event, the military aggressor would use bio-agents on battlefield situations against enemy troops during ground conflicts, and not on civilian populations. But air dispersion will always be a potential risk to civilians during this type of silent war campaign.

The kind of covert bio-warfare where aggressors can get away with the attack and not be identified is labeled the *silent war*. This means that the one who executes the attack will leave trails that lead away from the attacker. A nation that comes up with a polished dispersal device technology, using a common strain of bacteria that does not give away their location or the material used, would fare well in confusing an enemy. The one attacked would be in a precarious spot as to how to retaliate if they are not positive who their attacker is. If genetically modified weapons are ever to be used in a covert warfare, they will be used very selectively and very carefully.

In some cases, using outdated or basic bio-agents in a silent war can be beneficial to weaken a nation, and an effective way to get away with an attack without leaving fingerprints. For instance, contaminating the water systems with water-borne pathogens or causing more intense "natural" outbreaks of diseases (such as influenza) geographically typical for the effected regions. Another strategy would be to instill fear in a nation to the point the people were filling themselves with antibiotics, thinking they are protecting themselves, when they are unwittingly weakening their immune systems and becoming vulnerable to a secondary bio attack. An example would be the anthrax scare that happened shortly after the 9/11 attack on the World Trade Center. After a few people died from inhaling anthrax sent through the mail, 20 million citizens ingested the Cipro antibiotic, mostly out of panic. Cipro is a potent antibiotic. If the attackers had wanted to hit again with a common bacteria, those 20 million people might have ended up being even more susceptible to the new germ.

A nation with a weak or untrained immune system would be an easy target for biological attack. Today biological war between nations is a process involving invisible steps at the onset and simultaneous multi-regional releases of highly contagious pathogens finalizing the process. Invisible steps include preparation of the enemy's immune system to be defeated by the final attack. These steps involve proper analysis of: what people like to eat and drink, their lifestyle, types of food processed, the geographical and historical locations of natural and typical diseases, pharmaceutical suppression against the immune system (such as habitual overuse of antibiotics), concern or lack of it by pharmaceutical giants for people's health, type of drugs used by the nation, concentration and amounts of these typical drugs or antibiotics, condition and styles of work with new epidemics, and the location of sensitive populations. These steps give the enemy a clear map of places to attack. Tactically they need to know what agent will be the best for what geographical area and population.

Terrorists or enemy nations who develop biological weapons know that hitting a densely populated city is going to accomplish much more then targeting a smaller area where people are spread out. It is interesting to note that God knew this information long before any scientists understood contamination and infectious spread. In Ezekiel 7, verse 15 the Lord makes it clear that cities are most susceptible to plagues: *The sword is without, and the pestilence and the famine within: he that is in the field shall die with the sword; and he that is in the city, famine and pestilence shall devour him.*

When there is an actual biological deployment used against nations, the big cities will be hit. In that hour, people will migrate out of them, psychologically afraid to ever return. If this happened today, a huge economic tailspin would result and ruin that city. As mentioned in the last chapter, I believe biological warfare will be used, but only when God allows it, as I believe He will during the great tribulation time. The book of Revelation, Chapter 16, verse 2 clearly shows that a God-given disease, or a man-made bio-weapon is being used against those who take the mark of the antichrist system: *And the first went (angel), and poured out his vial upon the earth; and there fell a noisome and grievous sore upon the men which had the mark of the beast, and upon them which worshiped his image.* Again, with such advanced weapons stored up, there is no way the antichrist system will not implement all of them to fight his wars. But, God again proves He is in control of all disease, no matter how many bio-weapons the antichrist system will use.

Revelation 11, verse 6 gives us this assurance: *These (the two witnesses for Christ sent by God) have power to shut heaven, that it rain not in the days of their prophecy: and have power over waters to turn them to blood, and to smite the earth with all plagues, as often as they will.* They have the power to use as many plagues as often as they want. This is pretty amazing. God can never be outdone by any man-made bio-weaponry.

Epidemics of diseases like smallpox which should have been eradicated have the possibility of resurfacing because of the bio-weapon technology that began in the Soviet era and still is being played out in the new Russian Federation.

We live in precarious times, yet amazing times, because we see that despite man's intentions to destroy one another, he has not yet been able to do so. It is God who gives life and determines the fate of every man and every nation. Let me end this chapter with this note of hope in Exodus 15: 26: *And God said, If thou wilt diligently hearken to the voice of the Lord thy God, and wilt do that which is right in his sight, and wilt give ear to his commandments, and keep all his statutes, I will put none of these diseases upon thee, which I have brought upon the Egyptians: for I am the Lord that healeth thee.*

The Terrorist Mindset

During the time I was stationed in Poland, November 1989, I was selected to attend a ten-month internship at a military medical hospital back in my hometown in St. Petersburg. When I got home, my wife was disappearing for long weekends to be with Alexander, who had gotten out of the service and returned to Moscow. This was the first time she was serious about another man, especially a buddy of mine, and it was hard to take. I felt alienated, not only from Lena, but from the goals and aspirations I had given up long before. A resentful disturbance catapulted inside me as my contempt towards military life also grew deeper.

After nine years in the army, I wanted out. I had no idea how my life would end up after I told the general what I wanted to do. It could destroy me. And in Russia, finding myself without a "cushion" might mean my downfall. As I look back on it, I see the Lord's hand in pushing me forward. At the time, I did not understand that propelling force. I had bowed to my parents, my in-laws and to my wife's affairs. Now I was planning to defy them all in order to do what I wanted to do.

I had to return to Poland in August 1990 to finish my last few months of service there. Before I left, I knew that I had to talk to my in-laws about getting out of the army or I never would have the chance again. Convincing my father-in-law to persuade all the other high-ranking officials to let me out of the military was like asking the army to allow women to serve inside Leningrad's all-male military medical academy.

Getting out of the Russian Army was almost impossible. Military soldiers and cadets unwilling to serve in the army ended up in mental institutions or the front lines of war hot spots. My request was only going to be successful through my connections. The fact I was a physician made things worse. The army had spent too much money on my training to let me go.

The only lawful way an officer could get out of the army was if his regiment became dismantled. According to Russian military law, if a regiment ends, officers can choose to remain in service and relocate to another division, or they can step down from full time service to active reserve officer.

I hoped the general's knowledge of Lena's affairs might make him bend to my plight. But I needed a boost to give me the courage to make such a request. A memory of the tin cross incident that happened in my first year of service helped inspire me. That tiny piece of tin represented something or someone far greater than I understood. Since it held the power to spark such heated reactions from Soviet officials, I wondered if this "someone greater than I" might hold the key to my gaining the strength I needed to get my life back. I had never prayed before, didn't know how to, but somehow hoped that this God might help me anyway. The magnitude of how much help I did get from God would not hit me until much later, after I came to know Him personally.

So it happened, the general agreed to pull the appropriate strings, but not before a relentless two weeks of badgering me to "think things over." He reminded me that I held a promising career "up the ladder." I didn't want that kind of life and bluntly told him so.

I returned to Poland, finished up my service, and then hurried back to Leningrad to await news concerning my requested resignation. My father-in-law knew of one military unit that harbored convicted soldiers in St. Petersburg that would be dismantling. After numerous interviews with military intelligence officials, I was stationed in Military Unit P.O. Box #11554. One year later the division disbanded and I was free to start working in the New Russia with my father.

It wasn't long before I found myself in some precarious situations, doing business nose to nose with some of the most malicious Chechen terrorists.

The war between Russia and Chechnya has been a long and bloody one, and terrorism had sprouted up from both sides. The Chechens are a colonized people who have been conducting a struggle against imperial Russia and the imperial Soviet

Union for more than 200 years. At the beginning of the 19th century, Chechnya, led by the legendary Imam Shamil, was conquered by the Russian Empire. Vladimir Lenin declared that development of Chechnya would be the primary target of the Bolshevik government. This promise, as was common with Lenin, was broken, and the communists destroyed the beautiful mountain country. Josef Stalin had a vision of ethnic and religious cleansing of the Northern Caucasian district. In 1944, in less then 30 days, he deported 493,269 Chechens and Ingush, herding them into trains like animals (thousands died), from their homeland to uninhabitable regions of Kazakhstan.

It was no surprise that Chechnya, as did 15 other nations recognized today by the United States and the world community, declared their independence immediately upon the collapse of the Soviet Union in December 1991. It is because Chechnya was denied its freedom that terrorism emerged from that country.

Terrorism is not new, nor is terrorism found only within Islamic societies. Terrorism has been around since the beginning of time when scripture first reveals the hateful mindset of a brother named Cain against his own brother Abel. Hatred, the driving force behind all acts of violence, stems from rebellion.

History has dealt out plenty of terrorism, and the book of Revelation is clear that terrorism will continue to be a part of the future. Beginning with the time jealous King Saul terrorized his son's best friend David, to the time shortly after Christ's ascension when believers were fed to the lions and sawn in half by the Romans, to the period of the inquisition when the Catholic church tortured anyone who would not adhere to their creed,

to the violent Hindu sects in India, to the 12th century in Iran
when the Shiite Muslims used brutality in order to purify Islam,
to the Russian revolution when hatred crushed freedom, to
Stalin who mass murdered the lower class, to World War II when
Hitler slaughtered the Jews, to the present fanatical groups from
Ireland, Israel, Japan, and Arab nations who use bombs to exact
vengeance—terrorism is an ongoing menace.

Yes, bombs can destroy more lives at one time, and biological threats are worrisome, but terrorism itself is no greater a
problem today then it was thousands of years ago. It just seems
so because of the televised pictures of blown-up buildings and
human executions coming into our living rooms daily. In reality,
today's terrorist acts are just as constant and atrocious as they
were in past civilizations. Torture is gruesome and ugly in any
form, in any century.

Terrorists are criminals, but not ordinary criminals; they are
political zealots birthed out of social problems. They are the
guerilla fighters who are the armed wing of a revolutionary
group or movement, trained to engage enemy forces in battle.
They are the revolutionaries who are focused on overthrowing a
government, and not necessarily by brutal means.

Blind patriotism, mind control, hatred, insecurity, false
religions, greed, political devotion, and cultural traditions can
all be reasons why individuals are susceptible to becoming
terrorists.

The logic behind terrorist strategies in general can be
varied: attempting to make a political statement, wanting an
immediate political change, a practice for violence, a test to
determine limits, or a reason to test the strength of governments.

Webster's dictionary defines *terrorism* as, "the use of force or threats to demoralize, intimidate, and subjugate, especially such use as the political weapon or policy."

Silent terrorists fall under the classification of state terrorism. They sneak in through the back door by implementing mind control and fear tactics on populations in order to overtake governments. These might not seem as bloody as those groups that torture their victims, but they are just as deadly because they work to kill the mind and control the masses, which allows them to eventually have the power to torture and kill whom they want.

Dictators often practice silent terrorism to deceive and scare their own citizens into accepting new laws, wars, or political changes. Countries that need a war or want to change their government's structure will often create or allow disasters, even if it means killing their own people to fulfill their wicked agenda. Soviet Russia, China and North Korea also fall under this kind of terrorism.

The Soviet Union used silent terrorism by convincing the entire Russian population that the "enemy," the United States, intended to attack them. They didn't actually stage a disaster, but they created a delusion so deep that people lived in fear. By doing this they were able to justify building a strong military police state and to solidify complete control over the people.

Totalitarian and authoritarian regimes don't typically have internal problems with terrorism once they have formed their controlled governments, because they have already terrorized the population into submission and now are able to filter out most crime. Soviet Russia is a prime example of this. They didn't begin to have internal problems with terrorism until after the fall of communism.

Some terrorist groups kill for money, or simply for revenge. These types are treacherous because they have thought out their plan thoroughly and effectively. They seldom make mistakes and will kill whoever is in their way in order to accomplish their goal. Their greed leaves no room for mercy.

International (state sponsored) terrorism appears when a government sponsors terrorism in one or more other countries. Usually international terrorism involves violent acts dangerous to human life that are a violation of the criminal laws of the (United States or any) state. These acts are intended to intimidate or persuade a civilian population, influence the policy of a government by coercion, or affect the conduct of a government by assassination or kidnapping.

Domestic terrorism is practiced within a country by people with no ties to any government. Trans-national terrorism occurs when groups in different countries cooperate with each other. According to the FBI, domestic terrorism is the unlawful use, or threatened use, of force or violence by a group or individual based and operating entirely within the United States or its territories without foreign direction, committed against persons or property to intimidate or coerce a government, the civilian population, or any segment thereof, in furtherance of political or social objectives.

Terrorism as a world-wide threat is almost always based on an excessive and blind devotion to either a political or religious cause, where many people can be influenced to participate, and hatred is the unifying foundation behind the force. Insecure people who lack self worth find these hate groups to be an appealing alternative. *Shahids* are common in terrorist cells because they are so loyal to their tribe and to their relatives inside the cell. Due to the close blood ties within these groups, law enforcement and military forces find them difficult to infiltrate and, thus, hard to eliminate. The 50 terrorists that terrorized the 900 people inside Moscow's Dubrovka Theater, on October 23, 2002, were part of this group.

Shortly after the second act of the famous "Nord Ost" musical, at approximately ten o'clock at night, three camouflage-clad men bounced onto the stage, waving Kalashnikov rifles and hand grenades high above their masked heads. Firing a round into the ceiling, they faced the audience and shouted, "Stop the Chechen war!"

Within seconds, 50 Chechen guerilla rebels, all heavily armed, were screaming from different sections of the theatre.

The leader, Movsar Barayev, a young man in his 20s and a known member of the Wahhabite sect (an extreme form of fundamentalist Islam founded in Saudi Arabia and imported to Chechnya by Arab volunteers), appeared onstage in front of the shaken actors—men, women, and children. His close-set eyes looked fierce as he yelled at the audience, "You are all my hostages now. Our demand is that the Chechen war be stopped and there be an immediate withdrawal of Russian troops out of Chechnya. If at the end of this week the Kremlin does not meet our demands, we will execute all of you!"

Movsar Barayev, also known as Movsar Suleimenov, was the nephew of the renowned warlord Arbi Barayev, who gained fame

by establishing a large slave-trading network throughout
Chechnya. After his Uncle Arbi was slain in the summer of
2001 in his home village of Alkhan-Kala, Movsar took command of most of his uncle's men and continued the kidnapping
in Chechnya. He seemed invincible as he dodged death, although Russian Federal Forces repeatedly claimed to have
killed him.

Raised in Argun, the war-torn town southeast of Grozny,
Movsar's generation was the first to live outside of the Soviet
mentality. He grew up hating Russians and chose to carry
submachine guns instead of schoolbooks. Movsar and his fellow
gunmen came to Moscow to bring death and destruction, and to
die in the process if need be.

The 18 women terrorists, covered head to toe in black,
ranged between the ages of 20 and 30. Each female stood guard
in her strategic area, and moved carefully with pistol in hand
towards the hostages. Their faces were hidden behind black
veils; and the tight cloth on their foreheads bore Islamic slo-
gans. Around their waists they wore bulky explosive belts; their
pockets bulged with hand grenades.

The entire takeover plot was accomplished with precision
skill. The theater had been penetrated days before the siege.
Mines and explosives were planted at exits and entrances.

"Why are you here?" A young woman, irritated at the
intruders, appeared out of a back door and yelled at the terrorists.

"Shut up or be shot!" Movsar hollered back at her from his
tactical location near the stage.

"So shoot me!" the woman bellowed back.

Three male terrorists ran down the aisle to the back of the theater. They grabbed the woman, pulled her into the foyer out of view of the hostages, and there they beat her with the butts of their rifles, and shot her. The murderers returned and, with angry shouts at the hostages, taunted them for an excuse to kill again.

Ishot Bakuvia and Sekeelot Aleyva, young women who grew up near the capital of Grosny in Chechnya, raised their pistols in salute at one another. They were standing on the same side of the theater, guarding the hostages.

Ishot, a serious looking young woman with a long face and square jaw, came from the village of Ilenovka and had owned a pharmaceutical business in Grosny. Her brother, Bayodi, a famous guerilla field commander, had been killed in 2000. Not long afterward, she lost two more brothers and a brother-in-law to the war.

What angered her the most was losing her favorite brother, 15 year-old Daout, who had been captured and tortured after he tried to place an explosive device inside a Russian-held building in Grosny. The refusal by the Russian authorities to return his broken body was done deliberately to disgrace her family and to mock the Muslim custom that demands that the dead be buried within 24 hours. Ishot also knew that the Russian soldiers raped their male captives with broken bottles in order to make them unclean for *shahid* missions. To a Muslim, rape is a far worse fate then death.

Ishot's neighbors did not like her. She had become too involved with the Wahhabite sect after the death of her brothers, and they understood that to her they were pagans. They had heard about the bomb young Daout had tried to plant inside the busy building, which would have killed many Muslims as well as Russians, and they were angered by his willingness to murder other Chechens. They steered clear of Ishot and her family. Ishot didn't care. She knew what she had to do. In the fall of 2002, she suddenly sold her business and moved to Moscow.

Sekeelot Aleyva was a thin, petite woman with attractive eyes. She graduated from the Chechen State University in 1998 with honors, a major in acting, and a degree in International Business Management. Her brother, Movsar, was 22 years old when Russian soldiers killed him in 2000. Disturbed at his death, Sekeelot partnered with her grandfather's Wahhabite friends. Her aunt on her father's side convinced her to attend a special course on Islam. Before long, Sekeelot gave up her love for music, dance, and acting, and turned to the Wahhabite belief, dressing in long clothing and avoiding her family on her mother's side. In the fall of 2002 she told her worried mother that she would secure her a place in heaven. She was ready to die.

Hour by hour the militants inside the theater followed their precise plan, taking turns sleeping and guarding. "Rat-tat-tat-a-tat-tat" was often played into the ceiling by yelling gunmen to control the audience.

Russia's President Vladimir Putin, unwilling to bend to a terrorist threat, called in 200 men from an anti-terrorist squad, the Alpha Force. There they set up listening devices and prepared the gas tanks they had brought along.

On the third day, after Russia refused the Chechen demands to pull their troops out of Chechnya, the rebel Movsar gave the

sign to start shooting. His allies seized a man and woman out of
the front row and shot them. They were the first ones to be
killed in front of the crowd. But the guerillas had no idea that
Russian Special Forces had already infiltrated the theater with
tanks of gas. Fumes began seeping out of the airflow ducts as
soon as the two hostages were killed.

At the smell of the gas, most of the crowd covered their
faces, but those who were closest to the vents lost consciousness
immediately, including some of the female terrorists. An explosion opened a hole in the theater wall and the Alpha team, safe
in gas masks, quickly burst through from their tunnel underneath the building. Two hundred Russian troops stormed inside,
and for the next 45 minutes they battled the remaining terrorists, finally taking out the male guerillas with bullets to the
eyes. Meanwhile, a select group from the Alpha team, with
special orders to prevent the comatose female guerillas from
going into convulsions and unknowingly activating the explosives, rushed up to the unconscious female terrorists and shot
them in the temple at point-blank range.

Sleeping hostages were dragged outside by the troops, feet
trailing in mud. Some bodies were left on the icy walkways for
almost an hour; others were loaded on buses to be transported to
hospitals. Many of them suffocated on their own vomit. A total of
129 hostages died; two from gunshot wounds amid the rescue
operation, and three who were executed by the terrorists. Seven-
teen of the dead were cast members. Six hundred sixty-four of
the hostages were hospitalized.

The callous treatment of hostages by the rescue teams after
the theater was secured and the explosives deactivated was

tragic. Most died several hours after they had been rescued (which shouldn't have happened if proper care had been given). Hospitals and medical staff had not been alerted before the operation or given a proper antidote to counter the narcotic gas.

To date, there has been no authorized information released on what kind of gas was used—typical of the secretive ways of past Soviet rule—but I know what it was. During my service, fentanilum cocktail and other powerful stable anesthetics in aerosol applications were developed at the Faculty of Military Toxicology inside my academy. They were tested on soldiers during the Afghanistan War and the Chechen conflict. When General Colonel Shevchenko, the chief of the former Ministry of Health of the Russian Federation, hinted on Russian news broadcasts that the gas used in "Nord Ost" was developed at my academy, it wasn't hard to figure out it was fentanilum.

Despite the grief-stricken relatives demanding answers to the way their lost loved ones were treated, the Kremlin claimed the rescue operation was a brilliant victory.

From the evidence gathered regarding the terrorists inside the Dubrovka Theater that October night in Moscow, it seemed possible that some in that group did not intend to die in that theater. All the male guerillas wore masks, except Movsar, the leader, who obviously wanted the Russian authorities to see he was not dead, as they had often reported. It is doubtful Movsar would want to end his life when he had inherited the famed "head honcho" position over his dead uncle's duties. The fact that all the other men hid their faces seems odd if they were planning a suicide mission. A few of the women might have had time to activate the explosive belts the second they began smelling the gas, but they did not do so. Yet, on the other hand, from researching Sekeelot's conversation with her mother before heading to Moscow, she was willing to die, and expected to die during that siege. Whatever and however each one thought individually, one thing is clear: they did what they were told to do; they followed their orders. Within every terrorist group, mind control is found at the helm.

Respecting the mindset of a terrorist is important. The woman who defied the terrorist thugs in the theater did not do so, and this mistake cost her life. She underestimated their state of mind and showed disrespect for their culture. Back talk from a woman in the Muslim society is prohibited, and women are killed and beaten for dishonoring a man in such a way.

If individuals find themselves hostage to a terrorist plot, remaining calm and avoiding risk-taking is important. Second-guessing the motives and heart of a terrorist will cost lives.

If there is a probable chance to escape, victims should look for this opening at the beginning timeframe when the terrorists are working to gain control. There might be enough commotion and confusion to grant some people access to getting away. If the confusion period passes, it is best to sit still and not chance an escape, unless death seems imminent and another opportunity grants the chance for survival. The ruffians will kill those who try to escape and fail. Terrorists spend months and sometimes years putting together a plan of attack. They are well trained and know all the entrances and exits better than the captives.

Never irritate a captor. Remember that God is in control of the situation; pray silently to Him. Staying alive will have a lot to do with understanding the enemy as a person *not* to reckon with. Don't take for granted that a terrorist holds any sympathy whatsoever, even toward children. If small children are present, speak calmly to them; reassure them everything is okay, and that God is with them. Keep them quiet.

During a siege situation where there are only a few hostages, the terrorist(s) might choose to converse with one or more of their victims. Stay calm, talk calmly, make eye contact (this lets them know you are not afraid), and if you have the opportunity, talk about your family. Sometimes letting them see you as a mother, father, sister or brother (because they have family and understand that bond), instead of seeing you as an enemy, might work in your favor.

But don't give out personal and detailed information. If they do not want to listen, stop talking. If they confide in you, listen, but don't sympathize.

Be aware of the Stockholm Syndrome—named from an incident in 1973 when four Swedes held in a bank vault for six days during a robbery became attached to their captors. There is never a good outcome for the hostage if they become sympathetic with the terrorist mindset.

I met Ibragim Djalilov, a middle-aged soft-spoken "business man," shortly after I left the army, outside the Hotel #1, the meeting point where my father and I were to purchase the cases of cognac. Ten of Ibragim's trucks were parked inside the hotel's gate, bumper to bumper against the brick wall when we arrived.

Ibragim knew my father from prior business arrangements and liked him. He greeted me with a strong handshake and firm pat on the shoulder. "I am happy to meet you, Igor," he said. "It has been good business for us. Your father has sold most of my product. He has good connections."

Dad's mouth curled up proudly as he exclaimed, "Igor is my new partner."

Ibragim replied, "Then let's celebrate. What better way to test my product; I brought good stuff. Let's crack open some bottles now!"

Ibragim's seemingly quiet demeanor and expensive suit masqueraded his terrorist mindset. Inside he wore his hatred as thick as his stocky arm muscles. Although he resided in Dagistan with his family and had worked quietly as an engineer for many years, Ibragim was born and raised in Chechnya. His lust to see his native land freed from Russia's tyranny motivated his every step. Everything he did since the New Russian Federation came into power was to help the Chechen rebels fight the Russians. What he sold us was part of necessary "formalities" to keep anyone from figuring out what his business really consisted of—sneaking weapons in and out of the Russian border. My father and I stayed neutral on such matters—our motivation was simply to make money.

The opening of Russia produced newly formed businesses. Transport convoys, mostly large trucks, chugged back and forth across the borders continuously, in and out of St. Petersburg and Moscow, all stocked with merchandise and food—and military type arsenals. It wasn't hard to get officially stamped documents from heavy metal and aluminum type companies wanting truck drivers to transport their goods across the border. These drivers, who took the job to sell weapons, were able to pass through Customs without being checked at all.

Ibragim's activities in chemical and radiological business paid off. His connections in Moscow with the government metal company called GERMET, got him past Georgian and Turkish borders, without Custom officials blinking an eye, and he was able to sneak through metals, especially palladium, platinum, gold, mercury, titanium, and red phosphorus from military and chemical bases. He paid the "Tombovsky" mafia for personal protection during his business excursions and hired plenty of his own armored "bulls" to secure the goods in his trucks.

Excited at my newfound freedom to work where I wanted, I grinned and followed Dad, Ibragim and two of his men to the back of the last truck. After Ibragim slid open the access door, I caught sight of some black painted-over containers in the corner, stacked away from the regular brown boxes. I recognized them immediately as military property. "Where is the booze from?" I asked Ibragim, my eyes still on the military stash in the corner.

He caught my gaze. "Too many questions, Igor." Ibragim removed his suit coat and handed it to one of his men, and then jumped into the back of the truck. His thinned-out silver hair made him look older then he was, but he didn't lack energy. The rest of us jumped inside the truck and sat on the boxes. Ibragim tore open one box, pulled out a few bottles of cognac, and passed them around. He wrung the lid off his bottle and raised it high. "To my people," he burst out in toast. "May they find peace!" His eyes flashed like hot coals and I knew his mind was not on the sale of alcohol.

After swigging the golden-brown liquid, and having a few laughs, Ibragim asked me to get his map from the front cab.

"Tonight I head for the Georgian border. I will show you where I go."

I jumped down and went around the truck to the driver's side, opened the door and slid onto the seat. My shoe caught on something as I climbed in, and when I reached down to check it out, my hand hit against cold metal. It was an AK-47 automatic rifle. At once I realized how dangerous this meeting was, and it sobered me. I grabbed the map from the visor and returned to the back.

Ibragim moved his finger down the map. "Turkey is our destination," he said. Then he asked my dad, "By the way, Vladimir, you worked in LOMO, the military factory where they build optics. Do you have any connections there anymore?"

I felt uneasy. I knew optics helped build nuclear submarines. I hoped my dad wouldn't get involved in that aspect of Ibragim's business.

"No," Dad replied. He had a way of putting people at ease, making them believe him. "No connections there anymore. Too much time has passed."

Ibragim didn't pursue the matter. Relieved, I took another chug of cognac.

Before we left the truck, Ibragim said to me, "Igor, you like this watch?" It was a Rolex.

"Sure," I said.

"You get one if you will work for me," he added, drunk, but serious.

Dad spoke up before I could talk, his blue eyes steely, and said, "Ibragim, he is *my* partner. I just got him back from the army. He works only for me."

But Ibragim turned to me, patted his wrist, and winked.

Four months later I heard about Ibragim's death from a few of his "bulls" at the Hotel #1. A dozen Mercedes cars had blockaded a small road near the Moscow airport. Killers had stepped outside them and stood there holding automatic weapons called "Bizons" underneath their long trench coats. A trade was taking place. Trunks flew open and suitcases full of money were exchanged for long stainless steel tubes, rumored to have been full of radioactive material.

As trunks were closing, guns started to show up. Gunfire erupted; bodies fell, and cars sped away. Five men were left behind dead on the street. Ibragim Djalilov was one of them.

Because the majority of today's terrorism threats are coming from Islamic groups, this chapter will conclude with focus on the "pro-Allah" mindset. The militant group that interrupted the "Nord Ost" musical with weapons belonged to the Wahhabi sect. This sect can be labeled as a severe and dangerous cult because the followers are excessive in their reasons to kill, and more apt to sacrifice children and young women to accomplish their goals. They are the bloodiest of terrorist groups and interpret the Koran more aggressively than general Muslims, believing it is a guide toward pro-Jihad, or holy war.

The Wahhabites are known to be involved with the politically powerful Sa'ud family of Arabia, and now have members stationed in Chechnya to fight against the Russians. They refuse to follow the governing rules of the land, and their allegiance to the cult precedes their loyalty to family members, a contrast to the mainstream Muslim culture. They are believed to be a puritanical version of Islam, diminishing the Islamic traditional role of the prophet Muhammad and condemning people who revere Muhammad, considering them idolatrous. A parallel would be American Puritans denying the importance of Jesus.

Ibn 'Abd ul-Wahhab, a nomad, founded the Wahhabi sect. He despised Christians and Jews, even though traditional Islam had long considered them protected classes within Islamic society. He also believed that Muslims who did not follow his belief should all be killed, their wives and daughters violated, and their possessions confiscated.

The Wahhabi code is one of the strictest in all of Islamic history, and can be compared to the Nazis. The code dictates almost every aspect of a believer's life, including the way they must dress. The men sport beards without moustaches and wear uniforms that include shorts and long-sleeved shirts. Unlike Chechnya women, the female members wear veils over their faces and completely cover their bodies.

These types of groups often branch out into other countries and seldom operate from one location. Although they use unsophisticated training techniques and equipment, like most groups, they are funded by crime and drugs and can accomplish effective plots to kill. These terrorists are void of emotion, and do not follow any moral law.

Psychology of all terrorism can include oversimplification of issues: the lust for risk taking, a lust for blood, social isolation, frustration, a need to be noticed, and utopianism. But Islamic terrorism, whether involved under extremist sects or not, is borne out of tradition, founded upon the book of Koran, and this is what makes it more precarious.

Islam, in a religious way, means submission to the will of Allah and obedience to his law. It is "a code of political, ceremonial, civil, and criminal law, as well as moral and religious precepts, all communicated in the name of Allah."

Allah in the Arabic language means "god," the creator of the universe. Muslims believe that Allah is in control of their entire history and, in the doctrine of predestination, an acceptance of destiny and resignation to fate. They believe that anything that happens is the will of Allah and done by him, and that in the day of the judgment when the world as we know it will come to an end, all men and women from Adam to the last person will be resurrected from death to stand their "final and fair trial." Individuals with good records will be generously rewarded and warmly welcomed to Heaven; those with bad records will be cast into flames of Hell.

Although the Wahhabites will not idolize him, Muhammad is the prophet that most Muslims believe was a direct descendant of Abraham through his firstborn son, Ishmael. Born in Saudi Arabia 570 A.D., Muhammad was in his 40s when the Muslims say Allah gave him divine revelations inside the cave of Mount Hira, in Mecca, Arabia. In 629, under the command of Muhammad, Muslims put the sword to the Jews of Khaybar as an example for all others who were refusing to accept Islam as their religion. In 630, Muhammad took over Mecca and hastily converted everyone to Islam. Muhammad died of poor health in Medina in 632, at the age of 62 and is buried in the courtyard of the mosque in Medina.

The Koran is the Muslim equivalent of the Christian's Bible, "holy scripture revealed by Allah to the Holy Prophet

Muhammad" through the angel Gabriel. According to Muslims, the Koran is "the last book of guidance from Allah" revealed to Muhammad over a period of 23 years in the Arabic language. It contains 114 Surahs, or chapters, and over 6,000 verses.

Islam's holiest book, the Koran, is eerily militant in its views toward Christians and Jews. Its account of Jesus Christ emphatically rejects his divinity as Son of God and mentions him only as one of the great prophets. It condemns Jews and Christians as idolaters, stating, "They have taken as lords beside Allah their rabbis and their monks and the Messiah son of Mary, when they were bidden to worship only One God." [at-Taubah 9:31]

From its inception 600 years after the death of Jesus, Muslims have imposed Islam on throngs of people with the bloody sword of Jihad. They justify Jihad by claiming it is confirmed in defense of Islam. However, the Koran makes exceptions for Christians and Jews: *Idolatry is more grievous than bloodshed ... fight against them until idolatry is no more and God's religion reigns supreme.* (Sura 2:91-93) *O ye who believe! Take not the Jews and the Christians for friends. They are friends one to another. He among you who taketh them for friends is of them. Lo! Allah guideth not wrongdoing folk.* [al Ma'idah 5:51.11]

In the Islamic culture there is a wide acceptance of peripheral religious writings that promise a grand place in paradise for those men who die while taking the lives of unbelievers. They willingly die, especially when they believe they will inherit a harem of 72 virgins.

These people are spurred on by their faith in Allah, a belief that cannot be conquered or exterminated by military force.

That is why Lenin feared the faith of true believers; he understood how the belief system worked, that it could not be beaten out of people. Unfortunately, Muslims don't follow the Gospel of Jesus Christ; this is what makes their belief system so deadly.

The Christian Bible teaches love; the Muslim Koran teaches hate. Here is a clear picture of the contrast between good and evil, God and Satan. Although many Muslims who are not terrorists claim their religion is kind and peaceful towards all people, the Koran's teaching does not agree. This is why evangelist activity by Christians is considered aggression against Muslims and is punishable with death in some Islamic states.

Any person or group who terrorizes in the name of a political agenda or religious cause does not adhere to Biblical principles, and moves opposite the will of God. They are driven by an evil force, that antichrist spirit, which cannot be eradicated by gunfire. There is no easy solution to end such terrorism, with the result that never in history since Christ has there been a pause in the plundering of human lives.

The young people in this last generation in Chechnya—people like Movsar, Ishot, and Sekeelo—have grown up around violent and senseless war. Their minds have been numbed against feeling emotion because of the numerous killings that take place around them. Once they get involved in a terrorist cult, they become lethal to civilization.

The most damaging reason behind this aggressive mindset is that their culture and religion invite them to kill. Many are vulnerable to belong, since they no longer have families. Others have lost so many brothers that they feel a need for revenge. This state of mind is like a tornado—you can't stop it, you can't

guess which way it will go, you don't know how much destruction it can cause or who will die in it. And you don't know when
it will end. In order to adequately discern the mind of a terrorist, one must view their mind as a tornado, and understand that
a mind bent on destruction is impossible to tame.

Hatred causes strife: murder, wars, and jealousy. It moti-
vates people to slander and curse, to belittle and destroy, to lie
and to cheat. This is the outcome of a people who deny Jesus
Christ as God's only begotten Son.

I John Chapter 4, verses 1 to 3 give warning to the earmarks
of false teaching. *Beloved, believe not every spirit, but try the
spirits whether they are of God: because many false prophets are
gone out into the world. Hereby know ye the Spirit of God: Every
spirit that confesseth that Jesus Christ is come in the flesh is of
God; And every spirit that confesseth not that Jesus Christ is come
in the flesh is not of God; and this is that spirit of antichrist,
whereof ye have heard that it should come, and even now already
is it in the world.*

A denial of Christ's deity is the first clue of a belief system
that will work to destroy the true Christian faith. Jesus' Gospel
is born out of the Father's merciful heart toward His creation.
"Turn the other cheek," "love our enemies," and "do good to
those that spitefully use us" are the threads that weave together
the true body of Christ. The Christian believer does not battle
with grenades and bombs, but with prayer, faith and truth. Some
might argue that the Old Testament God promoted terrorism. If
we look back to the beginning, in the garden with Adam and
Eve before the fall, we see that God's intentions were never to
have a world full of evil, violence, war and hatred. The Father

did not place the first man and woman in a war zone. He gave them a beautiful lush garden home, with everything provided to live a wonderful, peaceful, and happy life.

Evil came into the world because of disobedience to God's Words, not because God was keeping score on a board of war games and enjoyed watching bloody battles. Satan gained control of the world through sin and upstaged God's goodness to bring about rebellion and war. God has been working ever since to undo what happened in the garden. He accomplished this spiritually through His Son's death and resurrection, and at the Lord's return we will see the physical completion of His plan.

Jesus Christ's sacrificial death for all humankind canceled out what Satan did in the garden, and He came preaching love and forgiveness. He did not come bearing a sword for physical battle to fight those who hated Him; instead he fought unrighteousness with the sword of faith. He came with the Father's heart to restore to humans what Adam and Eve lost. His message is not to kill unbelievers, but to love our neighbors and our enemies. And this is where we see the difference with most other religions, especially the Islam faith.

When Jesus faced his executioners after they nailed his hands and feet to the wood, He did not spiel hatred and curses at them. Instead He said, "Father, forgive them; for they know not what they do." His disciples did not go around blowing up the homes of the malefactors who drove the nails into their Lord's body. Instead they preached forgiveness and love and hope and mercy. In this world of terrorism we must be cautious that we respond to our enemies with love and not hatred. We are representatives of Christ, and we need to act with His heart.

Young David took on the giant terrorist, Goliath, by faith, never once doubting that God was in control. The same weapon of faith that David used is the best defense against terrorism. Although one bomb may destroy one city, our prayers are to stop four other bombs from blowing up four other cities. We do not always see what our prayers produce. If we could, we would be amazed at what they do to save lives.

A believer in Christ should be careful that unresolved arguments do not turn them into terrorists against the Gospel of Jesus Christ. Any time we hate other people and manifest that anger through our mouths to slander them or physically abuse them, we are not walking after Christ's Gospel, but rather giving in to the mindset of a terrorist. *Whosoever hateth his brother is a murderer: and ye know that no murderer hath eternal life abiding in him.* (I John 3: 15) This applies as well in marriages. The battering of a spouse by a professed Christian is never justified. Terrorizing one's own family is as grave a terrorist act as those that brought down the World Trade Center.

I mentioned earlier how overwhelmed I was at the factual reports I received at my job that implied how supernaturally protected America is. Without God's protection, no nation, especially America, would have made it this far. In order to face today's threats around the world, citizens must not look at today's events without seeing the big picture. This picture is told in the Bible from beginning to end, from the time sin first came into the world to Satan's undermining of God's goodness to make the world corrupt, to God's plan to restore humankind to Him through His Son's death on the cross, to our eternal place with Jesus when He rules the earthly nations. Biblical history and prophetic Revelation is given to us in scripture so that we do not live in fear and forget our destiny in Christ's soon-to-come kingdom. Yes, bombs will continue to destroy lives, and terrorists will kill women and children—but the end will come, Christ will return. Those dark forces will be judged for their evil, and those lives that were lost here on earth, throughout every century, will be revenged. Then we will rule and reign with our Lord. What a great time that will be. And it will be.

When we look at how far the world has come, and how short a time it has left, and what the future holds, our minds can be comforted, our losses can be dealt with, and our fears can be diminished.

Once out of the army, I had the freedom to do what I chose to do. Yet I was still a prisoner in my marriage. The general seemed distant to me after I left the army, and when I agreed to work with Joana's "lover" on weekends to help build her a summer cottage, Joana became my target of blame for Lena's loose behavior. On top of that, my business with my father irritated my in-laws because they were losing their grip on me, and disliked my dad's contacts with the mafia. But I liked the work because I was able to make my own decisions, something I hadn't been able to do in a long time. I supplemented my income by taking a job at Sanitary Unit #122 at the former KGB Hotel #1, which also gave me more independence and control over my life.

Then things worsened for me. Lena surprised me one day and told me she was pregnant by Alexander. Soon he was practically living with us at her parent's flat, and I felt even

more estranged from them for allowing Alexander to sleep there
while I was expected to accept the "boyfriend." Although the
prison door had opened for me, I still stood inside that cell,
unwilling to walk out. I felt as though I had allowed a "dirty"
bomb inside my heart. I feared that if I didn't come up with a
quick plan of evacuation for myself soon, I would blow up and
the outcome might ruin me. But I waited too long, and my mind
exploded and I became murderous, like the terrorists and mafia
groups I had worked with. The next few weeks were spent in a
fog, planning how to kill my wife.

Lena had been gone for months with Alexander in Moscow.
My plan was to travel there and do it. On a warm Saturday
afternoon in August, I went to the depot and bought a ticket for
the next day's train ride to Moscow. I returned home to pack,
and was relieved that Lena's parents were out. I walked into my
bedroom and noticed the old icon of Jesus on the wall. It had
hung there for as long as I could remember, but I never really
took much notice of it before. Now it seemed to be looking
straight at me. Remembering the tin cross, a flood of emotion
choked me, and I unexpectedly slid to my knees and awkwardly
cried, "God, I need your help." Deep moans escaped me and I
sounded like loose shutters when a windstorm hurls them
against the house. Soon, drained and confused at my reactions, I
rose from the floor and went into the kitchen for a smoke.

The next day God was not on my mind. I boarded the train
for the long ride to Moscow, impatient, aloof and obsessed with
revenge. I nervously fondled the sharp switchblade in my jacket
pocket with every intention of murdering my wife. By the time I
arrived at Alexander's house in Moscow I was beside myself. I

put my fist through the kitchen window and ignored Lena's frightened look when I pushed my way inside the apartment. I was faster than her boyfriend and, clutching the knife, I grabbed my wife by the hair and pushed her down to her knees. Alexander froze as I yanked up her chin and pushed the blade against her throat, drawing blood.

Chapter Nine
Keep My Floors Clean
No Matter What!

I don't have any other explanation as to what stopped me, except that God took me up on my prayer the night before. In that split second when my hand should have moved to finish off Lena, it didn't. The deep anger inside me was gone. Suddenly I didn't want to kill anyone. I just wanted to walk out those prison doors and get on with my life. Alexander would have to deal with my wife now. That was enough satisfaction. I released Lena, and slumped down at the kitchen table. Alexander poured two glasses of cognac and sat down beside me.

Early the next morning I returned to the newly named St. Petersburg. The conversation with my in-laws was strained as I packed my belongings. The general seemed to understand, but

Joana pleaded with me to stay; but it was over. I left, taking only
the clothes I needed, and moved in with my folks. I never saw
Joana or the general again.

Three months later my divorce was final and I turned to
vodka to numb the constant melancholy hanging over me. My
life had taken a complete turnabout. I was not only getting used
to life outside both the military and my marriage, but I was
adjusting to the changes inside the new Russia. Still, no matter
how much money I made or how well I performed at work, I
could not shake the shroud of despair weighing me down.

Living with my parents was also painful. I had alienated
them during my marriage, partially because I had blamed them
for my sour life and partially at the request of my ex-wife who
strongly disliked my mother. The wounds sandwiched between
my folks and me were thick, and more so because they were
never discussed. The evenings alone at home with my parents
were difficult times.

The profound changes in my life seemed to unleash emotions I had been suppressing for the last ten years. I felt power-
less to control those new feelings and wept often, which I felt
showed weakness. After a few weeks of losing the battle to the
turmoil inside me, a thought came to me, almost as if a voice
had whispered in my ear, *Write your feelings on paper*.

As a young boy I had been a dreamer. I would gaze at the
stars for hours through the window and wonder how they got
there. My parents worked long days, and I was left alone to
ponder such big issues as how the universe came to exist and
who made it all work so perfectly. The memory of "Him"
charged into my head—the title of the first poem I wrote in

school about a mysterious "being" who made the world. The teacher, although uncomfortable with it when I read it in front of the class, gave me a high score. I continued writing poetry for a few months until I moved on to other interests.

I got out some paper and sat down at the small desk in our hallway. With pen in hand, I wrote verse after verse about my ambitions and desires, my troubled past and questionable future, and the mysteries of God. I couldn't stop; it was as if there was a wind inside me, pushing those feelings out of me onto the paper—like art. As the poems took shape, the pain, frustration and loneliness that I had amassed from the torn relationship with my parents, my marriage, and military life began to dissolve. Within a week, calm and hope settled over me. The Holy Spirit again supernaturally intervened in my life to comfort and guide me. Later on I would find out that God did the same for a king named David whose heart-felt poems, born out of pain, were added to the holy scriptures as "Psalms." It wouldn't be long before I would meet this "Him" and find out how personal He really was and how utterly unprepared my life had been without Him.

Heart preparation is vital to cope with whatever life throws at us. And I wish I had it during my training in the military back in the late 1980s when our class teamed up with many civilian clinics and isolation wards in Leningrad to work firsthand with various contagious diseases—adult measles, adult chicken pox, and drug resistant tuberculosis.

My first contact work started at Botkinsky Barracks, the famous civilian infection control hospital, where my classmates and I spent weeks being exposed to diseased patients. Three levels of isolation protection were always present in that hospital; the highest was level three and considered a highly contagious ward area. Patients were stationed in single rooms, no more then two patients per room, with a proper negative-pressurized ventilation system.

Medical training was directed to the effects after potential use of biological, chemical and nuclear weapons. Since the Soviet government concluded that the U.S. was also developing similar biological agents as offensive weapons against Russia, it was important to them that military physicians could recognize first symptoms of human-created infectious diseases.

Soviet philosophy was that an incurable weapon was the best weapon. Dedication to Soviet bio-weapon research followed this idea. New drugs, cures or vaccinations, which could be developed to counter weaponized diseases, was received as a major threat to their national security. Instead of developing new drugs against common diseases, scientists in military research facilities worked hard to develop original unknown forms and change known strains.

My suspicion at that time was strong that my academy was partially involved in developing slow-going weaponized agents for silent wars with other nations. If they could keep the enemy's minds focused on "natural" outbreaks they could possibly bankrupt a society. We needed to overcome capitalism, and the military planned every strategy available to do so.

Most of my military professors believed that the origin of the AIDS virus came from United States labs, and that it was developed and tested as a bio-weapon in Africa. They viewed it as a failure because the incubation period of HIV sometimes takes years before it starts killing its victim, the same as leprosy and TB.

Even with our limitations to classified information and WMD military plans, cadets were expected to know the coded list of potentially useful biological agents that were available both for war and peace time. That code contained 80 microorganisms and their toxins in weaponized forms.

Since we were so well vaccinated during training, we were advised that it was not necessary to wear protective gear. We were not given the truth that relying solely on vaccinations as protection while treating contagious patients is risky. The army hoped we were too naïve to figure that out, because our role involved more than learning how to treat such diseases; we were also human "guinea pigs" for the military to study the effectiveness of their own vaccines.

In 1988 while I was working with active tuberculosis patients inside one of the TB centers in central Leningrad, wearing only gloves and a surgical mask, I caught enough of the bacillus to show a positive TB reading. Luckily my vaccinations protected me from developing the disease, but a few medical cadets were not so fortunate and developed active tuberculosis. One cadet lost his right lung and was discharged from service. At times some vaccinated cadets in training caught meningitis, diphtheria, and adult chicken pox.

Another reason our professors preferred we did not wear PPE (Personal Protection Equipment) was that they believed physical and psychological stimulation of the immune system was important for troop protection.

During my training I had to find a psychological peace within myself during contact work with highly contagious patients. I understood the risk of catching the disease, especially when we worked around germs such as Siberian ulcer (a cutaneous anthrax), glanders, adult measles, chicken pox, diptheria and military chemicals such as nerve agents VX and Soman. We worked with microorganisms specifically based on the bio-weapons available in Russian stockpiles. The military was always willing to risk their own to gain insight into understanding those viruses or bacteria that they planned to deploy as weapons. This stress took its toll on some medical cadets who ended up in the military mental institution.

We were never allowed to discuss the use of bio-agents against civilian populations. If we asked too many questions, we were carted off to spend time with the *politruk*, who would set us straight on how to act *politically* proper.

During the Afghan war, many soldiers and officers recovered at our academy after developing mental and nervous system diseases due to the new chemical testing of agents, particularly novitchoke-5. The Russian military academy was constantly involved in discovering new generations of drugs or super immune system stimulators for the troop's protection. One involved the use of highly concentrated hormonal extracts from different glands (thymus gland, for example). In some cases the use of human aborted fetuses was a common way to test new applications on the immune system. Extracts of blood from a stillborn baby's umbilical cord held a high concentration of young hemoglobin, along with material from the bone marrow. This program was developed under the Brezhnev regime in the late 1970s and 1980s. The main idea at that time was to develop youth type agents and super immune stimulators for military special operations and nuclear/biological/chemical troops, as well as for high officials in the communist party. Boris Yeltsin received one of those shots during his presidency. Intense research was also going on to create barrier-proof creams for temporary skin protection of troops during bio-warfare as well as to develop anti-biological non-penetrative light suits. Today the Russian Federation is just as active in its research.

The hospitals where I trained were safeguarded in every way against spread of disease (except for us trainee guinea pigs). The staff was trained in every aspect of quarantine and decontamination procedures.

In emergencies, hospitals are the first place sick people end up. A contagious outbreak of any form would collapse a hospital system within the first week without proper training procedures in place to handle a mass casualty epidemic. Today in the United States, the majority of hospitals, except for a few military hospitals, do not have the experience, training or means to deal with long-term isolations of mass numbers of highly contagious patients. This means medical personnel and hospital staff would become infected by the time they figure out they are dealing with a modified biological agent, possibly reducing the staff help in half, while pathogens spread within hours and days to each of the hospital floors. A shortage of medical staff, isolation rooms, drugs, and PPE gear would cause the facility to plummet out of control. If the outbreak is due to a bio-weapon (such as the hypothetical cruise ship release of genetically modified pathogens of plague/smallpox mentioned in Chapter

7), the situation becomes even more dire. Hidden pathogens would surface later in supposedly treated patients who doctors have released back into the city, creating multiple outbreaks and overtaxing the hospital system even more. Hospital planning cannot be ignored when biological technology developed for warfare is as advanced as it is today.

During a large outbreak, a hospital staff initially would face possible flocks of panicky healthy people showing up at the emergency room for observation, adding stress to the staff's already hectic schedule. Hospitals would lose the services of frightened health care providers who might refuse to come to work, allowing for an even greater shortage of medical staff.

A positive response should be rapid, effective, balanced, well coordinated, and timely. It would coordinate health care departments, especially labs, with hospital officials and heads of the local community emergency planning division. Good preparation means controlling the spread of contamination by using proper decontamination processes, having plenty of isolation rooms, keeping enough PPE gear on hand, stockpiling plenty of drugs and antibiotics, preparing autopsy rooms, and having enough containers for the remains of the deceased.

The first thing that our military hospitals did in Russia was to quarantine the entire area of people, including hospital staff and anyone who had come in contact with the disease. (If an outbreak occurs in the United States, the Center for Disease Control should be contacted immediately.) The entire facility was then disinfected. All residents who had potential contact with the infected patients were put under observation for at least three days past the incubation period of the disease. This means that a particular group at the hospital needed to coordinate the history of each of the patients over the previous few weeks, then contact the possibly infected people so they could be immediately vaccinated and isolated for observation. Such contact had to be permanent and constant during the entire length of the outbreak. Ambulatory teams of physicians trained to deal with highly contagious diseases and the use of proper PPE were on-call to follow up with possibly infected resident physicians.

Both non-medical and medical employees wore complete protective gear in all contaminated areas dealing with any type of virus or bacteria—which protected them against the toxic chemicals used to disinfect the facilities as well as the microorganism. Each shift worked two hours long, trading off with one of the two standby teams. Both groups were completely disinfected at the end of each two-hour rotation.

Hospital Quarantine

Hospitals must be ready for potential illnesses and mass loss of life developed within a short time frame. They must also be prepared for unknown and combined bio-weapons working at the same time. They need to know how to work with victims who are receiving unusually high concentrations of bio-pathogens and who might be extremely contagious. Planning for clear control must be established with safe isolation measures during the evacuation of patients from the primary to the secondary medical facilities. If a hospital is dealing with an unknown disease, no one should leave the building for at least three days, until clinical laboratory diagnosis is established.

Inside the hospital facility at my academy, the first contagious group of patients remained in the same room until a
special brigade of prepared transporters, each wearing an anti-
plague level suit, removed patients to the final proper infection
ward, either in another room on another floor or another facility
outside the hospital. (Infection wards had to be set up to handle
highly contagious diseases.) Complete disinfection was then
necessary for the rooms and modes of transportation.

Multiple isolation wards were organized outside the hospitals in one-story buildings on the outskirts of the city, with
controlled entrances, exits and roads. The wards were a fair
distance from other property and not too far from the main
hospital. Medical personnel were trained specifically to respond
to these wards at the time of need. In America, camp areas that
have numerous buildings or cabins on the grounds would be a
good choice for isolation wards.

Every hospital should have a blueprint plan ready. The
architects and construction companies who built the hospital
are the ones to let hospital directors know the best containable
areas, floors, and rooms usable for the restricted zones. If a
hospital is not built and properly sealed for a bio event, a
complete spread of pathogenic microorganisms through walls
and floors could result, infecting the patients who are under
care for other reasons besides the epidemic. Since today's
American hospitals are not built to contain mass numbers of
contagious patients, the best recommendation to combat unnecessary spread of disease is to designate at least two (based on
the size of the city) specifically sealed and active hospitals with
properly trained staff, on the outskirts of the city. Each should

be ready to be activated and used in the event of a highly contagious bio-release. People showing symptoms and those under suspicion of being in contact with contagious patients should be separated and directed to those hospitals, and not allowed visitors.

Once a hospital becomes contaminated, the decontamination process can be complicated and costly. The ideal solution is getting the government to prepare in advance by building architecturally sound facilities, or restructuring existing buildings, that can hold mass numbers of victims without allowing for release of pathogens outside. Multiple isolation rooms should hold between 500 and 2,000 patients. A secure organization of transport and ambulances to move victims to these special sites is a must.

Most early symptoms of infection by bio-agents are flu-like—fever and chills, increasing toxicosis, headaches, light-headedness, increased weakness, sometimes nausea and vomiting, and swollen and painful joints and muscles. During the initial exam, some folks might already show signs of increased respiration, coughing and sneezing. This is why doctors can become victims themselves. Two categories of victims will be present: those with developed symptoms (possibly contagious), and those without symptoms who are considered suspicious because of the fact they had full or partial contact with the contagious victims. Both groups must be isolated and under intense medical observation.

Those patients who are most susceptible to spreading the disease are the ones with signs of respiratory impact, pustules on mucous membranes in the mouth, or watery diarrhea with the possible presence of blood. These people have to be isolated from other patients, even if a diagnosis has not yet been given. If patients do not have clear symptoms, they should not be transported in the same ambulances used to transport those patients who are showing symptoms.

Exposure to biological agents does not mean that everyone develops the disease. Clinical diseases depend on many factors, such as the dose of organism inhaled, the strength of the immune response of the person, and the initial depletion of white blood cells (needed to fight infection). Of course a person will get sick faster if the initial dose of microorganisms is in an optimal size. If the initial dose is less then necessary to develop the disease, the person will not become ill at all. With spore related anthrax, it takes a large number to develop the disease, at least between 3,000 to 50,000 inhaled spores. But with a weaponized smallpox virus, 15 to 20 inhaled viruses will be sufficient. Soviet-made Marburg type U virus needs only two to three inhaled viruses to develop the disease. This means there is a 100 percent ability to develop the Marburg virile disease to everyone exposed.

In Russia, as soon as officials recognized mass casualties coming through the doors, the hospital designated separate pathways: one leading to an emergency room, one leading to a room with the new patients who showed full symptoms, and another leading to an area for people who were under suspicion but not showing symptoms. Emergency rooms were broken down into two rooms and never crossed each other during the receiving of victims. Each area was sealed off, with only authorized personnel wearing PPE allowed access. The room that took the first symptomatic patients remained in use just for symptomatic patients since this room was already contaminated and considered a hot zone.

In the event of virile infections and highly contagious diseases, like the plague for instance, regular hospital patients already inside the hospital were to be evacuated outside to a separate building before the first plague victim was brought in, unless the hospital was confident it had a secure isolation unit.

Russian hospitals were prepared for dramatic work and shift changes during quarantine. Surgery rooms dealt only with the contagious patients. The normal daily emergency cases were directed to other facilities and the hospital did not take in any patient that was not a victim of the bio-microorganism. When the disease was finally subdued, the entire facility was disinfected inside and outside before being allowed to return to its normal function mode.

We were trained in an outbreak of smallpox, to recognize three groups of patients. The first group includes those who come into contact with the infected patient; the second group is everyone inside the same building with the infected patient, no matter how big the building or how many floors; the third group is everyone else in surrounding buildings within a perimeter of at least a block.

The first group must be under quarantine for 14 days and have immediate vaccinations. If a person reacts to the live vaccine, anti-smallpox immunoglobulin would be administered. The second group is next on the list for vaccination, and would be quarantined for 14 days with complete isolation in a different building. The third group would be last for vaccinations and must remain under observation for potentially being in contact with contagious people.

Two separated isolation wards would be set up. One ward would be for patients displaying fever and external rash on their skin; the second ward for the patients exhibiting fever but no external rash. Two times a day, the medical staff inside these facilities would have to be checked and controlled with a documented registration of temperature, and examined by the lead doctor before their shift started. This is important because some medical workers might develop smallpox during contact work with contagious victims.

Organization of the pre-emergency room waiting area, or sorting area, is absolutely necessary to handle registration, medical triage, sampling, immediate medical care, sanitary processing, transportation to the isolation ward, and disinfection of all people, clothing, and stretchers. The sorting area would need at least two evaluation rooms with one sanitary entrance, as well as a separate room for medical professionals on duty. At least one or two doctors and a nurse would have to be present at all times, and better if they were infectious disease specialists. A storage room had to be set aside for clean clothing for patients, and a decontamination area set up outside for transport equipment. If a medic transports a potentially contaminated victim to an evaluation room, the ambulance and the medic would have to undergo disinfection, which is a lengthy process.

Inside the rooms where the active smallpox patients lie, medical personnel would need to wear level B suits with air connectors. Level C suits and gas masks would need to be worn outside the facility. Daily decontamination is necessary for the staff at the end of each shift, when they take breaks, or use the restroom. The staff who works inside the quarantine zone would not be able to leave the area after work and go home. Instead they have to remain stationed in special clean rooms and rest areas inside the quarantine zone for as long as they are in contact with the outbreak.

The first medical personnel to respond to an epidemic in any hospital, anywhere, are considered the "first responders" and are the first to be exposed to the contagious patients. The area where the first contagious victim is found must be immediately considered a contaminated casualty collection point for all future cases showing similar symptoms, at least in the beginning of the response. These victims must remain inside this area while hospitals prepare to receive them into their facilities.

This area may be a quick care clinic or a family practice office. The biggest mistake a physician can make once plague is suspected is to send the sick person to the hospital. The physician must also bear in mind that the medical staff and everyone in the waiting room would be suspected carriers of plague, and would be quarantined inside the facility.

Quarantine includes these rapid actions: shut down all ventilation or heating systems, close down all connections between floors, tape windows, and use only one controlled entrance and exit. The room where the victim is diagnosed must be completely isolated from other rooms. Creating a list and getting in touch with all people who have been in contact with the sick person must be done immediately so they can also be isolated. No clothes or items can leave this facility.

Hospital personnel should not work around patients if they have skin damage on their face, hands, or other uncovered body areas. It is necessary for each staff worker to be checked by physicians for abrasions, cuts or development of flu-like symptoms before their shifts start. All people without proper PPE who have any contact with an infected patient must be isolated for the incubational time and put through an intense prophylactic course of antibiotics. Decontamination must be performed on all patients and hospital personnel and their personal belongings, and any place this person has worked, shopped, slept, or urinated.

Spore forming bacterial pathogens, like anthrax and compared to virile infections, will have different type of isolation precautions. In the event of an anthrax release in a city, decontamination points must be set up outside the hospital with the properly trained medical staff. Checkpoints for contaminated victims should be multiple and set to receive people before they ever reach the hospital emergency room. External contamination with anthrax spores will be a serious threat for an internal hospital setting. The good news is that strict isolation precautions are unnecessary for those patients; they are not contagious, like plague and smallpox. Yet, all the fluids coming from their bodies during hospitalization must still be subject to controlled collection and disinfection. Unfortunately people with anthrax will contaminate their own homes without even knowing they are doing so. All these residences will need to be decontaminated.

In the event of an actual dangerous pathogen release, vaccination teams should be available in most central and accessible locations (airports, train stations, bus stations, and schools). Keep in mind that if it is a genetically modified bio-agent, vaccinations are futile. The city would be under quarantine and citizens would not be able to leave their homes. Traveling would be prohibited and roadblocks set up to keep the epidemic from spreading outside to other parts of the country. Those who do not follow quarantine orders may be detained for violation under the new MEHPA law (Model State Emergency Health Powers Act).

MEHPA

United States citizens should be aware of—and concerned with—the Model State Emergency Health Powers Act which was fortunately rejected by most state legislatures and, unfortunately, passed in Florida.

Portions of the MEHPA were incorporated into the Homeland Security Act and provide for forced vaccinations and confiscation or destruction of personal property under the *mere threat* of an outbreak. Buried inside the 500-page Homeland Security bill, the provisions give federal health representatives virtually unchecked power to declare health emergencies—actual or potential bio-terrorist emergencies—along with power to force *countermeasures* that include vaccines to individuals or whole groups, and to indefinitely extend the emergency declaration. The MEHPA gives state governors broad powers to suspend civil liberties and use militia to *influence* the population—which nullifies the freedoms sanctioned in the U.S. constitution.

Please read the following very carefully. A few of the worrisome provisions include:

- Granting the governor of each state power to declare a "public health emergency" as defined in the act, with or without consulting anyone (Article IV, Section 401).

- Requiring medical examinations and/or tests and forced isolation or quarantine if it is deemed that refusal "poses a danger to public health" (Article VI, Section 602(c)).

- Requiring treatments and/or vaccinations and "isolating or quarantining" those "unwilling or unable" to do so (Article VI, Sections 603(a)(3) and 603(b)(3)).

- Constituting as a misdemeanor "failure to obey these provisions" (for examinations, testing, isolation or quarantine), (Article VI, Sections 604(a) and 604(c)).

- Providing that there be no liability for any "state or local official" causing harm to individuals in their efforts to comply with the provisions of the act, unless there is "gross negligence or willful misconduct" (Article VIII, Section 804(a)).

- Providing for similar absence of liability for "any private person, firm or corporation" and their "employees" or "agents" (Article VIII, Section 804(b)(2) and 804(b)(3)).

- Allowing for destruction of properties without compensation if "there is reasonable cause to believe that [the properties] may endanger the public health pursuant to Section 501" (Article V, Sections 506 and 507).

- Limiting legal recourse (Article VI, Section 605).

- Allowing for "the public safety authority (to) request assistance from the organized militia in enforcing the orders of the public health authority" (Article IV, Section 404).

Americans should utilize their constitutional rights before willingly and blindly handing themselves over as "sheep for the slaughter." If there were a major biological release due to a natural outbreak, terrorism, or war, strict isolation and quarantine rules would go into place, stripping the population of normal daily freedoms and imprisoning them inside their own homes, with laws possibly forcing the public to relocate to isolation wards or camps.

Tread carefully in the event there is sudden breaking news of an epidemic in your city. Make sure the news is legitimate and that there is a real threat before surrendering your freedoms. Being imprisoned inside your home or a camp and being forced to take vaccinations and antibiotics, knowing such vaccinations are a possible dangerous health risk, is not something any person should submit to without proof that their life is indeed in danger.

PATHWAYS OF TRANSMISSION

Smallpox isolation wards in a hospital does not guarantee that contamination will not spread to other floors. There are three possible pathways of transmission that can occur inside a medical ward. The first is if the patient was a victim of a bio attack and exposed to a high concentration of material and still has the contaminant on their clothing. The second occurs with patient contact in the form of droplets from sneezing, coughing or talking. The third transmission happens from contagious clothing, sheets (damp sheets and blankets can house live smallpox virus for weeks), newspapers, walls, and every possible surface in a room through the form of dust (partial dry forms and a "nucleus" stage of transmission, which is a completely dry form). This last one is the most difficult to control. If victims in isolation rooms are stationed on the first floor, for example, and visitors are allowed to come into the health care facility for other reasons, they have the possibility of catching smallpox within 15 to 20 minutes of standing in the stairwell area. In some cases, if other healthy people are on the same floor with the isolation ward, there is a strong possibility that they can get sick, even if they never entered the isolated area. The nucleus phase moves on the dust by airflow and can get through the smallest openings.

There is at least an 18 percent chance that transmission of smallpox will spread to all floors in any hospital setting. This is why an analyst of the airflow inside a hospital is important. A smoke test is a good way to check the security of the rooms. Smoke will reveal where the contaminated dust can travel. Usually the fastest spread of aerosol smallpox in a hospital will be from the patient's room to the corridor, and from the corridor to the elevators or stairwells. If any window is partially open in the hospital, the convection flow of contamination can reach the windows, go outside and waft back inside other open windows in other rooms or to other floors. Walking too fast in the corridors might create a secondary release of dust if contamination has found its way outside the room. Low humidity inside the hospital can also support transmission by allowing the virus to stay alive longer in air.

After removing a sick person from a room, contamination is present in this room with stable aerosol. If the room is not disinfected properly, it can contaminate other rooms in the facility with convection flow. The nucleus stage of aerosol can stay in the air for hours and travel long distances. Keep in mind that smallpox bio-agents are specifically prepared for the environment and can travel for miles after a professional air release. It is stable enough for a potentially secondary inoculation to other people.

During my so-called suspicious "measles" at the academy (before our class even had a chance to work around contagious patients of any sort), I had to clean up all surfaces that I had touched with wet disinfectant towels under the watchful eye of the nurse. Only authorized hospital staff was allowed in our room. There were no door handles on the doors, only keyholes. The medical staff who were allowed to possess keys had to go through sanitized corridors and doors before they could enter our room. Strict isolation regimes are vital during an outbreak and must be put in place and made ready long before an epidemic might surface.

PROPHYLACTICS

In the Soviet military hospital setting, prophylactics was an important part of hospital preparation against bio-warfare. There were two types of prophylactics: general urgent and specific urgent.

General urgent was a combination of medical methods used to prevent the *unknown* origin of infectious disease based on distribution of pharmaceutical drugs that have large spectrums of affects against at least a few pathogenic microorganisms. Distribution was to be done immediately after a biological attack was known, since the effectiveness of the prophylactics is based on the speed of the distribution of the drugs and the incubation period of the disease. In most cases, groups of antibiotics, such as tetracyclines, doxycycline, pephlocycline, and rifampicin should be used. This distribution was to be done in no less than five days if the pathogen still had not been identified.

Specific urgent prophylactics were a combination of medical methods used to prevent infectious diseases of *known* origin, and were based on the distribution of the most effective pharmaceutical drugs against a specific pathogen. Distribution started only if the hospital knew the specific microorganism they were dealing with. The speed of the drugs and the incubation time were important too. If symptoms of the disease developed, the process of taking the drugs then became *treatment* instead of a prophylactic. The groups of drugs in those cases might be antibiotics, antiviral drugs, or chemo-prophylactic drugs. The drugs selected would have to be effective protection properties against known pathogens, with a usual course of ten days or longer.

Immunization was a part of immune-prophylactics and was necessary if it had not been done previously. Everyone who had a high risk of getting infected would need to have immunization, as well as everyone who responded to a bio-incident. Drugs with a fast immune response and rapid stimulation of the immune system would have to be administered in no longer than two to three weeks. It was possible to start a course of urgent prophylactics at the same time as immunization against botulism, smallpox, typhoid fever, and cholera. Administered vaccinations against plague, tularemia, Q fever, and anthrax could have been done two days after urgent prophylactics, and 14 days after urgent prophylactics against the disease brucellosis (if negative serological results occur). Unfortunately most American hospital personnel are not immunized against anthrax as medical professionals were in the Soviet military infectious hospital wards. In Russia the best protection against anthrax exposure was taking the vaccination a year prior with STI vaccine.

Prophylactics used inside a quarantine zone should include a temperature check twice a day. In the instance of smallpox, thermometry needs to start on the sixth day after exposure to the agent. In the case of plague and other contagious pathogens, thermometry needs to start at the moment the quarantine is established.

The effects of any type of biological warfare release would continue over a period of months, so a rapid and accurate outbreak investigation is necessary. If genetically modified agents are released and the pathogenic properties of the microorganism are misdiagnosed, the health system will be causing harm to large numbers of people. This mistake would cause a complete collapse of the response system and the highest mortality rate possible, with a potential endemic throughout the country. If a silent biological plan was activated previously by enemies and not recognized by health authorities, this would cause an unusual negative response toward the urgent prophylactics and initial treatment of typical infectious diseases. The immune system, already weakened by antibiotics, would have a poor response to the surprise germ attack.

For bio-weapons that are not genetically modified, the earlier the treatment starts the better the results will be. Again, there would be no treatment for genetically modified agents (as of today's technology), and only proper quarantine is the answer. Virile outbreaks may start with a few victims in the beginning. However, within just a few days, the health care system might be dealing with thousands of infected patients. If the hospital is not prepared, it will collapse.

Hospital preparedness is important to stop the spread of disease and save lives, but what my training did not offer us interns was preparation of the heart. Cadets landed in the psychiatric ward all too often because they did not know how to deal with the emotional aspect of facing potential death.

All the evacuation plans, quarantine procedures, and external scrubbing of contaminated bodies is futile if we are not spiritually prepared. Sin bottles us up inside and stops us from the spiritual readiness that can only come from a committed relationship with Jesus Christ.

Jesus said in John 14: 6, *I am the way, the truth, and the life: no man cometh unto the Father, but by me.* By acknowledging Jesus, God's true Son, as our personal Lord and Savior, our great creator, and our civil defense planner, we have a wonderful future guarantee that no matter how many times we stumble He will forgive us.

The subject of death should never be ignored. Eternity is too close. Folks spend great amounts of money and time purchasing cemetery plots and bountiful life insurance policies, but spend little time preparing for the afterlife.

If there is a WMD incident, everyone wants to know where to go and how to get to the safe zone. We should desire that same route even more for our own soul before it ever leaves our earthly body, unexpectedly or not. Eternity separated from God is not a risk worth taking.

Our heavenly Father has put together a secure and glorious escape plan through the death and resurrection of His beloved Son Jesus. *For God so loved the world, that he gave his only begotten Son, that whosoever believeth in him should not perish, but have everlasting life.* (John 3:16). If we choose to prepare our hearts and give our life over to Jesus for care, the Bible is full of beautiful promises and depictions of what life in heaven will be like. *In my Father's house are many mansions: if it were not so, I would have told you. I go to prepare a place for you.* (John 14: 2).

Chapter Ten

Are We Ready?

PREPARATION FOR WMDS
THREATS IN TODAY'S WORLD
U.S. PROTECTION
SAFETY UNDER GOD

Mobster gangs pulled into the Hotel #1 square in black limousines and black sedans all day, every day. I was used to seeing them. So when I saw an old red and white bus pull up and hiss to a stop that balmy September day in 1992, I was curious. I leaned against the outside brick wall and took a long drag on my cigarette. My medical students wouldn't be arriving for another 20 minutes, so I waited to see who would step off the bus. I was curious.

The bus door swung open. I chucked the simmering butt to the ground and shoved my hands inside the pockets of my leather jacket and watched as an excited group of young men and women streamed out. I perked up immediately. They were Americans!

This was the first time I had come across Americans since Russia had reopened its doors. I kept a sober face as the prattling troop passed by me sporting wide grins.

I don't know whether it was the colorful American flag jacket she wore, or her stride that first caught my attention, but my gaze fell upon a pretty blond woman who I guessed was the leader because of her take-charge manner. She walked by me and said, "Hi."

I was dazzled by her shining smile, but replied with a stone face. She returned several times with her gabby group to unload the boxes and luggage from the bus. Each time she passed me, she smiled.

The vibrant bunch was a stark contrast to the reserved way Russian people acted in public. Although I thought their behavior odd, I was inwardly amused, and found myself hanging around longer than I needed to. I even sauntered into the lobby and watched them stack box after box against the wall.

"Who are these people, another mafia group?" I jokingly asked the receptionist, an older lady I knew well.

"They are from America! They call themselves missionaries," she whispered.

"What is in the boxes?" I asked.

"Bibles. Can you believe it?"

This surprised me because the hotel had been built for the KGB, and never before could *believers* come here. I figured I would nose around the lobby over the next few days and find out more about these missionaries, their Bibles, and maybe even her—the blond with the smile.

What should I do if there is a WMD disaster? What preparations can be made? And what actions should be taken to live through such a disaster? These are just some of the questions that people all over the world today should be able to answer.

In the late 1940s and early 1950s nuclear air raid drills were the norm for American schoolchildren. As the cold war between the U.S. and the Soviet Union escalated, anxiety of a nuclear war increased. The United States backed up its civil defense program, confident of group shelters that would be ready to handle 50 million people and arguing that simple defense procedures would protect them. They put out a nation-wide alert campaign using booklets and films to reassure people and convince them that simple precautions would help them survive a nuclear attack. Walled-off corners of basements were to be stocked with two weeks' rations and a radio. Children were taught to "duck and cover" under their desks or hide in school basements during the drills, as though this was enough to protect them. Many Americans who did not feel confident took survival into their own hands by digging bomb shelters in their backyards. Worries came into play about friends and neighbors who neglected to build bunkers of their own. Building contractors were often ordered to construct their shelters in the dead of night so snooping neighbors wouldn't see.

Those folks that built the bomb shelters and constructed them properly were wise. The U.S. civil defense at that time was not solid and would not have saved many lives in the event of a nuclear attack. School children hiding under their desks or in the basement would be dying or dead if they were inside the bomb's target or in a contaminated Red Zone and not evacuated in time. The few scattered air-raid shelters, some built for the purpose and most improvised in basements and subways, were not sufficient to protect people, especially large populations. With today's serious concerns of nuclear/biological/chemical (NBC) attacks, the United States should have a strong civil defense program. However no such program exists today.

A U.S. civil defense poster put out in the 1950s best sums up the responsibility of both nation and individual. It reads, "The best way to survive the hazards of radioactive fallout, or any other threat an enemy may use against us, is to be pre-pared—know the facts—learn what to do, now!" Unfortunately without a good civil defense program in place, many people will die in the event of an actual WMD attack. I could write until I am blue in the face about stocking up on food, water and duct tape, but without WMD-proof underground shelters, these things are worthless in themselves.

The Soviet Union, in comparison, had an excellent civil defense program in the large cities, prompted into reality after the bombing of Nagasaki and Hiroshima, before the cold war. Russian citizens did feel confident they had protection in the event of a nuclear attack. (All of this makes the Chernobyl incident so disturbing. The Russian government, focusing on attacks from America, seemed oblivious to the dangers of civilian nuclear plants outside the big cities).

The multiple bunkers and underground systems built in the large cities protected most of the population. Soviet subways were built extra deep so they could be used as safe zones. Those people who lived within an 18-mile radius of a radiological plant or a two-mile radius from chemical factories were individually provided with PPE equipment. Every employee in factories where there was the presence of radiological, chemical, or biological agents had protective gear not far from their workstations. Stockpiles of food, water, individual medical kits, and full gas masks for almost the entire population were stored underground in special stations away from potential target areas. The medical kits contained pharmaceutical drugs and anti-chemical pads for partial degassing and deactivation of chemical and bio-agents.

Soviet cities built after World War II were architecturally engineered to withstand WMD attacks, especially nuclear. Large buildings, institutions, factories, theaters, hospitals, and schools had multiple underground bunkers with complete sets of masks and medical kits.

Industrial factories were protected by being built outside the city limits. Inside the city, streets were built wider to handle mass evacuation. The distance between tall buildings and streets was far enough so that if a building collapsed, it would not block the street.

Good civil defense can be gleaned from the Soviet Union's defense program. Still, during an attack, if the stockpiles and underground shelters are not utilized, another Chernobyl tragedy would probably happen.

America needs a good civil defense program, but that plan should never include eliminating people's freedoms as the Soviets did with their citizens. Citizens who are willing to give up their freedom out of fear will receive fascism as a reward and greatly regret it later.

A 2004 article in The Associated Press reported that Russia's nuclear forces prepared their largest maneuvers in two decades, an exercise involving the test firing of missiles and flights by dozens of bombers in a massive simulation of an all-out nuclear war. The exercise, though it had its problems, resembled a 1982 Soviet exercise dubbed the "seven-hour nuclear war" that made the West nervous at the time. President Vladimir Putin personally oversaw this latest exercise to demonstrate to the world the revival of Russia's military might. The maneuvers involved Tu-160 strategic bombers test-firing cruise missiles over the northern Atlantic, which analysts described as an imitation of a nuclear attack on the United States.

We know that the Russian Federation has not stopped working on perfecting its biological warfare program either. And we know from intelligence sources that enemy countries have been able to purchase top-secret WMD information and materials from Russian laboratories and stockpiles, and from other countries. The quest for power by evil men who desire to rule the world will always ensure development of bigger and better weapons of mass destruction.

Igor Ivanov, Minster of Defense for the Russian Federation, stated in 2003: "We are planning further development of the strategic complex Topol-M and all strategic rocket bases, with the main goal to keep our nuclear trinity more effective than anything else. Topol-M has the potential ability to break through the anti-missile systems of the United States up to 65 percent, but it will be 87 percent, I promise." He then went on to say, "We have no interest in the reaction of foreign governments; we must worry about our own safety."

In light of this statement, how can anyone think the cold war is over? Especially since the Topol-M is one of the newest Intercontinental Ballistic Missiles built with the ability to completely duck detection and destruction by any anti-missile system, due to its unique flight pattern and construction.

During my classified tactical training at the academy I learned about the strategic military doctrine of the Soviet Union and the operational applications of this doctrine during nuclear/biological/chemical warfare. Large color-coded global maps lined the walls in our classrooms showing specific European and American territories as possible targets for the execution of nuclear and biological weapons. We were trained how to use incapacitating bio-weapons against enemy troops in European areas with the use of short range and low flying cruise missiles, as well as learning the effects of those agents. Deployment of strategic ballistic missiles, such as the SS-18s at that time, was specifically oriented around nuclear warheads. They could carry ten warheads, each carrying 500-kiloton devices. In the mid-1970s the Soviet military had already developed technology for intercontinental ballistic missiles that could reach U.S. soil; WMDs were aimed at the heavily populated U.S. and European cities.

The Soviets understood how damaging a radiation disaster would be for the United States. That is why ICBM's were, and probably still are today, directed to hit all American nuclear plants. Devices, such as neutron bombs and biological weapons, were planned against the important key cities to save city structures and eliminate human life, thus allowing their military forces to penetrate U.S. territory.

WMD is no longer a "Russian" thing. Production of WMD is on the rise in many foreign countries. Currently the U.S. has gone on a huge and fast-paced biological science spending spree, funding massive new bio-defense research efforts, redirecting up to $10 billion toward projects related to biological weapons such as anthrax. High-security nuclear weapons labs have begun to conduct genetic research on dangerous pathogens; the academic world is receiving government monies to build high-tech labs equipped to handle deadly infectious organisms; and Fort Detrick, Maryland is about to build two new high-tech bio defense centers. A good number of microbiologists, nonproliferation experts, and former government officials fear the pump-up of bio-defense might simply produce the next generation of killer germs, adding to the worldwide bio-weapon explosion instead of stopping it.

Even more disturbing and mind-boggling is that in the midst of these huge WMD arsenals threatening the world, the United States of America has not yet secured its borders and built a solid civil defense system for its people. America is an unprepared nation in every aspect. Few hospitals have programs in place for biological emergencies of any kind. Gas masks, vaccine stockpiles, and bunkers don't exist for civilians in the event of a nuclear, chemical, or bio-attack in the majority of U.S. cities. People in general are clueless of any evacuation and decontamination procedures that might be available. Borders and ports remain an open invitation to "come on in."

Six million containers enter America's seaports each year; the majority get through without anyone checking what's inside them. Ninety-five percent of the $827 billion of trade done with countries outside of North America comes in by ship. That is 7.6 percent of the $10.4 trillion of goods and services consumed annually in the United States. In addition, the $104 billion worth of oil imported yearly in the U.S. comes in by ship. For all of this, U.S. Customs and the Coast Guard still are not privy to intelligence information, nor do they have the effective systems in place to exchange accurate information on the ships, crews and cargo heading toward a port.

Commercial ship transports must submit a manifest that lists all the cargo it is carrying, because this system is built on trust, shippers can put down whatever they like on this key report. This determines which ships it should ask the Coast Guard to stop at sea and inspect, and which containers it should inspect upon arrival in a U.S. port. Usually, just days before a cargo vessel enters an American port, the lists of a ship's crew are faxed to the Coast Guard. Many times the document is unreadable, which means names can't be checked against an immigration database, or the captain of the ship can submit any names, even fictitious ones.

Therefore nuclear devices or bio-weapons could easily be sneaked into America through ship containers, ferries or small boats. Ports serve railway lines and roadways. If a weapon-filled container makes it past Customs, it could be transported within days to almost anywhere in the country. Even with armed sea marshals checking more ships than ever at the nation's busiest ports, recent studies and investigations of seaport security show how critically vulnerable they still are.

This nation's borders are out of control. Anyone—job seekers, criminals, disease carriers, or foreign agents—can

easily cross either the Mexican or Canadian borders today. The
U.S. and Canadian border is 5,525 miles long and the U.S. and
Mexican border is 1,989 miles long. The borders and entry
points to the United States are like leaky colanders, offering the
nation little protection against possible terrorists who want to
enter the country. Even the Agriculture Department's inspector
general, as reported by the Associated Press, says that the
Forest Service, while not the lead border security agency,
oversees nearly 1,000 miles of boundary "that are potentially
vulnerable to infiltration by terrorists, smugglers and other
criminal agents." The Forest Service manages 460 miles of land
bordering Canada, oversees 450 miles of land between Alaska
and Canada, and also manages 60 miles of land on the U.S./
Mexico border. Despite the 196 million acres of land the Forest
Service is responsible for, only 620 officers monitor that acre-
age, and just a small number patrol some 520 miles of border-
land, with 450 miles that are not patrolled at all.

With such gaping holes in this country's borders and ports,
and with the escalation of terrorism, it seems peculiar that
American troops are sent all over the world to guard other
nation's borders, but not their own. Yet, when we look back at
America's lack of homeland defense during the cold war and see
how protected this nation was despite Russia's lusty bio programs and notorious nukes, it isn't too hard to grasp the supernatural magnitude behind why America has not been obliterated
thus far.

Isaiah 45, verse 7 says: *I form the light, and create darkness:
I make peace, and create evil. I the Lord do all these things.*
Simply put, God decides who to protect and who not to protect.

No matter how many weapons are pointing our way, they cannot move unless He allows it. Was it 200,000 U.S. troops positioned at America's ports and borderlands that protected this nation from Russian warfare coming from Cuba in the 1960s? No, they were not necessary, because God did the job well enough.

What are the reasons that impel God's decisions to either "make peace" or "create evil?" And how can we be confident He will want to protect us? God is clear in scripture that a nation who forsakes Him will lose its protection. Biblical Israel is the greatest example of what happens to a people that forsake God. Their enemies defeated them numerous times because they turned from the Lord and compromised their faith. They did not protect their borders from idolatry and they polluted God's Holy Temple with demonic artifacts and lifestyles. God is serious about His take on idol worship. He abhors it because it shows great disrespect and dishonor to who He is. It is an awful slap in His face to give something or someone else credit for His creation and His goodness.

When Moses communed with God up on the mount to receive the Ten Commandments, it was bad enough that the people convinced Aaron to build the golden calf, but when they begin to worship the image and thank it for bringing them up out of Egypt (Exodus 32:4) this was worse than the fashioning of it, especially after all the open miracles God performed publicly to get them out of Egypt. For this God judged them with plague to let them understand idol worship was a serious problem with severe consequences: *And the Lord plagued the people, because they made the calf, which Aaron made* (verse 5). Judgment is exacted on any nation and people who meddle with Satanism.

People might insist that their statue-like idol or religion is not a worship of the devil, but scripture is clear that Satan authors the worship of anything or anyone besides the Biblical God. It has always been the devil's plan to be as God and convince people to turn from the truth. *I (Lucifer) will ascend above the heights of the clouds; I will be like the most High* (Isaiah 14: 14). This is confirmed in Revelation 13: 15 when Satan causes everyone to worship his image (or the image of his system).

With all the evil in the world today it is not hard to understand the spiritual battle that is going on for our souls and for the nation. It is no mere coincidence that we see the same conflicts against God as were recorded in Biblical times. For those folks who refuse to believe in God or the validity of His Son Jesus, a quick read through Revelation shows that those descriptive visions given to John in A.D. 95 by Jesus are too comparable to today's current events to be mere coincidence.

People that take a neutral stand will not be saved from the great tribulation talked about throughout scripture. A choice will have to be made for either God (good) or Satan (evil). There is no such thing as an in-between or lukewarm position, and that is the greatest con Satan has brought upon the world so far—to make people think that if they close their eyes to what is going on around them, or avoid getting involved, they will somehow be exempt from the responsibility of the wrath that is coming. The one doing nothing is just as guilty as the one doing wrong. It is no wonder God remarks in Revelation 3:16: *So then because thou art lukewarm, and neither cold nor hot, I will spew thee out of my mouth.*

Thus it is necessary to be spiritually prepared as well as

physically prepared for all that the future will bring. It is not terrorism and weapons of mass destruction that Americans need to fear, but God's judgment. Numbers 33: 55, 56 says: *But if ye will not drive out the inhabitants (of idolatry) of the land from before you, then it shall come to pass, that those which ye let remain of them shall be pricks in your eyes, and thorns in your sides, and shall vex you in the land wherein ye dwell. Moreover it shall come to pass, that I shall do unto you, as I thought to do unto them.*

Whenever Israel repented and worshipped God, God graciously gave them back their city. And He will respond to any nation that will do the same.

The unsecured borders of the United States today simply symbolize the spiritual condition of this country, a nation whose love for material wealth and self-gratification have overridden the love of the Gospel on which it was founded. Without securing the borders of our hearts, we can never feel safe in any country. Protection begins with our relationship with the Lord Jesus Christ. Allowing Him to be Lord of our lives, and standing up for holiness is what will make Him choose peace for us.

Except for the faithful believers who continually fall on their faces and cry to Him for mercy, this country would be under severe judgment. This is true when we compare America with so many other nations today who are besieged by wars, economic tailspins, and natural disasters.

Judgment can come in different ways to this country, and it may not be by an outside enemy takeover. It could happen through an internal undoing of the constitution, whereby all citizens would lose their freedoms. With the troubling new laws passed by government in the last few years that have destabilized the constitution and chipped away at personal freedoms, all citizens and non-citizens alike should be praying hard. This is the beginning of sorrows for every free person living in America.

Patrick Henry, a great patriot, did not let fear rule his agenda. His statement, "give me liberty or give me death," exemplified bravery and trust in God. Without his frame of mind and the many other courageous Americans who fought for this country's glorious constitution, America would have succumbed to the British. If Henry were alive now, he would be the first one fighting to keep the constitution in this country safe.

The memory of those dedicated soldiers of the past, along with the historical accounts of horrible murderous dictators like Hitler and Stalin should encourage all Americans to shake off slumber and fight for their liberty—both spiritually and constitutionally. Evil did not end with the cold war; it is still working hard at the highest levels to undermine anything morally good. Conspirators are not part of fantasy; proof lies in the way the world is heading today. As U.S. patriots, we cannot afford to ignore the signs of judgment and lose this nation's core foundation as "one nation under God, indivisible, with liberty and justice for all." Russia kicked God out of its government, and look at what it became.

Compromise always gives the enemy a 50 percent edge. Standing for truth, even if it means standing alone, is a gutsy move, but one that will be rewarded with God's promise in Psalm 37: 37, 39: *Mark the perfect man, and behold the upright: for the end of that man is peace... But the salvation of the righteous is of the Lord: he is their strength in the time of trouble.*

Throughout this book I talked about the strict schedules I had to follow in military life. Every hour, each day I was responsible to make sure my job was performed perfectly, and in unity with my fellow cadets and commanders. During our training there was no room for mistakes—a mistake could cost lives. The same strict rule and pattern applied in Russian preparedness against all WMD incidents. Without a unity in planning among all departments, there is no success in dealing with an enemy attack. A good defense is required to defeat the enemy. This rule also applies to the spiritual part of our lives. If we do not keep a good defense plan intact, there is no way we can elude the fiery darts and piercing arrows coming at us. To properly keep our lives clean of demonic intrusion, we cannot work alone; we need a strong unified defense plan with others.

This is why the church today is suffering and weak, because there is a great lack of unity in the ranks. The "if it feels good, do it" attitude in America has infiltrated the very core of the church. The exploitation of the supernatural through extra-biblical esoteric experiences seems to be more common than the need for repentance. Churches are being persuaded by get-rich type doctrines instead of holiness messages. Mind control is an epidemic causing people to shirk their responsibility to read the scriptures and stay abreast of current events—a big mistake when there are so many antichrist views infiltrating governments and lands. There is no way we can escape deception if we are not aware of the enemy in our midst. Closing a blind eye because we would rather live the good, easy life and avoid anxiety or fear is a dangerous position to be in.

An actual army must take the offensive in order to win a war; they must use good and accurate intelligence information to understand the enemy and be wise enough to know his tricks. The army of God is no different in their duties. We must not rely on mainstream media for our source of intelligence, but be wise to search for the proper sources that will not dilute the truth. The Bible commands us to be watchmen, and warns us to "guard our salvation with fear and trembling." God knows the devil is like a roaring lion seeking to devour anyone he can, and that he will do so to anyone who is naïve enough to think they can live life in a passive state without securing their spiritual borders.

Jesus gave us the book of Revelation so that we as people can discern current events and be aware of the plots and ploys of Satan. He works to deceive; if we do not have the correct information necessary to thwart him, he will fool us. II Corinthians 11:14, 15 tells us, *And no marvel; for Satan himself is transformed into an angel of light.*

In Soviet Russia the military hid their ICBMs from U.S. satellites by using mobile nuclear re-entry vehicles. They transported these missiles constantly on big trucks from station to station, and hid them under foliage in different parts of the Siberian forests or in special warehouses. We should never underestimate the enemy, and certainly not allow our minds to be distracted from Christ's command to "watch and pray always."

The Bible says "the effectual fervent prayer of a righteous man availeth much." The great thing about God's army is that His warriors do not need to be lined up physically side-by-side to win a war. They can be scattered all over the world, alone or in groups, strategically set to combat the evil forces through steady intercession. It is a spiritual uniqueness that makes this army strong, something the adversary finds difficult to block. As a well-fed society we need to remember to walk in faith and stay awake, be willing to suffer with Christ, and pick up our crosses daily and follow Him.

The world faces new threats and new types of warfare every day, and concerns about how to deal with them are necessary. There is a greater issue at hand, and that is the realization that Christ is coming soon. Preparedness for His coming is vital because the book of Revelation prophesied that weapons of mass destruction will be a part of the great tribulation period preceding the time of the Lord's return. There is a great hope for those who choose to let the Lord Jesus be in charge of their lives. Revelation 22: 20 lets us know that God will be worth standing for: *And, behold, I come quickly; and my reward is with me, to give every man according to his work shall be.*

Jesus and His saints will smite the nations with a rod of iron, and Christ's reign will begin. The end is clear; the winner is the Lord and no amount of nuclear, biologic or chemical warfare will stop His coming or defeat His position. Revelation 19: 11: *And he shall rule them with a rod of iron ... And he hath on his vesture and on his thigh a name written, KING OF KINGS, AND LORD OF LORDS.*

We don't need bio-weapons developed in the U.S. or fiercer nuclear missiles erected. We can get away with open borders again if we do one thing: repent, turn back to God, and allow Him to be our civil defense planner, as He so promises in Psalm

91: *He is my refuge and my fortress: my God; in him will I trust.*
Surely he shall deliver thee from the snare of the fowler, and from
the noisome pestilence ... His truth shall be thy shield and
buckler ... there shall no evil befall thee, neither shall any plague
come nigh thy dwelling.

A few days after I first saw that old bus, I ran into the blond
missionary in the hotel foyer. She smiled again and
handed me a Bible and introduced herself as June. This time I
smiled back and accepted her gift. Through June's translator I
discovered the missionaries belonged to a ministry called,
"Christian Airline Personnel Missionary Outreach," and that
they were all airline employees. June had established the
ministry during her involvement with the international Christian
organization, "FCAP (Fellowship Christian Airline Personnel),"
and put the group together in order to bring the Gospel of Jesus
Christ to the Russian people.

What a thrill it was to learn that the God she preached about
was the same God I had prayed to a year earlier in my loneliness. God *had* heard me. Now, standing before me was someone
who *knew* Him and could tell me all about Him.

June possessed something that I had never seen before, a
genuine love and concern for other people. I was deeply at-
tracted to her because of this. However, our language differences kept me from telling her with words; therefore, I tried to
let my eyes show her what I felt. Two members of June's group
misread my bold eye contact and would later complain to June
that I exhibited a lustful eye towards her. June understood the
language barrier and had seen past the surface of my eyes, deep

down into my soul. Just like God was seeing me. I was amazed at her ability to understand me, and I knew it was because she had God's heart for me.

Another eight months passed before I saw June again. She returned with another group, and it was then that I made my decision to know the same Jesus she did. I asked Him to forgive me for all my wrongdoings, all my failures, all my selfish attitudes, and I asked Him to come and dwell inside me and cleanse my sin-soaked heart with His love.

He did, and I became a new person. June's group left and she remained behind at the invitation of my parents. God had been working on her heart that entire time we were separated, and she knew I was to be part of her life. I proposed marriage and she shocked me by saying yes!

A week before our wedding, I was water baptized in one of the American churches that had sprung up in Russia. On May 15, 1993 June and I were married at the Marriage Palace in front of my parents, our friends, and my American pastor. That was the most beautiful day of our lives—because Jesus now had blessed my life. The joy I felt was so complete that I no longer felt the need to drink or smoke. All I needed was God.

Six months after marrying June, I relocated to her hometown in Seattle, Washington. June resigned from the airlines in 1994 and together we opened a small coffee business. That job was a blessing, not only because it helped me to develop English quickly, but also because it enabled me many free hours each day to study the Bible. I soon learn about my Heavenly Father and His Son Jesus, about my Jewish heritage, and about the eternal future awaiting me.

I faced new trials in my life, but this time I understood their purpose and leaned upon God, allowing Him to strengthen me through the difficulties. I had a lot to learn about His mercy and love, and God used those difficult tasks in my life to reveal those amazing attributes of Himself. The most important lesson of all was learning to love my neighbors as much as I loved myself—one of Christ's greatest commandments.

As we face threats of WMDs and of possible future wars, the nation's obedience to this greatest command will bring unity and purpose out of chaos. Emergency responders of all departments—whether doctors, police, paramedics, or firefighters—could not do their job without having this important decree burned inside their hearts. They need our prayers because they will be the most important people in our lives in the event of any disaster, sometimes sacrificing themselves to save us, a feat that takes the heart of Christ to be able to do.

In 2001 God gave me the great opportunity to assume the work of developing programs and training emergency responders on all aspects of WMD for the Combating Terrorism Program at Bechtel Nevada. Everything I gleaned from my military career is now being used to prepare U.S. emergency responders. I am glad God is able to take my undesirable past and use it for good.

The Lord has been more then generous to me, saving me from earthly and eternal devastation worse then any weapons of mass destruction sitting in the Russian stockpiles today. There are no words that can adequately express how very glad I am that He never gave up on me.

Although the technologically advanced WMDs in the world today are a terrifying possibility, what is even more frightening is being unprepared against the epidemic of immorality and sin that threaten to separate us from the Lord Jesus Christ. Accepting His sacrifice and making Him Lord of life, individually, corporately, and as a nation, is our greatest vaccination against all weapons that could be stockpiled against us.

Instruction for You and Your Family

ESSENTIAL EMERGENCY AND EVACUATION ITEMS FOR THE HOME

There are essential items every household should stockpile. Don't be without them. If an attack occurs, no one will have time to run to Wal-Mart. These items should be together, preferably in a suitcase for easy transport and set aside in an easily accessible area. If you evacuate, take all these things with you.

- Canned food and bottled water, enough for two days for your whole family
- A manual can opener
- Scissors
- Two rolls of duct tape

- A box of HEPA (high efficiency particulate air) filter masks or surgical masks, enough for three per person
- Safety glasses for each family member
- Extra clothing for each family member, including underwear, light cotton gloves, a box of latex gloves, hats, and socks
- Long raincoats (the inexpensive fold-up kind are good) and galoshes
- Battery-operated radio and flashlight with extra batteries
- Medical kits containing KI (Kalium Iodine) Potassium iodine (Iodine needs to be placed in containers)
- Compass
- Ten plastic bags
- Baby shampoo
- Fragrance-free hand lotion and soap powder
- Shower caps for each family member
- Non-alcoholic baby wipes, regular cotton pads, washrags, sponges, and towels
- Talc or baby powder
- Small individual sized boxes of plain corn flakes
- Oversized umbrella
- Toilet paper
- Bottle of hydrogen peroxide
- Radiation Detector (available in keychain form to monitor and alarm presence of radiation. Can be purchased at http://www.nukalert.com.)
- This book

AFTER A REPORTED BIOLOGICAL RELEASE

Wherever you are, cover the most sensitive parts of your body, especially the respiratory tract and the eyes. If you are outside, quickly seek indoor shelter; remaining outside is dangerous for high exposure of a virus or bacteria. Remember, you cannot see the microorganism, but it is deadly and should be treated like a visible attack.

Evacuation is not an option during this type of disaster because people might become infected through normal breathing by the time they reach a safe zone. Do not bring clothes inside your home or shelter. If possible, undress before entering and put worn clothes in a sealed container and leave outside.

If the release is known, everyone inside the potentially effected area would be under suspicion for future development of the disease.

Listen to emergency radio stations for directions. Moving prematurely if you are in a contaminated area will bring on unnecessary spread of the disease and cause epidemics. Isolation in a prepared underground facility is the best answer for germ warfare.

Contact your local government and find out what options are available for your city in the event of a bio-release.

The important things to remember are:

* Turn off the air conditioner and heat systems.
* Tape windows and all openings shut.
* Immediately take a hot shower with a temperature of 104 degrees and use hydrogen peroxide on all open skin areas, including the neck, face, eyelids, and lips.

- Use plenty of soap and shampoo (no conditioners) and keep eyes closed during the wash, especially while shampooing the hair.
- After the shower, put on and wear masks, or anything that can cover your nose and mouth.
- Do not go outside.

Evacuation of people by air is possible. If a biologic or chemical is released by cruise missiles through bomblets, flying out of infected areas would be much safer than going by land.

AFTER A NUCLEAR EXPLOSION OR RADIOLOGICAL INCIDENT

A nuclear plant mishap will allow for immediate and organized evacuation. Whereas, with a surprise nuclear detonation, there is more confusion and no time for immediate evacuation. At the impact of a nuclear explosion everyone needs to turn away from the blast, lie face down, and wait 20 seconds for the shock wave to pass over. Cover your face the best you can and do not look at the blast!

Afterward brush off as well as you can and find stable shielding. One thing to remember is that the walls of wooden construction can weaken ionizing radiation two times, brick walls up to ten times, basements up to seven times, and basements with concrete walls up to 100 times. Your best bet is to be in the concrete basement. But don't go into basements if there is a fire above it.

There are three types of aggressive actions that should be made available to the population for any WMD attack. This can only happen through a solid civil defense program in place for the city. Ask your city to provide the following:

1. Safe bunkers. If the government has been forewarned of an impending attack, the first action is to find a safe bunker because you will not know where the missile might hit.
2. Personal protection gear and medical supplies for all people.
3. A good evacuation plan. This would include ways to evacuate at least four miles outside city limits—but only if it is safe outside to do so. Manuals for WMD instruction should be made available to all citizens so they have a list of what food and medical supplies they will need for a five-day evacuation, and the location of collective points (such as schools) where they would be meeting to commence the evacuation.

After an attack, evacuation can be partial or complete if there are safe bunkers for shelter. In a partial evacuation, senior residences, nursing homes, schools, and other institutions need to leave first, along with people that are not involved in the manufacturing or handling of necessary production. Workers who are needed to operate a nuclear plant or electrical station should try to stay behind as long as they can to maintain city safety.

There should be enough underground bunkers to protect and feed part of the population for three days, house the IC (incident command) and administrative government personnel, contain a mobile electrical unit, and harbor a medical facility.

The size of these buildings should vary from a small size that holds up to 150 people to the largest size to accommodate over 450 people. They must have proper ventilation/filter systems because isolation is vital.

It is possible to have pre-built or fabricated above-ground safe houses erected within an hour. These systems would work only in certain conditions: the levels of radioactive dust must be low, the filter/ventilation system provided needs to be effective against the chemical or biological agents released, and the facility must be far enough away from fires. Hiding time in these bunkers in fire areas will usually be no longer then seven hours. Coal mines and metro stations are good places to use as bunkers. One-level buildings with basements also are workable.

Anyone taking shelter in a bunker or basement after a nuclear blast where the level of radiation exceeds between 8 to 80 R/hour cannot remain longer than 24 hours. If the level of radiation is between 80 to 240 R/hour they should remain up to three days. And if the level is over 240 R/hour they are safe in their bunker more than three days. If your bunker is damaged by the shock wave or in any other way, do not wait for rescue teams; get out fast. It is difficult psychologically and physically to live in bunkers for days.

After four days the radiation is settling, and this is when folks can leave their bunkers and quickly relocate to other enclosed buildings. Do not stay outside. If you have to be outside, don masks. Once inside a secure building, tape windows and do not activate air or heat systems. Eat only canned food, and touch nothing that has been sitting out. If transportation comes to the rescue, get on that bandwagon.

Potassium iodine (KI), available over the counter, should be stockpiled and included in your medical kit because it has the potential to protect the thyroid gland against radioactive iodine up to 95 percent. (CAUTION: iodine can cause allergic reactions.) KI needs to be taken right away, at least 130 mg a day as long as you are exposed (65 mg for ages three and 18; 32 mg for ages one and three; and 16 mg for ages birth to one). Waiting to take the iodine six hours will drop that effectiveness to 50 percent. An 11-hour wait will not work at all. The Chernobyl incident released so much radioactive iodine in the air that thyroid glands blocked completely in six hours.

Saving lives means preparation. Without it, people will die unnecessarily. Citizens in their city and state should fight tooth and nail to get their local politicians to provide a strong and effective civil defense program.

EVACUATION

Being educated about what to do in the event of a disaster can save your life. Keep your head and move with knowledge, not with fear. Evacuation will be first and is important to understand. A proper evacuation is organized removal of the population from dangerous areas to a safe zone far enough away from radiological or certain chemical contamination. It is effective when done in a timely and organized manner.

Evacuation in large cities can be done either by using public transportation systems, including airplanes, or by leaving the city in cars or on foot. Public transportation is the best way to go, especially because masses tend to get confused. City drivers would have better specifics and knowledge of the best route to get out of the city and into the safe zones. If a person chooses to drive their own vehicle, they must know where to go; otherwise they can end up driving toward the hot zone instead of away from it, and dangerously contaminating themselves and their family with high levels of radiation or chemicals.

Everyone should keep a battery-operated radio in their home because this will be valuable for the safety of your family in knowing what to do and where to go. A good compass should also be in your supplies in case the city is destroyed and your sense of direction is muddled. Walking is the fastest way to evacuate a hot zone if traffic jams clog the roads and slow down the process. Having proper clothing is a must in this case if you are in a contaminated area.

The most important mindset to assume during this kind of crisis is that you are not alone; you are part of a unit, working with everyone around you. No one gets left behind; you work together to reach your goal. This attitude will diminish panic and accomplish a great deal more.

In the case of a nuclear plant incident, evacuation will be much easier because the city would not be a mangled fireball. (The personal response of evacuation and protection mentioned in the next few pages applies to a post-nuclear explosion as well. Radionuclides inside the fallout after a nuclear detonation and after a nuclear plant incident differ, but the principles of protection against radioactive fallout are the same).

Boats should not be used as a source of evacuation if the body of water is near the destroyed nuclear plant; the water surface will be heavily contaminated. Avoid walking on soil or grass. Travel on asphalt roads if possible and avoid gravel roads that harbor dust. First responders and federal organizations have the survey equipment to analyze radiation levels and should be giving out information on the safe and unsafe routes to use. Again, keep the radio close at hand.

Before evacuation starts and before leaving home:

- Block every opening in your house, including the space underneath doors, with wet towels to ensure the best protection against radioactive contaminants. In Pripyat, after the Chernobyl incident, the people who did this procedure did not lose their furniture and belongings to contamination.
- Unplug all electrical utensils and shut off the gas.
- If your property has an outdoor water well, cover it.
- Tune into the television or radio emergency stations for instructions.
- If you have been wise and stockpiled, put on the mask and do not remove it as long as you are in evacuation mode.
- Don long sleeved shirts; turtleneck tops are ideal. Wear pants and long socks, high shoes (boots are best).
- If you are near a highly contaminated area, tape shut all openings and gaps, such as the area between your boots and your jeans, or gloves and sleeves. Cover all skin with clothing as much as possible.
- Before putting on latex gloves, first sprinkle talcum powder on the hands, add cotton gloves, and lastly add the latex gloves. Face coverings should be wet.

- Shower caps are excellent for protection of hair against radioactive material.
- Lotion applied thickly to the face will help keep radioactive material from penetrating the skin. Do this whether you plan to use public transportation, your own vehicle, or if you are walking.

In a large WMD event, expect to lose belongings, property, and cars—but don't look back. Stay focused on saving your life, not your material goods.

EVACUATION BY VEHICLE

Grab your stockpiled suitcase (the openings should be taped) full of emergency items and place it with you in your vehicle. Heavy-duty trucks that sit up high from the ground are ideal protection to use for evacuation.

Once inside the vehicle, seal off all the vents, all openings under the dash, and around the windows with duct tape. The air conditioning and heat systems must be turned off and remain off. This will limit the presence of dust sneaking inside your vehicle as you drive.

Once you determine which way to leave the city, do not open the car or stop until you arrive at a safe destination. Stay close to the car in front of you, tailgate if possible, so that radioactive dust cannot fly up and possibly find its way inside. Avoid traveling through forest areas because the density of the foliage protects and absorbs the concentration. Drive away from the radioactive fallout cloud, and avoid rainfall if possible.

Do not eat or drink, if possible, until you reach the safe
zone. If you or your children need water, take small drinks, but
do not remain without face covering for a long time. Use only
bottled water; do not drink water from a faucet or well. Usually,
if a mass evacuation is going smoothly, safe zones are four to six
hours away. It is best to wait to eat or drink until you arrive at
your secure destination.

Clean zones might become contaminated due to a shift in
weather, and evacuation to another zone might be necessary.
Keep this in mind.

An effective emergency plan of evacuation by government
officials would include regional breakdowns so that people in
predetermined districts or neighborhoods would have ready
public transportation available.

Children and pregnant women should go first, since they are
most sensitive to ionizing radiation, followed by the elderly. No
one should be left behind.

Change face masks during evacuation at least three times
and wipe your face down with alcohol-free baby wipes when you
do this. Expect delays and be ready for them.

Evacuation by Foot

If you are stuck in the city, especially if you are walking, stay in
the middle of the road and away from buildings that may be
heavily contaminated. If it is raining, do not walk through rain
puddles that might be heavily contaminated. Shield yourself as
best you can, and use a raincoat. Avoid unstable crowds; the
last thing you want is to get caught inside a panicky group. Do

not go through parks; avoid grass and trees. One evacuee from Chernobyl who wore shoes, used a bicycle, and rode through grassy fields, ended up in the hospital with third degree radioactive burns on both feet.

For evacuation by foot, 1,000 people should be broken into ten groups, with each group having one leader. The leader should be in charge of the map and the radiological and chemical survey instruments, with proper instruction on how to use them to check contaminated ground levels as they walk. These groups need to head away from the city with haste, but with carefulness so as not to shuffle and kick up contaminated dust.

Evacuation of pets applies the same as for humans. Pets need to be covered (especially their paws), washed, and even shaved if possible. Evacuation of animals from farms should take place after the people.

PERSONAL DECONTAMINATION

When you arrive at the safe zone, decontamination stations should be set up to survey and wash skin and change clothes. Place used masks and worn clothes in doubled plastic bags and dispose where instructed. Also collect belongings like watches, rings, wallets, and money in separate labeled bags to allow responders to survey the belongings later to see if they could be decontaminated. If no decon stations with showers are organized at your safe location, this can be a problem, because the most important thing is that you shower and wash thoroughly. Radioactive contamination has the ability to become fixed on the skin; delaying removal by shower might be dangerous. In these cases techniques of removal can only be performed in a hospital setting.

If at all possible, have someone help wash your hair because it will be the most concentrated area of contamination and the most challenging area to clean. You may want to cut hair short to avoid the difficult job of cleaning, then dispose the hair in bags. Do not use shampoo combined with conditioner, or rinse with conditioner, since conditioners can bind the proteins of your hair follicles with the radioactive material. Use baby shampoo.

Before tackling your hair, wash your hands thoroughly with a shampoo and water mixture, then slip on waterproof gloves and wash your face and eyes with the same. Do not use soap. Use wet swabs to clean the ears and nose.

Gargle and spit out, using a 3.6 percent hydrogen peroxide solution for your mouth. Brush teeth well, including the gums and tongue. Flush the eyes, keeping them wide open. Use direct water flow, starting at the inside corner of the eye. Blow the contents from your nose into a tissue.

Cut fingernails and toenails and clean under them. Dispose used items into plastic bags. Wash any small "hot spots" or tender areas (like underarms) with wet soapy pads in a spiral motion beginning at outer areas to the center. With large areas, wash with downward strokes and never backtrack over that cleaned area with the same pad. If you have no cleaning pads, use sponges or tampons.

Do not re-use washing aids after rinsing. Three percent strength of lemon extract is a good way to remove radioactive contamination and can be mixed with shampoo and water.

As you wash the hair, do not let any water splash into the face. It is best to sit on a chair and keep the head back at all times. Do not open the eyes or mouth. Use little water, mostly shampoo, on the hair; wash and rinse at least three times. Make sure you or your helper wear waterproof gloves.

Finish showering your entire body, using shampoo and water mixture, and use a soft brush or sponge over the skin. Then, dry off with a towel.

Afterward, if you have the items, take dry unscented soap powder and mix it together with plain corn flakes to make a thick paste. Apply it heavily all over your hair using little water; then brush it in well. Rinse, shampoo, and rinse again two more times. Use soft brushes and pads to comb hair. Hair dryers are okay to use. This method of cleaning is an awful ordeal, but necessary to decontaminate.

Despite all this showering you still cannot be sure that some radioisotopes did not penetrate the skin or still remain inside the hair.

Dispose all worn clothes, utensils, towels, shampoo, and brushes into the plastic bags.

A good way to remove contamination from the skin on the hands is to use a perfume-free lanolin or skin cream and cover with plastic while they sweat. Leaving this on the skin for at least three hours will be effective in destroying almost 40 percent of external contamination. Remove the lotion with pads, preferably non-alcoholic baby wipes, and do not use water. This process should be done twice.

The bad news in washing in private homes is that the bathroom will more than likely become contaminated. The best place to wash is in special showers assigned for the task by city officials. There should be checkpoints of irradiation for people to make sure the decontamination process is efficient. This is the reason a good emergency plan is a necessity in every major U.S. city.

If there are open wounds on your skin and radioactive material has possibly gotten inside them in liquid or solid form, you have only 15 or 30 minutes until this material enters the peripheral blood. Depending on the chemical structure of the radionuclide, they would be concentrating in different "critical" organs. Therefore irrigating the wound as soon as possible with water is important. If there is arterial bleeding, you need to put a tourniquet two inches above the wound (use cloth underneath the tourniquet to protect the skin from bruising), then flush the wound. Cover the cut with sterile pad, but do not close the wound.

Once inside the clean safe house, do not get lazy. Everyone needs to consistently wipe down walls and surfaces with wet towels daily, just in case the radioactive dust has touched down in your area.

Be Wise

Today's media are neither psychologically prepared nor educated for large-scale WMD events. This means that various news broadcasts might give out a lot of confusing information.

For instance, if first responders would be establishing decon stations across the city, the media may report incorrectly that your life is in immediate jeopardy from radioactive fallout, and may forget to inform you that only three or four stations are open in a city of one million. Long panicky lines would result, exposing everyone in the line to unneeded doses of radiation.

Proper decontamination of skin and clothes by responders takes at least ten minutes or more per person. Only four or five people being washed in one hour within one shower, makes a slow, slow process. Don't stand outside in stalled lines; it is better to delay the shower and stay shielded from the fallout than to take on double doses that could be worse for you, shower or not.

Use wisdom during these times, and depend more on emergency broadcast news stations than the major television news networks.

To correctly prepare evacuation pathways, open mobile gas stations should be set up by responders in PPE gear to pump gas so that people do not have to get out of their cars and face exposure to radiation again. These gas stations should also be opened in the safe zones as special points for deactivation of transport and decontamination of people.

The government should have enough of these stations to accommodate thousands and thousands of fleeing people. Personal monitoring equipment for radiation levels at these stations is crucial. Then responders can know who to send on their way, and who to keep back for decontamination.

DEAD ZONES

If a nuclear accident happens of the size of Chernobyl, or a large-scale nuclear detonation or biological attack occurs, many people will lose their houses forever. Replacement will be necessary in new clean zones (which will be a serious financial impact on the country). After such catastrophes, "no go" or dead zones will need to be erected and put in place around the most severely contaminated areas for decades because they will be impossible to decontaminate. If more than half the United States is contaminated, populations will have no choice but to live inside contaminated zones.

In Belarus and the Ukraine, nearly two decades after Chernobyl, three million people are living in contaminated zones and will do so for the next 80 years or more. The biggest dangers for these people are that their immune systems do not respond to small doses of radiation; they are prone to receiving carcinogenic effects on the bones; and they could suffer genetic instabilities, which can transmit to future generations. They have become ultra sensitive to all types of allergens, antibiotics, vitamins, pharmaceutical drugs and chemical products, such as bleach. The effects of radiation on humans also cause people to age fast. A Chernobyl responder's life expectancy today is about 49 years.

During a nuclear plant explosion, a shortage of water supply would occur quickly; most underground waters would become contaminated in the first week. Don't rely on home water filter systems for protection. A destroyed nuclear reactor will continually contaminate surrounding regions on the topsoil and in underground waters as long as it is alive and leaking radioactive material. It has been 18 years since the Chernobyl incident, and radioactive substance is still leaking from the destroyed area and poisoning nearby rivers.

Today, still, every autumn in Belarus, certain responders have the task of collecting contaminated leaves from trees before they can fall to the ground and blow to other areas. It is a sobering fact to know that there is nothing earthly normal or fixable about radioactive contamination. Gaining knowledge of radiation and putting into effect a good family preparation plan are the first and most important steps in staying alive during a radiological catastrophe.

Key Points for Emergency Responders

Five Nuclear Zones
Initial Response
Evacuation and Processing Casualties
Pre-Decon Triage
Hot Zone Decon
Warm Zone

FIVE ZONES TO WATCH FOR IN A NUCLEAR PLANT DISASTER

A development of five zones will come into play in the event of a nuclear plant disaster.

1 The zone of radiation danger.
2 The zone of reasonable contamination.
3 The intense contamination zone.
4 The dangerous contamination zone.
5 The extremely dangerous contamination zone.

These zones are categorized to give knowledge of levels of radioactive dose rates and the evacuation speed needed to move away from the zones. For example, if there is a development of a radioactive plume and future fallout with the wind speed of 16 feet per second, with a 50 percent release of activity from the destroyed nuclear core into the atmosphere, the first zone will be 362 miles long and 26 miles wide, with a dose rate inside the zone at 0.14R/hour, developed in the first hour after radioactive release.

The second zone will be 118 miles long and 7 miles wide, with a dose rate inside this zone at 1.4 R/hour, developed in the first hour after radioactive release.

The third zone will be 29 miles long and 1.5 miles wide, with a dose rate of 4.2 R/hour in the first hour after the incident.

Inside the border of the fourth dangerous zone, the exposure rate is 14 R/hour. This means the responder can collect a full yearly occupational dose limit within 20 minutes. The average occupational limit for responders in the United States (DOE) is 5 rem a year. So this dose received in 20 minutes is what should normally take one year to get if they were inside this zone. The fourth zone will be 15 miles long and .5 mile wide.

Finally, most dangerous for responders is the fifth zone. It will be 6 miles long and .5 mile wide, with dose rates going up to dozens of hundreds of R/hour, and this means people can develop ARS within minutes and hours if they are exposed and delayed in evacuating.

For each one of these zones, evacuation of the population is critical.

KEY POINTS FOR NUCLEAR PLANT INCIDENT

- Be prepared to deal with highly radioactive debris including fuel, core components, structural items of the destroyed building, the plume of smoke and radioactive fission products, and heavy debris deposited close by (which will develop a large radioactive field around the nuclear plant). Impulsive releases of radiation in the atmosphere may seriously change response time and effort, and put responders in an unpredictable risk at once. Until the crater is closed, low amounts of radioactive materials will be released from the core as long as up to 40 days. Keep yourself inside the shielding areas during this time.

- During actual response, make sure all members of your team have personal dosimeters, which can also detect the dose of gamma waves you are receiving. Keep your dosimeters and other equipment covered so they will not get contaminated from radioactive dust and liquid.

- Doses must be counted carefully and realistically; do not second-guess the situation or the monitoring equipment; prepare yourself for the worst in order to make sound judgments.

- Response after a nuclear detonation involves problems with high dose rates from the exposure area, making it difficult for responders to move toward ground zero until the radiation levels drop.

- DOE limits adopted by responders today are 5 rem/year, following the level of exposure by gamma radiation.

Keep in mind this is not a realistic dose level when responding to a Chernobyl type incident because some responders can collect their 5 rem/year dose within minutes or hours of response.

- Civil defense meters are the best to detect the levels of radiation around or inside a reactor.

- Don't use level A suits in these operations. In cases dealing with overheated highly radioactive liquid forms, like steam cloud, use a breathing apparatus and regular gear, taping all possible openings (gloves and boots), and use baby powder on feet and hands before donning cotton gloves and socks. Cover the cotton gloves with rubber gloves. Make sure boots are the correct size; avoid using brand new untested body gear, especially boots. (If you develop blisters and get radiation burns, it will be an open door for a secondary infection.)

- Avoid drinking any alcohol the night before or during the response. If food and water supplies will be brought to you by trucks, make sure this food is not contaminated with radioactive dust. It may happen if drivers used contaminated roads.

- After a nuclear plant incident with complete destruction of the plant structure, responders must know this is an extreme danger. Be ready for casualties and for making tough choices. Critical response will lead to extreme and dangerous situations around and inside the destroyed reactor. An entire nation's survival will be based on fast and complete enclosure of the crater. Responders face a risky job knowing they will not be able to avoid high

doses of radiation and accomplish the task at hand at
the same time.

- Be ready for surprises. Reactors in many critical situations are unpredictable. Clear and correct information
from nuclear plant employees on the condition of the
reactor must be known before response.
- Treat thermal fires as potentially radioactive fires. When
radioactive fallout starts contaminating the surface of
the buildings, they will become hazards to responders.
- Use monitoring equipment to check the level of radiation exposure from the walls. Remember that the level of
radiation after a nuclear blast will be going down, but
the level of radiation after a Chernobyl style accident
will be going up in surrounding areas—as long as the
crater of the destroyed reactor is open to the atmosphere
and releasing radionuclides.
- If the reactor core is completely destroyed, quick work
must be done to control the area from constant release of
radionuclides into the atmosphere. Bear in mind that a
disaster like this can contaminate at least half of the
U.S. territory and bring financial collapse to the nation.
- Many clean up operations will have to be done by hand
due to electromagnetic impulses (from intense gamma
umbrella).
- Use long sticks or handles to keep radioactive material
distanced from hands.
- Work in rotation so you can leave the area and take
plenty of breaks. Do know that after you get your yearly
dose of 5 rem, you are not obligated to return to work.

- The best bet is to use unmanned aircraft to cover the hole of the crater to eliminate health risks to pilots. If pilots are necessary, helicopters need to be lined with lead shielding on the sides and floor to help protect pilots from gamma waves. Complete personal protective gear (PPE) in the form of light suits, HEPA filter masks, and rubber gloves must be worn by the pilot.

- Be cautious of the steam cloud from vaporization of the water pool, as exposure rate will be at least 1,000 to 1,500 R/hr. You can operate no more than five minutes in this condition because ARS can develop in about ten minutes, and death can occur in about three to four weeks after a one-hour exposure. HEPA filters will not work in steam conditions.

- No matter how difficult the situation, do not compromise safety principles during response.

- NEVER lose sight of each other.

- Every evening after work and every morning on the following day examine your body for unusual puffiness or redness of the skin. If these symptoms are present and there is no feeling when you touch the area, this is a beta burn. Consult a physician.

- Any unusual symptoms, such as nausea, weakness, or intensifying headaches need to be reported to your IC immediately. Leave the area as this might be the first signs of ARS.

- Re-use heavy-duty equipment (bulldozers, fire trucks, and ambulances) as long as possible until radioactive contamination hits unacceptable levels. Pressurizing steam is the best way to decontaminate the vehicles. Use lead shielding in the driver cabins of bulldozers.

• Use water trucks constantly to spray roads against radioactive dust before transporting.

KEY POINTS DURING INITIAL RESPONSE FOR NUCLEAR DETONATION

• Do not use monitoring instruments to survey victims *inside* a radiological active hot zone. They will not give accurate readings. The number one concern is saving lives.

• Separate clean stretchers from the contaminated carriers and designate one person to oversee carrying equipment. The contamination level on the stretcher needs to be checked after every fourth victim. If the level of contamination on the stretcher is higher than the level on the victim, the carrier should be separated from the rescue teams and stored in a secure area for decontamination.

• Mark stretchers with visible tape after each victim is transported to avoid confusion about how many times the stretcher was carried in and out of the hot zone.

• Keep in mind, when picking shielding areas, brick buildings protect the decon station from high background radiation levels at least ten times as well as from radioactive dust or rainfall. A concrete building protects up to 100 times. Decon stations need to be set up in low level radiation areas.

- A large warehouse-type building is ideal for the decon station. This way there is good control of all entrances and exits and plenty of space to set up open decontamination lines and decon tents inside.

- Undressing victims before bringing them inside the decon building/station will limit contamination. Once inside, victims can be directed to the emergency medical treatment areas. Entrances and exits should never be crossed, keep victims going in and out the same way throughout the entire evacuation process.

EVACUATION AND PROCESSING OF CASUALTIES BASED ON MEDICAL TRIAGE SYSTEM

Externally contaminated victims need to be selected with these medical triage principles (based on the standard triage four-color tag system, which is used by responders during any type of response). Tags are used for eight different situations based on the presence of radioactive external contamination:

1 Walking (ambulatory) patients who are externally contaminated are tagged green (minor injury).

2 Walking (ambulatory) patients who have no external contamination are tagged green (minor injury).

3 Immediate category, stretcher-carried patients, who are externally contaminated are tagged red.

4 Immediate category, stretcher-carried patients, who are non-contaminated are tagged red.

5 Expectant category of victims, stretcher-carried patients, externally contaminated or not, who are dying with no

chance of survival, are tagged black. They are to be placed in a contaminated casualty collection area not far from the hot line.

6   Delayed category of victims, non-ambulatory stretcher-carried patients, who are externally contaminated, but show stable vital signs, are tagged yellow. These patients are able to wait for the next available vehicles to evacuate them to the hospital.

7   Delayed categories of victims, non-ambulatory stretcher-carried patients, who are not externally contaminated and show stable vital signs are tagged yellow. They, too, can wait for the next available vehicles to evacuate them to the hospital.

8   The deceased are tagged black and should be left in the hot zone area for further criminal investigation teams.

Responders should have certain select areas set up for smooth evacuation of victims. (See Graph 1 for details.)

KEY POINTS TO REMEMBER IN THE PRE-DECONTAMINATION TRIAGE AREA

The pre-decontamination triage area is where triage officers and medics identify the medical conditions of the victim and check for external contamination. This area is set up in front of the hot zone of the decon station. (See graph 1, Box 11)

•   In large mass casualty situations where there are thousands of victims, there is little time for survey and decon. Responders in this situation should survey only

open skinned areas, especially on the walking victims. If
no contamination is found on skin surfaces, decon teams
at the hot zone area should instruct the victims to
undress and don clean clothes or blankets.

- If during a rapid survey, which should take no longer
  than 60 seconds, a triage officer's meter starts showing a
  dose rate at more than two backgrounds of radiation,
  there is no need for further survey. This victim is externally contaminated and needs to be moved through the
  appropriate corridor or pathway. Hopefully at this same
  time another medic will be making decisions on the
  victim's health condition. Working together keeps the
  process of triaging running smoothly.

- Responders coming from the hot zone will have external
  contamination on boots, gloves, and masks. If there is a
  large response team waiting for the doffing process,
  responders shouldn't waste time, but immediately start
  surveying one another at the triage area using their own
  instruments. Make sure the instruments are not contaminated after working inside the hot zone. If gear is non-
  contaminated, the responder can head for the clean
  corridor. In most cases responders will be externally
  contaminated, so they will need to head for the decon
  line specifically set aside for responders.

- Dry swabbing of both nostrils on all victims is necessary
  at the triage area, otherwise radioisotopes will be moved
  down to the tracheal and bronchial areas and swabbing
  will not show accurate levels of contamination. Place
  swabs in zip-lock plastic bags, one bag for each nostril,

labeled with the time the swab was taken, and the
victim's name. This valuable information will help labs
estimate the internal doses from inhaled radioactive
material as well as the chemical properties of the radio-
isotope.

- If any contamination is found on the victim's face,
  quickly wipe that area with non-alcoholic wipes (baby
  wipes are good), starting at the forehead, avoiding the
  eyes, and going down to the chin. Flush the eyes with
  water, from tear ducts outward. Afterward apply the
  HEPA filter mask on the face for protection. A mask
  with eye shields is best protection from splashing during
  decon process. A delay in cleaning eyes can cause
  radioactive material to be absorbed internally.
- If vomiting occurs at any time, collect the victim's vomit
  in a labeled disposal bag and send to the lab for evaluation.

KEY POINTS TO REMEMBER IN THE HOT ZONE OF THE DECONTAMINATION STATION

The hot zone is part of the decon station, where victims and
responders undress and prepare to enter the warm zone inside
the decon building. (See graph 1, Small Ovals 6-A, 7, 8)

- Brushes are not good for removal of radioactive dust
  from clothing and skin. Brushing spreads dust and
  creates a secondary release of contamination in the air.
- Before the victim removes clothing, responders need to
  spray them all over (except the head area) with water

(garden hoses are good, but don't use heavy-duty fire truck hoses as this method will spread contamination over the victims' bodies), or use prepared wet blankets to put around them. This keeps the radioactive dust from spreading.

- After cutting and rolling off victim's clothing, alcohol wipes or vinegar should be used to clean the scissors.
- Make sure to constantly remove the pile of contaminated, bagged clothes away from the work station; otherwise the background of radiation will rise to high levels.
- Keep in mind that summertime produces more skin exposure, meaning more skin will be exposed to contamination. This means that only 40 or 50 percent of contamination will be removed along with the victim's outerwear. In colder weather, 95 percent of contamination will be removed because the victim has on more clothing.

THE WARM ZONE OF THE DECONTAMINATION STATION

The first detailed radiological survey will take place inside the decon building at the first warm zone station. The warm zone is the area for the wet decontamination process. (See Graph 1, A Building)

- Keep in mind most radioactive contamination will be present on the victim's skin in the form of spots. All measurements of contaminated spots are to be documented on personal survey forms.

- A second and final survey should be done at the last warm zone station after finishing the wet decon process and towel-drying the skin.

- Hair should be cut short if radioactive contamination is found during survey at the first warm zone station. Double bag the hair and remove as radioactive waste. If the victim chooses not to lose their hair, they will need to go through an extensive hair-washing procedure using shampoo without conditioner (see Appendix 1). The longer the hair is not washed the more fixed the contaminant will become on hair and skin.

- In some cases concentration of radioactive dust may be so intense and radioisotopes inside the dust so active, it will be hazardous for responders. After a nuclear plant incident like Chernobyl, radioactive dust can give exposure rates in dozens of R/hr (a responder can get a dose of 5 rem/year within 12 minutes), so responders can work only in short rotation times.

- After finishing the decon procedure, a final analysis with instruments on the fixation of contamination on skin needs to be done by swiping the affected area with a pad. If the pad shows contamination readings, then contamination on the skin is loose (is removable). If the pad shows no contamination, then the radioactive material is fixed to the skin. All spots with loose contamination must be covered and taped; otherwise these spots can be a hazard to transporting medics or responders.

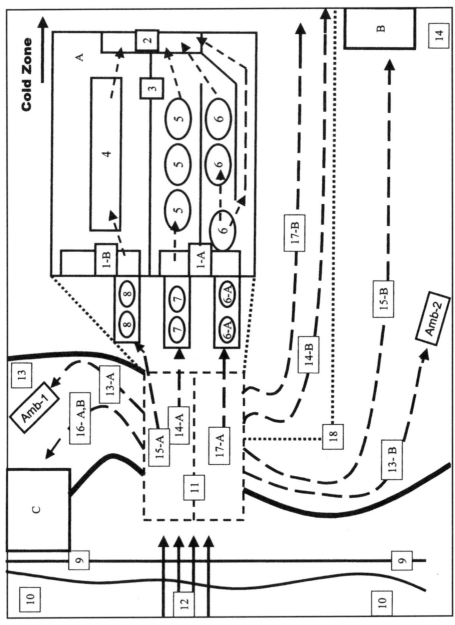

Graph 1

*EVACUATION PATHWAYS AND DECONTAMINATION STATION
FOR MASS CASUALTY SITUATIONS*

- If contamination is still present on the victim's hands after a complete wet decontamination process, apply lanolin or another barrier cream thickly on hands and cover with gloves. Tape them shut. After the victim leaves the decon station, have them keep gloves on for at least four hours. Survey the area and repeat the whole process. (In Russia this sweating technique is applied to the other parts of the body as well.)
- All victims should be covered with blankets after leaving the decon station.

A Building—This building is the warm zone for decontamination and is used as a shielding against any negative environment condition, like radioactive fallout or rainfall, or high natural background of radiation.

B Buildin —This building is dedicated for the casualty collection area and is used to clean delayed (non-ambulatory) and post-decontaminated delayed patients.

C Building—This building is dedicated to live but expectant categories of victims, contaminated or not. The entire facility will be contaminated inside when mass numbers of dying victims are stationed here. Medical personnel taking care of these patients should wear all necessary protective gear.

Box 1-A Entrance Door—This entrance is for ambulatory contaminated victims with minor injuries and contaminated responders who finished their work at the hot zone of incident.

Box 1-B Entrance Door—This entrance is for non-ambulatory contaminated victims. Control of contamination inside the building is accomplished only by opening doors after victims have completed undressing and are ready to proceed into the warm zone.

Box 2 Exit Door—This exit is for victims (including walking wounded) and responders who have completed the decontamination process and are ready to enter the cold zone (clean area outside decon station shown on graph) EMT station area for necessary medical treatment. This exit area should be separated in two parts, for walking and non-walking patients. Strict control of this site may not be necessary.

Line 3—This line represents the separation of decontamination lines inside building A so there is no cross-contamination during the decon process.

Long Box 4—This box is the area of one warm zone non-ambulatory line inside the building.

Three Ovals 5—These represent one ambulatory line for externally contaminated walking wounded inside the warm zone.

Three Ovals 6—These represent the line for responders who have external contamination and need to be decontaminated. Separating the responders from victims is wise because the responder's doffing (undressing) process is completely different from victims.

Small Ovals 7, Small Ovals 6-A and Small Ovals 8—These areas show the location of hot zones of the decontamination station where victims and responders undress before entering the warm zone. Minor injured walking victims with external contamination (Box 14-A) who are tagged green will be sent by the triage officer to this hot zone, which is the designated area in front of the decon building A. They will be directed into the ambulatory line (Small Ovals 7). Small Ovals 6-A is the tent area for contaminated responders and Small Ovals 8 is the area for non-ambulatory victims.

Box 9—This is the hot line of the pre-decontamination area and should be established by responders based on radiological survey of the area.

Box 10—This is the location of the hot zone of the incident.

Box 11—This box inside the dotted line area represents the location of the medical triage and first quick radiological survey. The dotted line separating the box represents the two areas for contaminated and non-contaminated victims on stretchers for prevention of cross-contamination.

Box 12—This represents the victims brought into the triage area by rescue teams from the hot zone.

Box 13—This represents the corridor or pathway for contaminated victims. This corridor should be set up before the decon operation starts.

Box 13-A—This is the line for immediate contaminated victims who are tagged red. These people must be immediately taken through the contaminated corridor (Box 13) and evacuated to the hospital for decontamination and medical treatment.

Box 13-B—This is the line for clean immediate victims, tagged
        red, and they are being evacuated through the clean
        corridor, Box 14. These patients are then taken by
        paramedics inside the non-contaminated ambu-
        lances (Amb-2) for immediate evacuation to the
        hospital.

Box 14—This is the clean corridor, established by responders
        for all non-contaminated victims, except expectant
        (dying) category. This corridor should be set up
        before the decon operation starts.

Box 14-A—This represents the line for the minor walking
        injured (green tagged) who have external contamina-
        tion and were sent over by the triage officer to go
        through the ambulatory line for a complete decon-
        tamination process.

Box 14-B—This pathway (inside the clean corridor) is for the
        walking minor injured, who are not externally
        contaminated, after they have been tagged green at
        the triage area. These victims will get medical
        attention at the cold zone (clean zone) EMT in
        another building or tent behind the decon station.

Box 15- A—This represents the line for the delayed (non-
        ambulatory) category of victims with external con-
        tamination who are tagged yellow. They should go
        through the whole decontamination process using
        the non-ambulatory decon line, starting with Small
        Ovals 8 at the hot zone of decon, entering through
        Box 1-B door and moving to the warm zone (Long
        Box 4). For a mass casualty situation there will be

numerous decon lines, some used for non-ambulatory and other for ambulatory victims. After complete decontamination these victims will be exiting
(Box 2) in Building A in going to the cold or clean
zone.

Box 15-B—This line is for the delayed (non-ambulatory) victims tagged yellow without external contamination.
They should be removed from the area by rescue
teams through the clean corridor (Box 14) to the
casualty collection Building B. They should receive
basic medical treatment inside the building and wait
for the next available non-contaminated ambulance.
Clean vehicles will transport these patients later to
the hospitals.

Box Amb-2—This box represents the area for the clean (non-
contaminated) ambulance service, which can be
used only for non-contaminated immediate category
of victims.

Box Amb-1—This is the location of the unclean (internally
contaminated) ambulance service, which can be only
used for contaminated immediate category of victims. In large size events, because contaminated
ambulances will not have a time for decontamination, paramedics need to wear complete personal
protection during transportation of contaminated
patients.

Box 16-A, B—This place is for both contaminated and non-
contaminated externally expectant category of dying
victims who are tagged black. These do not need to

be decontaminated, and rescue teams should bring
them through the contaminated corridor (Box 13)
into the separated Building C, where they will be
placed under supervision by medics in complete
PPE.

Box 17-A—This represents responders who are coming back
from the hot zone after finishing their job. In most
cases they will have presence of external contamination on their gear and hands. If after complete
doffing of gear (in the Small Ovals 6-A area), the
first survey (inside building A, Oval 6) shows no
external contamination, they will not need to go
through a wet decon in the warm zone of building A.
A temporary plastic shield should separate the warm
zone from the clean responder's walking area so they
can safely exit from Box 2 door.

Box 17-B—This route is for responders who have no external
contamination present on their gear and can proceed
through the clean corridor.

Box 18—This represents the line (made of cones or caution
tape) inside the clean corridor (Box 14) to separate
the non-walking victims from the walking victims.
This line is necessary because rescue teams will be
bringing victims on stretchers into the clean areas,
and contamination control of the rescue team's boots
is important. Boots should be checked before entering the clean corridor at the triage station. If your
team has enough people support (which in reality is
rare during a large-scale emergency), have an extra

team waiting in the cold zone so they can go through the clean corridor and take non-contaminated victims on stretchers back to the cold zone. If there is no extra team available, rescue teams bringing victims in from the hot zone who have external contamination on their boots will need to cover them with clean plastic shields before taking the victim inside the clean corridor (Box 14).

(NOTE: Only the externally contaminated, delayed, and minor categories of injured victims go through the complete decontamination process.)

Pre-Hospital Decontamination Process in the Event of a Biological Incident

LAYOUT FOR HOSPITAL
DECONTAMINATION STATION

In the event of a large-scale biological release of any kind on the city (from a terrorist attack or war), decontamination procedures should be set up outside the hospital setting before ever stepping foot inside the hospital or prepared clinic. This ensures that the inside hospital setting will be safe from unnecessary contamination.

Inside hospital preparation plans are vital for a complete overall control of epidemics. Since there is no room in this book to add such detailed blueprints, this appendix will remain focused on ways to follow the proper decontamination procedures outside a hospital.

On the following pages, a graph and detailed explanations provide the location and purpose of each decontamination post.

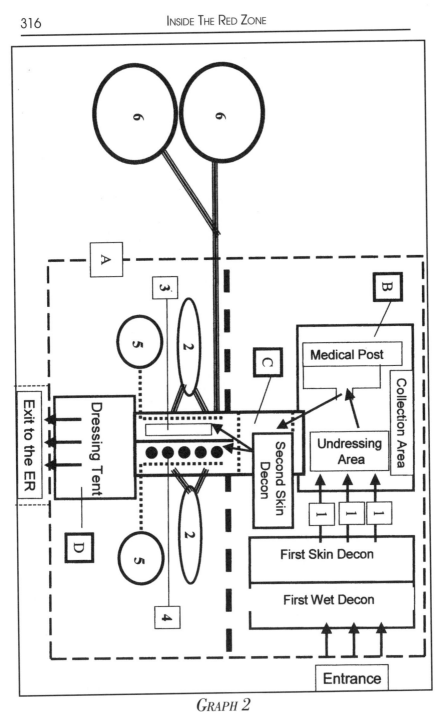

GRAPH 2

OUTSIDE HOSPITAL DECONTAMINATION STATION
FOR LARGE-SCALE BIOLOGICAL INCIDENT

Box A—The perimeter of this dotted square is located in the
          parking lot in front of the hospital and keeps the
          decontamination process secured. It should be
          roped off in order to keep the entire setup con-
          trolled. It is best put together on concrete or
          asphalt 65 feet from the entrance of the emer-
          gency room. Every person who is arriving at the
          hospital from the hot zone of a biological incident,
          including responders who might have compro-
          mised their Personal Protective Equipment (PPE)
          gear, must have complete decontamination before
          they enter the hospital setting. This means
          decontamination tents should be set up outside
          the hospital. Each section of the decontamination
          area should have its own work staff dedicated to a
          certain specific area or tent. This will ensure they
          are not walking back and forth to different sta-
          tions and cross contaminating areas.

Box Labeled "Entrance"—This is the entrance to the outside
          decontamination area. Only one single entrance
          should be open and secured at all the time during
          a biological response. A 24-hour security patrol is
          necessary at this opening to maintain safety and
          control. Most civilians who are coming from the
          hot zone do not have proper respiratory protec-
          tion. At the entrance gas masks should be given
          to these victims before they start going through
          the decontamination process. Recommendation
          for all victims before placing a mask on their face

is to clean the skin using non-alcoholic wipes (see Appendix 2 for detailed instruction on putting on mask). All responders must keep gas masks on.

Box Labeled "First Wet Decon"—This is the first "wet" area for decontamination, using showers. Because of the fixation of contaminated material to clothes and skin and partial decontamination of microorganisms, this procedure must be done first. All victim's clothing and masks should be sprayed with disinfectant (using a solution of 6 to 10 percent hydrogen peroxide works well to kill spore-forming microorganisms like anthrax). The liquid waste must then be collected and mixed inside specifically organized containers using strong bleach type disinfectants.

Box Labeled "First Skin Decon"—The first "skin" decontamination area comes right after the initial "wet" decontamination process is complete. This is where all open skin areas must be cleaned with large pads that are saturated with 2 percent chloramines solution. (All responders who have gone through the first wet decontamination process wearing their complete PPE gear skip the decon process at the first skin decontamination area and move onto the pre-undressing tent (Boxes 1) area).

Boxes 1—The pre-undressing tent area is where boots and shoes of victims and responders must be cleaned

with wet disinfectant solution before entering the
undressing tent (Box B).

Box B—The undressing tent has three separate stations: the
collection area, the medical post, and the undressing locality. This next procedure comes after
partial decontamination is finished. [Partial
decontamination is the entire process that happens before entering the undressing tent (Box B).]
The undressing tent is internally contaminated
during processing of externally contaminated
victims and responders; this tent must be closed
at all times, except when victims or responders
are ready to enter the tent. All personnel inside
this tent must be wearing proper PPE and work in
shift rotations no longer than three hours.

Box Labeled "Undressing Area"—Inside this area of the tent all
wet clothes from the victims should be carefully
cut off and rolled down off the body from inside
out. Masks should stay on faces until all clothing
is removed and contained inside double bags or
lid containers.

Box Labeled "Collection Area"—Containers and storage for
contaminated clothing should be located in this
area of the tent as well as victims' documents and
personal belongings. All wet clothing and belongings must be sent to the autoclave cameras for
complete disinfectant process.

Box Labeled "Medical Post"— This is the location where medical evaluation is performed by attending physicians and nurses. All medical personnel will be in protective gear and masks. If there have also been explosions taking place during this terrorist or war attack, any wet bandages present on the victim's skin after the previous decontamination process will need to be changed by physicians inside the medical post area and covered with plastic. This should be done before victims enter the second decontamination corridor (Box "Second Skin Decon"). The plastic covering can be removed after the next decon showering.

Box C—This locale is the final decontamination tent for the Second Skin Decontamination corridor and multiple shower stations for both non-ambulatory and ambulatory victims.

Box Labeled "Second Skin Decontamination"—This is the pre-shower corridor were the victim's nude body, face, hair and genital areas must be disinfected with disinfectant solutions using large pads or sprays. Responders should use this station for skin decontamination if their PPE was compromised.

Ovals 2—These are the fresh water tanks used for the showers.

Large Ovals 6—These are the water trucks (or water towers) for constant water supply to the water tanks (Ovals 2). The trucks are parked outside the decon station perimeter (Box A).

Box 3—Non-ambulatory decontamination showering area. The roller system is the best method to move victims from beginning to end of this decontamination line. (The washing process starts with the hair.) At the end , dry victims should be placed on a clean stretcher and moved to the dressing area.

Boxes 3 and 4—The shower area must have a trench, or pipes, erected underneath for collection and removal of contaminated waste. This water is collected and taken outside the dressing tent to Ovals 5 area.

Ovals 5—Waste collection areas for disposal of contaminated water. Used water is mixed with bleach solutions for deactivation of contamination. (After finishing decontamination for victims and responders, all contaminated material liquids must be mixed with disinfectants.)

Box 4—Shower stations for ambulatory victims. Each shower station should be designed for two people. Victims should be given 30 minutes to complete the decontamination process here (5 minutes for undressing, 20 minutes for washing, 5 minutes for dressing). With five shower stations inside the tent, 20 people in one hour should get processed.

Box D— Dressing tent. After completing the shower, the victims dry off and enter this tent to put on fresh clothing. From here they are directed to proceed into the hospital. (Inside the dressing tent staff needs to wear only a light Tyvek suit, HEPA mask, and gloves.)

Box Labeled "Exit to the ER"— This box represents the exit from the decontamination area. From this secured area victims proceed to the emergency room of the hospital. After complete decontamination, secured pathways are important in and out of the hospital so there is no chance of cross-contamination.

Acknowledgments

I want to thank my wife June who labored long hours and months writing my story. She was able to catch the essence of my story and relay it onto paper so accurately and vividly because she is one with my heart. This book would not be here if it were not for her willingness to put up with my prattle for long stretches at a time.

June and I want to thank Val Dumond, author/editor and friend, for her patience and support during this project. It is because of Val's encouragement that this book went forward and is now completed. She tirelessly answered our many, many questions, which in turn kept us focused on the task at hand. Her brilliant skills as an editor made the completion of this book smooth and painless.

I also want to express gratitude to my parents, Vladimir and Albina, for all of their efforts in getting me accepted into the Leningrad Military Medical Academy. Without that career move this book would not exist, nor would my job today entail WMD preparation. But mostly without that path taken in my life I might never have come to know Jesus as my personal Lord and Savior.

About the Authors

IGOR V. SHAFHID, M.D., is presently employed by Bechtel
Nevada /Martin Lockheed as
Senior Medical Scientist and as a
Domestic Preparedness Consultant in Las Vegas, NV. He works
with the Department of Counter-
terrorism Operations Support
(CTOS) /Nevada Operations, on
behalf of the U.S. Department of
Energy.

Dr. Shafhid develops and implements training programs for
CTOS, training physicians, first responders, SWAT teams, law
enforcement, FBI, counter-terrorism units, fire fighters, paramedics, civil support teams (National Guard), U.S. Customs and
other military and government agencies. He trains teams to be
prepared and to react quickly to foreign and domestic terrorism
and weapons of mass destruction, through the use of exercises
for nuclear, radiological, chemical, or biological attack.

A graduate of the Russian Military Medical Academy in St.
Petersburg, Russia, as a military officer and general practitioner
(internal medicine), Dr. Shafhid studied military training on

principles and tactics of Strategic and Ground Forces, and performed large chemical/ biological military field exercises in casualty collection units and organization of infectious disease control field hospitals, including military exercises known as "Nuclear Winter."

During the Chernobyl Nuclear Plant incident of 1986, Dr. Shafhid, then a medical cadet, studied the affects of radiation on overexposed military responders with acute radiation syndrome and chronic radiation illness. He also completed military training practices in the Strategic Rocket Division of Kapustin Yar Nuclear Test site in Russia. His studies included hands-on experience dealing with most military chemical agents and their effects on the human body. He received specialized training inside military infectious disease clinics on aspects of isolation precautions and contact work with contagious and non-contagious patients.

Dr. Shafhid's medical studies included aspects of military strategies and tactics of WMDs, along with programs on military toxicology, principles of military epidemiology, infectious disease control and prevention, as well as aspects of military and civilian quarantine. During his ten-year career in the Russian Army, Dr. Shafhid trained military personnel in all aspects of WMD, performed ambulatory services, and worked in the emergency extreme response program. He was involved in epidemiological control for overseas Soviet Military Special Service battalions and Ministry of Internal Affairs civilian employees.

Born and raised in St. Petersburg, Russia, Dr. Shafhid speaks excellent English. Since coming to the United States in

1993, Dr. Shafhid has consulted with many military, government and private business groups dealing with prevention and control of WMD, and protection for civilians against terrorist threats. He became a citizen in 1995 and currently holds a secret security clearance.

June Summers met Dr. Shafhid in 1992 during a group mission's trip to hospitals and orphanages in Russia. She had founded and formed the international "Christian Airline Personnel Missionary Outreach" ministry. She lived in Seattle, Washington, and was employed by Delta Airlines.

The Shafhids were married in 1993. Currently June is a busy mom, writer and helpmate for her husband's work on counter-terrorism. They have one daughter.

Index

Quick Order Form

Please send me _____ copies
of *Inside the Red Zone.*

Name:_____

Address:_____

City:_____State:_____ Zip:_____

Telephone: _____

Email address: _____

Please send more free information on speaking/seminars: Yes ___ No ___

Cost per book: $19.95
Sales Tax: Please add $1.50 for books shipped to Nevada address.
Shipping and Handling: $4.00. Add $2.00 for each additional book
International: $9.00. Add $5.00 for each additional book.

Payment: ☐ Check (*payable to Global Strategic Resources*) ☐ Credit Card

☐ Visa   ☐ MasterCard   ☐ Discovery

Card number:_____

Name on card:_____ Exp. Date:_____

Signature of cardholder as appears on card:_____

TO ORDER:

Website: http://www.globalstrategicresources.com

Fax: Send this form to: 702-259-9579.

Email: is@globalstrategicresources.com

Postal orders:
Global Strategic Resources
1725 S. Rainbow Blvd. Ste. 2, Box 171
Las Vegas, NV. 89146
Telephone: 702-259-9579